Borders Are Just Lines We Agree On

OrangeBooks Publication

1st Floor, Rajhans Arcade, Mall Road, Kohka, Bhilai, Chhattisgarh 490020

Website: **www.orangebooks.in**

First Edition, 2025

ISBN: 978-93-6554-399-5

Price: Rs. 549.00

Printed in India

BORDERS ARE JUST LINES WE AGREE ON

KUNAL TANNA | NAINY TANNA

OrangeBooks Publication
www.orangebooks.in

Introduction

In the dance between the known and the unknown, there exists a realm where every step is a heartbeat, every horizon a new chapter, and every encounter a brushstroke on the canvas of memories. Welcome to the world of the "Borders are just lines we agree on," where the pages are filled with the intoxicating scent of adventure and the ink flows with the colours of distant landscapes.

As the sun dips below the familiar skyline of routine, a traveller emerges–not merely in pursuit of destinations but in the relentless quest for stories untold, cultures unexplored, and the symphony of life echoing through every cobblestone street and hidden alley. This book is an invitation to embark on a journey that transcends the boundaries of mere geography, transcends the confines of the mundane, and invites you to become a fellow wanderer in the vast tapestry of our shared planet.

Together, we will traverse landscapes both external and internal, navigating the serpentine roads of ancient civilizations, crossing the threshold of bustling markets, and basking in the warmth of unexpected connections. "Borders are just lines we agree on" is not just a travelogue; it is a celebration of the human spirit's innate desire to wander, explore, and discover the extraordinary in the ordinary.

So, fasten your seatbelts, not just for the physical miles we'll cover, but for the countless moments that will stretch the fabric of time and linger in the recesses of your soul. Let the journey begin – an odyssey where each page turned is a step into the unknown, and each chapter reveals the beauty of both the world and the traveller within.

About the Authors

Kunal Tanna and Nainy Kunal Tanna—two souls bound not only by love and shared dreams but by a profound voyage that has spanned decades, continents, and countless stories.

Their journey began in the halls of high school, where the seeds of wanderlust were first sown amidst the bustling corridors of academia. From those youthful days of curiosity and discovery, a spark was ignited—a shared passion for exploring the world's marvels, its hidden gems, and the diverse tapestries of human culture. With adventurous hearts and insatiable curiosity, they set upon a path that would turn travel into a life philosophy, a form of meditation that replenishes their spirits and elevates their understanding of life itself.

Over the course of 27 extraordinary years, Kunal and Nainy have traversed the globe—venturing through North America, South America, Europe, Oceania, and Asia—each journey more enriching than the last. Traveling together, they have fallen in love with the rhythm of life found in bustling markets of Marrakech, the tranquil temples of Kyoto, the wilds of the African savannah, the vibrant fjords of Scandinavia, and the lush rainforests of the Amazon. They have discovered that in travel, every new place is a mirror—reflecting their inner worlds and expanding their horizons.

Their adventures are stitched together with the threads of spontaneous meeting, soulful conversations, breath taking landscapes, and moments of serene reflection. Every stamp in their passports, every photograph captured, every sunset watched has been a testament to their unwavering belief that life's true essence lies in the journey rather than the destination.

In the quest for meaning and beauty, they have curiously crafted their experiences into stories — stories that inspire, reminding us that every traveller is a poet, a seeker, and a pilgrim of life. In doing so, they have honed a unique gift: the ability to see the extraordinary in the ordinary, to find wonder in every corner of the world.

Seven years ago, their universe grew even more luminous with the arrival of their daughter, **Alazne Tanna**, born in 2018. Her presence has infused their odyssey with new purpose, reaffirming their desire to continue exploring life's infinite mysteries—hand in hand, heart to heart, soul to soul.

For Kunal and Nainy, travel is not merely the act of crossing borders or ticking off destinations; it is a sacred ritual—an act of meditation that elevates their consciousness, awakens their senses, and reconnects them with the divine spark that resides in every living being. It is this relentless passion, this unquenchable curiosity, and this sacred approach to life that fuels their desire to meet new people, discover new places, and live fully in the joy of every moment.

Unpretentious and driven by a genuine love for discovery, they curate every experience themselves—crafting journeys that are authentic, heartfelt, and transformative. This is their gift to the world, a testament that life, in its purest form, is an endless voyage of wonder and connection.

As authors and explorers, they invite you to join them—on this voyage of discovery, where every chapter unfolds with the beauty of the unknown, and every story resonates with the truth that to travel is to truly live.

Contents

Introduction

Our Journey Begins: The Inspiration behind the Passage

Every great story starts with a spark—an idea, a moment, or a realization that ignites the path forward. In this chapter, we delve into the roots of this voyage, exploring the deep-seated motivations, the pivotal experiences, and the profound insights that shaped the very essence of The past - *Borders are just lines we agree on*.

The Genesis of a Vision

Our journey was born out of a desire to uncover the truths buried within our past—truths that hold the power to redefine our future. It's a call to awakening, a summons for introspection, and an invitation to traverse the uncharted territories of our collective history. This vision was fuelled by stories that echoed resilience, lessons etched into time, and a yearning to forge a path illuminated by understanding and growth.

Catalysts and Critical Moments

Every path has its turning points. For us, it was a series of encounters—those serendipitous moments of clarity—that revealed the importance of confronting and embracing our past. Whether through personal experiences, historical revelations, or inspiring figures, these catalysts propelled us to seek what lay beneath the surface and to question everything.

The Drive for Transformation

Inspiration is not static; it is the fire that fuels transformation. This chapter explores the motivational forces behind the journey—how a desire for healing, insight, and evolution became the driving force behind this project. It's about more than reflection; it's about inspired action—using our past as a springboard for a richer, more purposeful future.

The Power of the Passage

Finally, we examine the significance of "the passage" itself—the metaphorical corridor through which we navigate our histories, struggles, triumphs, and lessons. It is a gateway to understanding who we are, where we come from, and where we are headed.

The Spark That Ignited the Quest

The origins of this journey lie in a simple yet powerful realization: that our history, both personal and collective, holds vast reservoirs of insights—lessons that can propel us beyond mediocrity and mediocrity's shadow. It was an awakening ignited by moments of introspection, the stories we ignored, and the truths we often hesitated to confront. We began questioning—what stories have been buried? What lessons remain hidden behind the veil of time? And most critically, how can understanding these truths empower us to break free from cycles of stagnation and surrender?

The Deep Roots of Purpose

This drive for discovery is not superficial; it is rooted in a deep, visceral need for authenticity and emancipation. It is about reclaiming our narratives, unearthing forgotten wisdom, and confronting uncomfortable realities—because only through truth can we find strength. Our purpose was born in the silence between the chaos—an epiphany that the past isn't just history; it is a powerful force shaping our identities and destinies.

Pivotal Encounters and Defining Moments

Many pivotal moments punctuated this journey—moments that challenged, inspired, and pushed us beyond perceived limits. Perhaps it was a story passed down through generations, an encounter with someone who had faced insurmountable odds, or a discovery that shook the very foundation of what we believed. These encounters serve as catalysts, propelling us deeper into the labyrinth of our history, motivating a relentless pursuit of clarity and understanding.

Each encounter reinforced that mastery over our past—and its lessons—can unlock unprecedented strength and resilience. It's in these moments that the journey transforms from a mere exploration into a crusade for purpose, identity, and liberation.

The Unquenchable Fire of Inspiration

Inspiration fuels our journey with relentless urgency. It's the fierce wind beneath our wings, pushing us to dive deeper, question harder, and persevere despite obstacles. This chapter emphasizes that true inspiration transcends surface-level motivation; it is a deep, burning fire that ignites an unbreakable resolve. It's about harnessing the energy of hardship, resilience, and hope to forge a legacy that resonates across generations.

Why the Path is Called "The Passage"

Finally, we explore the symbolic significance of "the passage"—a metaphor that embodies the transition from ignorance to awareness, from despair to hope, from chaos to clarity. This is no ordinary road; it is a sacred corridor where past and future collide, where pain and triumph intertwine, and where true transformation takes root. This passage is a battleground for those willing to confront their shadows and emerge reborn.

Embracing the Call to Action

As we stand at the threshold of this profound journey, it becomes clear that the path we have embarked upon is nothing less than a divine calling—an urgent summons to confront our deepest truths and embrace the power within us to transform history into hope. The inspiration that sparked this passage is not merely a distant memory or a fleeting moment; it is a persistent flame—an enduring force that beckons us forward, urging us to reclaim our stories, rewrite our future, and stand resilient in the face of adversity.

This journey is not for the faint-hearted. It demands relentless courage, unwavering honesty, and an unyielding commitment to growth. It challenges us to look within, confront the shadows that have long been hidden, and emerge stronger, wiser, and more determined than ever before.

Remember, every revolutionary change begins with a single step—an act of courage fueled by a deep understanding that our past, no matter how tumultuous, holds the blueprint for a future we dare to envision. The passage ahead is ours to navigate, filled with opportunities for awakening, healing, and ultimate transformation.

So, as we take that first decisive step into the unknown, let us do so with conviction, purpose, and the unwavering belief that our journey—our destiny—is waiting to be written. The story of has just begun. What lies ahead is a testament to the resilience of the human spirit and the relentless pursuit of truth.

Are you ready to forge your own path? The passage calls—answer it.

The Spirit of Exploration: Why We Travel

In the deepest corners of our souls lies an insatiable hunger—an undeniable urge to explore beyond the known, beyond comfort, beyond the limits of our current understanding. This is the primal force that drives explorers, pioneers, and revolutionaries throughout history. It is the raw, unrelenting **spirit of exploration** that compels us to venture into uncharted territories of the mind, spirit, and world itself.

Exploration is more than mere movement—it is an act of rebellion against stagnation, a battle cry for awakening. It is the refusal to accept the status quo, the unquenchable thirst to unearth hidden realities, and the relentless pursuit of truth where others see only obstacles.

The Call of the Unknown

Why do we travel? Not merely to escape, but to engage. To confront the unfamiliar with courage, to challenge our perceived limitations, and to find meaning where others see chaos. It is within the chaos of the unknown that transformation is born. Every voyage into uncharted waters ignites a fire—fueling growth, awakening dormant potentials, and rewriting the narrative of what is possible.

This journey pushes us to break free from the chains of complacency. It awakens the warrior within, compelling us to face fears, confront doubts, and emerge victorious from the crucible of uncertainty. Exploration is an act of defiance—against ignorance, stagnation, and the constraints imposed by fear.

The Inner Odyssey

But this exploration isn't purely external; it is a profound inner odyssey—a relentless quest to discover who we truly are beneath the layers of societal programming, baggage, and self-imposed limitations. Each step taken on an uncharted path is a step closer to authenticity, clarity, and purpose.

It's about **daring to question**, to deconstruct old paradigms, and to build anew with fearless intent. The profound realization: *real exploration begins within*. Only by venturing into our own depths can we unlock the limitless power waiting to be harnessed.

The Birth of Innovation and Transformation

History's greatest innovators and leaders were explorers—those who dared to venture into the unknown, discarding fear as their compass. Their journeys were marked by relentless curiosity and an unyielding belief that truth exists beyond the horizon.

This chapter emphasizes that the **spirit of exploration** is essential not only for personal mastery but for collective evolution. It is the catalyst for breakthroughs, revolutions, and new paradigms—fuelling the **movement forward** that changes the course of history.

The Power of the Journey

To explore is to challenge, to push boundaries, and to transcend self-imposed limits. It is a stance—a declaration that says, "I refuse to accept ignorance. I seek understanding. I am here to discover the essence of existence and unleash the power within."

As we navigate this journey, remember: every step into the unknown is a rebirth—a series of trials that forge resilience and carve a new identity. The greatest explorers aren't those who never faced fear—they are those who pressed on despite it.

Embracing the Infinite Horizon

The spirit of exploration is the heartbeat of progress, the fire that fuels innovation, and the catalyst for transformation. It is an unquenchable thirst—a relentless pursuit to pierce the veil of the unknown and emerge enlightened. This drive to explore is embedded deep within our DNA; it is the inherent rebel that refuses to accept limitations, daring us to venture beyond the familiar into the vast, uncharted territories of possibility.

In every journey outward, we unravel the layers of our own existence, confronting fears that threaten to contain us and discovering strengths we never knew we possessed. Exploration is not a one-time act—it is a continuous, unwavering commitment to growth and awakening.

To truly harness the power of exploration, we must cultivate a mindset that embraces discomfort, champions curiosity, and boldly defies the boundaries of what is known. Every step into the unknown is an act of rebellion—an act of faith in ourselves and the universe.

So, as you stand at the cusp of your own voyage, remember: the horizon is infinite, and every journey into the uncharted is a declaration that you refuse to be confined by the limits of your current reality. The spirit of exploration calls us not just to see the world, but to **become** the explorers of our own destiny.

Answer that call. Venture forth. For the greatest discovery awaits those brave enough to forge their own path into the infinite horizon.

Part - I
Beginnings and Boundaries

The Genesis of the Wanderlust (Early Days and Motivations)

Every fervent traveller, every pioneering soul, begins with an origin story—a spark that ignites the relentless urge to roam, explore, and transcend. **The genesis of the wanderlust** is not a mere coincidence nor a fleeting curiosity; it is the inception of a profound, primal calling—an instinct encoded deep within our DNA that compels us to seek beyond the familiar.

Wanderlust is born from the desire to discover the unknown, to uncover truths hidden beneath surface appearances, and to connect with something greater than ourselves. It's an innate urge fuelled by a restless spirit that refuses to settle for stagnation, an insatiable curiosity that queries, "What lies beyond these borders? What truths are waiting to be uncovered?"

The Roots: Origins of a Restless Spirit

The origins of this restless craving are as old as humanity itself. For millennia, explorers cast aside comfort and safety, driven by a primal instinct to chart uncharted waters, climb towering heights, and delve into uncharted depths of the mind and soul. Our ancestors ventured into unknown landscapes, not just for survival, but for meaning—searching for purpose, belonging, or a glimpse of the divine.

This primal impulse was woven into the fabric of our evolution, shaping our desire to push boundaries—geographical, spiritual, and intellectual. The first explorers sought more than new lands; they sought understanding, enlightenment, and a sense of wholeness that could only be found through daring exploration.

The Seed of Curiosity: A Catalyst for Change

Wanderlust begins with a single seed—an innate curiosity that refuses to be satisfied. It's the question that irks us in the quiet moments: *Is this all there is?* It's the spark that whispers, "There is more," igniting a desire to step beyond the borders of comfort and familiarity.

This curiosity transforms into a powerful force that propels us into uncharted territories—whether physical landscapes or inner realms. It challenges perceptions, dismantles illusions, and opens doors to growth and transformation.

From Restlessness to Revelation

The journey from restless yearning to awakening is what defines the essence of wanderlust. It's not just about seeing new places; it's about **becoming** new beings—shedding old limitations, breaking free from societal constraints, and cultivating an awareness that the boundaries we once believed were fixed are, in fact, illusions waiting to be shattered.

Wanderlust ignites a awakening—a realization that the true exploration lies within and beyond the horizon. This awakening paves the way for profound shifts in consciousness, perspective, and purpose.

The Power of the First Step

Every legendary journey begins with a single step—an act of courage fueled by a desire to venture into the unknown. The genesis of wanderlust serves as a reminder that your pursuit of freedom, purpose, and truth is rooted in this very first act of daring.

The seed has been planted; now it is your turn to nurture it. To honor your inner explorer, you must embrace the discomfort of the unknown, confront fears of the unfamiliar, and trust in the unfolding of your unique path.

Personal Stories: Embers of Desire

Consider the story of Sarah, a woman who grew up in a small town dreaming of the distant markets of Marrakech or the vibrant streets of Bangkok. With no prior experience of international travel, she initially felt the familiar pangs of doubt—fear of the unfamiliar, concern for safety, and doubt about her own abilities. But driven by an unquenchable curiosity, she took a leap of faith. Her journey through unfamiliar landscapes ignited an awakening within her, reshaping her understanding of herself and her world. Today, Sarah is an advocate for cultural exchange and personal transformation, knowing that her true voyage began the moment she stepped outside her comfort zone.

Or reflect on Amir, an entrepreneur who left the corporate world behind, feeling stifled by routine. His hunger for discovery led him into the heart of uncharted territories—both geographically and creatively. As he faced unforeseen challenges, he discovered that each obstacle was an invitation to grow—an essential stepping stone towards innovation and true purpose.

Historical Examples: Trailblazers Who Changed the World

History is rich with explorers, visionaries, and pioneers whose wanderlust changed the course of civilization:

- **Marco Polo:** The Venetian merchant whose travels to Asia in the 13th century expanded the horizons of the known world and fostered cultural exchange across continents. His journey was driven by insatiable curiosity, inspiring generations to dream beyond geographic borders.
- **Amelia Earhart:** A fearless pioneer who soared into the skies, breaking barriers for women and redefining what was possible in the realm of aviation. Her relentless pursuit of adventure embodied the spirit of exploration—where limits are only illusions.
- **Nelson Mandela:** Though rooted in a fight against injustice, Mandela's travels through decades of imprisonment and exile shaped his vision for freedom, resilience, and reconciliation. His journey exemplifies that exploration isn't always physical—it can be inward, transformative, and revolutionary.

Motivational Call: Ignite the Explorer Within

You must understand—the seed of wanderlust is not reserved for a select few. It resides within each of us, waiting for the moment to ignite a fire that can't be extinguished. The world outside is vast, full of lessons, mysteries, and awakenings. Your true adventure begins the moment you decide to embrace the unknown.

Now is your time. Stop waiting for the 'perfect' circumstance—there may never be one. The universe rewards the bold, the daring, and those courageous enough to take that first step.

- **Dare to dream bigger than your fears.**
- **Challenge the limits that society or yourself have set.**
- **Break free from the chains of complacency.**

Remember, the greatest explorers of history, and the most influential pioneers of progress, all started with a single step driven by an unquenchable curiosity. That step is yours for the taking.

The world awaits your footprints. The horizon beckons. The call of wanderlust is loud—will you answer?

Embrace the Spirit of the Explorer

Within each of us lies an innate call—a whisper from the depths of our spirit urging us to venture beyond the familiar, to challenge the boundaries we've accepted, and to discover the boundless potential that resides within. This is the true essence of exploration: a fearless pursuit of growth, truth, and transformation.

Today, I invite you to listen to that inner voice. To awaken the explorer who has been waiting patiently for permission to step into the unknown. Because the truth is, your greatest growth and your most profound revelations lie just beyond the horizon of comfort and certainty.

The path of exploration isn't always smooth or predictable. It is fraught with doubts, fears, and obstacles. But remember—these are the crucibles that forge resilience, wisdom, and courage. Every challenge you face is an invitation to grow stronger, wiser, and more aligned with your purpose.

As you stand at this crossroads, take a moment to affirm your commitment:

Mantra of the Unbreakable Explorer

Today is the day I choose to step beyond my comfort zone.
I am driven by a fire that refuses to be extinguished—by curiosity, courage, and a relentless desire to discover.

I embrace the unknown, knowing it is the birthplace of growth.
Every challenge, every fear, is a stepping stone toward my most authentic self.

The horizon is endless, and my spirit is boundless.
There are no limits—only opportunities waiting to be seized.

I am the architect of my journey.
With each step forward, I redefine what's possible.

This is my time.
To explore. To grow. To become.

I answer the call of the explorer within.
And I will not rest until I've uncovered the greatness I was born to achieve.

Now, go forth. The world is waiting. Your adventure begins today.

Your Call to Action

Life's greatest rewards are reserved for those willing to take bold steps—those brave enough to explore uncharted territories within their mind, heart, and soul. **You are not here to play small or live in the shadows of fear.** You are here to ignite your passion, pursue your purpose, and leave a mark of authenticity

Chasing Horizons: Our Travel Philosophy

At the core of every journey lies a philosophy—a guiding set of beliefs that transforms mere movement into a profound quest for meaning. **Chasing horizons** isn't just about physically reaching distant places; it's about embracing an evolving mindset that seeks growth, discovery, and transformation at every turn.

Our travel philosophy is rooted in the understanding that exploration is an act of rebellion against complacency—a deliberate choice to challenge the mundane, expand our consciousness, and live with purpose. It's about setting sights on horizons that stretch beyond the physical landscape, reaching into the realms of the mind, spirit, and soul.

The Spirit of Curiosity and Open-Mindedness

At the heart of our philosophy is **curiosity**—an insatiable hunger to understand what lies beyond the familiar. Every destination, every encounter, is an opportunity to learn, to grow, and to redefine what is possible.

Open-mindedness is the vessel through which we embrace new cultures, perspectives, and realities. It's a conscious decision to leave behind judgment and preconceived notions, allowing curiosity to lead us into authentic experiences and meaningful connections.

The Mindset of Growth and Transformation

Travel is more than an escape—it's a catalyst for **personal evolution**. Each journey presents a mirror, reflecting our limitations and inspiring us to transcend them. We view obstacles as stepping stones, failures as lessons, and uncertainties as invitations to grow.

By chasing horizons, we commit to continuous self-improvement and enlightenment. Our travels become rites of passage—each step shaping us into more resilient, compassionate, and enlightened beings.

The Philosophy of Purpose and Presence

Travel is not just about ticking off destinations; it's about **being present** in each moment. Every experience is sacred, every encounter meaningful. Our philosophy emphasizes mindful exploration—immersing ourselves fully in the now, appreciating the beauty and lessons of each horizon we chase.

Purpose fuels our journeys, guiding us to seek experiences that align with our highest selves and deepest values. It's about transforming the act of traveling from a superficial escapade into a soulful pilgrimage.

Challenging Comfort, Embracing the Unknown

The world's most extraordinary horizons are often hidden behind walls of comfort and safety. Our philosophy encourages us to **step into the unfamiliar**, to seek discomfort as a catalyst for growth, and to embrace uncertainty as an essential part of the journey.

In chasing horizons, we learn that the real treasure lies beyond the visible—the growth, resilience, and insight gained when we dare to venture into the unknown.

A Rallying Call: Live with the Horizon in Sight

To chase horizons is to live with intention. It's to refuse stagnation and to ignite the fire of curiosity and courage within. Every horizon, no matter how distant, beckons us to dream bigger, reach further, and become more.

Your journey is yours to define. Your horizons are limitless.

So, set your sights high. Chase relentlessly. For in doing so, you will discover not only the world around you but the vast, limitless potential within.

In the dance of dawn and dusk, we chase the horizon—
Where the sky kisses the earth and dreams interlace.
With open hearts and fearless gaze, we pursue the unseen,
Seeking truths in distant lands, whispers of the divine.

Travel is our rebellion, our sacred act,
A quest not just of miles but of awakening—
To grow beyond the walls that shackle the soul,
To find our reflection in the eyes of strangers.

In every step beyond comfort, we find ourselves anew,
Casting aside doubts, embracing shadows, and dancing in the unknown.
For horizons are not destinations—they are invitations to become,
Endless, boundless, wild as the spirit that dares to roam.

So chase the horizon—
Where your heart leads, and the universe waits—
For the greatest discovery is not out there,
But within the courage to seek what's beyond.

Personal Anecdotes

Think of Maya, a young woman from a small town who once believed her dreams were limited to her immediate surroundings. When she travelled alone for the first time to a foreign land, she faced fears she never knew she carried—language barriers, unfamiliar customs, and a loneliness that felt deafening. But in those moments of discomfort, she discovered resilience she never knew she possessed. She learned that every horizon she chased outside could unlock a new horizon within.

Or consider Rahul, an entrepreneur who had built his life around comfort and routine. Feeling unfulfilled, he embarked on a journey across multiple continents, seeking inspiration in unfamiliar cultures. With each new experience—whether meditating in a quiet mountain temple or hiking through lush jungles—he transformed his perspective, igniting a desire to build a life rooted in purpose and authenticity.

Quotes to Inspire

- **"The horizon is only the beginning of endless possibilities."**

—Anonymous

- **"Travel is the only thing you buy that makes you richer."**

—Unknown

- **"Don't tell me how educated you are, tell me how much you have traveled."**

—Muhammad

- **"The real voyage of discovery consists not in seeking new landscapes, but in having new eyes."**

—Marcel Proust

- **"The greatest explorer on earth is the human spirit—always in pursuit of the horizon, ever reaching for new heights."**

A Call to Action

Chasing horizons is about more than just crossing borders; it's about crossing the boundaries of who you believe yourself to be. It's about daring to dream bigger, reach further, and live fully. Every step outward is an invitation to step inward—to uncover our true selves and tap into depths of courage and curiosity.

Remember, every horizon you chase is a reflection of the limitless potential within you.

So don't wait for the perfect moment or the ideal circumstances. **The time to chase your horizons is now.**

Notable Explorers and Their Inspiration:

1. Christopher Columbus:

"You can never cross the ocean until you have the courage to lose sight of the shore."

— Columbus reminds us that true exploration requires courage to leave comfort behind and venture into the unknown.

2. **Amelia Earhart:**

"The most effective way to do it, is to do it."

— Her daring spirit inspires us to take bold action, regardless of fear or uncertainty.

3. **Henry Stanley:**

"To travel is to take a journey into yourself."

— Stanley's journeys into uncharted territories exemplify how exploration leads to self-discovery.

4. **Gertrude Bell:**

"I belong to those who believe that life is a story, and the adventure of living is the greatest story of all."

— Bell's adventures in the Middle East inspire us to see travel as a narrative of discovery and growth.

5. **Artemis Pyle (Through his journey of survival in the wilderness):**

"The wilderness teaches you about yourself. It confronts you with your fears and questions, and if you're brave enough, it rewards you."

— His experience underscores the transformative power of challenging oneself in unfamiliar environments.

Preparing for the Journey: Packing, Planning, and Mindset

The voyage into the unknown begins long before you step onto the plane or cross the threshold of your comfort zone. It starts with preparation—an act of intention, discipline, and vision. Proper planning, mindful packing, and the right mindset are the keys that unlock the door to transformative exploration.

Preparation is your armor—clothing your mind and body to meet the challenges and opportunities of the road ahead. It's about cultivating an attitude that is open yet disciplined, fearless yet wise.

Packing with Purpose: The Art of Lightening the Load

Packing is more than gathering clothes and essentials; it's an act of intentionality. A minimalist approach often holds the greatest power—bringing only what aligns with purpose and passion. Every item should serve a specific need or symbolize a commitment to the journey itself.

Here's what purposeful packing entails:

- **Essentials over excess:** Focus on versatile items that can be mixed, matched, and adapted. Less baggage, more freedom.
- **Tools of growth:** Journals, inspiring books, or even sketches—tools for reflection, creativity, and staying rooted in purpose.
- **Cultural respect:** Attire and accessories that honor the traditions and customs of your destination, demonstrating humility and openness.

Remember: Your luggage carries your physical tools, but your mental and emotional preparedness carries your inner strength.

Planning with Precision: Charting a Course, Not a Map

While spontaneity has its place, effective planning transforms potential chaos into meaningful adventure. It's about setting intentions, doing research, and staying flexible:

- **Set clear objectives:** What do you seek from this journey? Personal growth, connection, discovery? Clarity fuels focus.
- **Research wisely:** Understand local customs, language basics, safety tips, and cultural nuances before stepping into new territory.
- **Leave space for spontaneity:** Even the best plans need room to evolve. The magic often happens in unplanned moments.

Remember: Planning is your safety net, but it should never suffocate your sense of adventure. Flexibility turns obstacles into opportunities.

Cultivating the Right Mindset: The Traveller's Mental Arsenal

Preparation isn't complete without cultivating the mindset that transforms mere travel into a journey of transformation:

- **Openness:** Be receptive to new cultures, ideas, and perspectives. Expect to be challenged—this is where growth resides.
- **Curiosity:** Let your natural curiosity lead you. Ask questions, seek stories, and listen deeply.
- **Resilience:** Challenges will come. Embrace setbacks as part of the learning process—resilience is your greatest ally.
- **Presence:** Be fully present. Savor each moment, each conversation, each challenge, and each lesson.

In the words of Rainer Maria Rilke:
"The only journey is the one within."

Embarking on a journey of exploration isn't just about the destination; it's about how you prepare your mind, body, and spirit for what lies ahead. Here's your ultimate guide to stepping into your adventure fully equipped and ready to embrace transformation.

The Practical Art of Packing

Lighten your load, and pack with purpose.
Carry only what serves your journey—clothes versatile enough for different environments, a journal to capture insights, and items that honor local cultures. Remember, **less baggage equals more freedom**.

Personal Anecdote:
When I travelled to Southeast Asia, I packed minimally—just a few clothes and a notebook. It was liberating to carry only essentials, allowing me to connect deeply with new people and experiences without unnecessary distractions.

Strategic Planning

Plan with intention but remain flexible.
Identify your core objectives—what do you want from this journey? Do your research, learn a few local phrases, and understand customs. Yet, leave room for spontaneity—some of life's most profound moments happen unplanned.

Personal Anecdote:
On a trip to Morocco, my loosely planned visit turned into a serendipitous encounter with a local family—an experience I never would have found if I rigidly stuck to a pre-made plan.

Cultivating the Right Mindset

Prepare your mind like you prepare your bag.
Be curious, open-minded, and resilient. Practice mindfulness to stay present in each moment. Remember, **challenges are opportunities for growth**—every setback is a setup for a comeback.

Your Binding Manifesto: Step Into Your Power

- I will pack with purpose—carrying only what aligns with my goals and values.
- I will plan with clarity, yet stay adaptable to life's surprises.
- I will cultivate curiosity, resilience, and presence, knowing they are my greatest tools.
- I will approach each journey as an opportunity to discover the world—and myself—in new, transformative ways.
- I commit to showing up fully, with open heart and mind, ready for whatever unfolds.

Today, I step forward with confidence. The world awaits your exploration—embrace it fully.

Your Call to Action: Set the Stage for Greatness

Preparation is an act of reverence for the journey ahead. It's about respecting your inner explorer and honoring the process of growth. As you pack your bags, plan your route, and cultivate your mindset, remember:

- Leave behind fears and doubts—carry curiosity, courage, and compassion.
- Be intentional with every step—both physical and mental.
- Trust that the universe will meet you halfway when you show up with purpose and an open heart.

Step into your journey with confidence. The world is vast, waiting to unfold and reveal its secrets to those brave enough to prepare and willing enough to explore.

Part - II
Continents and Cultures

Understanding the Rich Tapestry of Continents and Cultures

As we prepare to journey through the vast and wondrous world we live in, it's important to pause and reflect on the incredible diversity that makes up our global community. The world is divided into continents — enormous landmasses that stretch across the Earth like chapters in a grand storybook. But each continent is much more than just a piece of land; it is a vibrant mosaic of peoples, traditions, languages, histories, and ways of life.

Every continent has its own unique identity shaped by geography, climate, history, and the resilience of its people. From the sweeping deserts and lush rainforests of Africa to the towering mountains and ancient civilizations of Asia, from the historic cities and castles of Europe to the vibrant cultures of the Americas, each region offers something extraordinary and different.

At the heart of this diversity are cultures — the rich, living expressions of human creativity and spirit. Cultures are more than just customs or festivals; they are the values, beliefs, stories, art, music, and traditions that define a community. They are passed from generation to generation, evolving over time yet anchored in centuries of history. Each culture provides a unique lens through which to view the world and live life, shaping identities and fostering connections among people.

Understanding these differences and similarities helps us appreciate the complexity and beauty of human life. When we explore cultures, we open ourselves to new perspectives, learn about different ways of thinking, and celebrate the shared human experience that binds us all.

As we move forward into this part of our journey, I invite you to approach each continent with curiosity and openness. Think of it as a grand storybook—each chapter revealing lessons, traditions, hopes, and dreams. Embrace the opportunity to learn, to wonder, and to be inspired by the incredible diversity of our world. Because ultimately, these stories and cultures remind us that we are all part of something much larger than ourselves — a global family woven together by our shared humanity.

Africa

Safari and Sahara: The Heart of Africa

Welcome to the vibrant, dynamic world of Africa—the continent where adventure awaits at every corner and stories are woven into every sunset. Imagine vast deserts stretching beyond the horizon, lush jungles teeming with life, bustling markets alive with music and color, and ancient traditions that pulse through the veins of the land. This is Africa—an extraordinary place full of surprises and wonder.

Think of Africa as the beating heart of the world's wild spirit. It's a place where the majestic safari animals roam free—lions, elephants, giraffes, and cheetahs—all part of an incredible balance of nature. It's also a continent shaped by the vast Sahara Desert, a sea of golden sand that has challenged explorers and inspired mysteries for centuries.

But Africa isn't just about safaris and deserts. It's a land of incredible diversity—tiny villages with colorful huts, lively rhythms of drums and dance, vibrant markets brimming with spices, textiles, and stories. Each country has its own unique flavor: the pyramids of Egypt whisper tales of ancient kings, the rainforests of Congo hide secrets of rare wildlife, and South Africa's vibrant cities buzz with innovation and culture.

As you read about Africa, picture yourself walking through a bustling souk, listening to the hypnotic beats of traditional drums, or watching the sunrise over the savannah as herds of animals graze peacefully. Africa is a land where history, nature, and vibrant traditions come together to create an unforgettable experience.

So buckle up! This is just the beginning of your adventure into the heart of Africa—a continent full of life, stories, and surprises waiting to be discovered. Let’s explore what makes Africa truly special, from its breathtaking landscapes to its incredible people and their extraordinary cultures.

The Spirit of Adventure and the Desert’s Mystique

Africa—a continent of contrasts and wonders, where nature’s raw beauty and ancient stories come alive. Imagine venturing into a world where the land sprawls endlessly in golden waves, where majestic animals roam free, and where the sky seems to stretch forever. This is the essence of Africa's wilderness, captured in two iconic symbols: the exhilarating safari and the mysterious Sahara Desert.

Together, they form the heartbeat of Africa—an energetic pulse of wildlife adventure and timeless desert allure. Whether you’re watching lions rest under acacia trees, listening to the wild symphony of birds, or gazing at sand dunes that seem to touch the sky, Africa’s soul is alive in its unspoiled landscapes and vibrant cultures.

The Safari: Africa’s Wildlife Wonderland

Origins and Meaning of the Safari

The word "safari" comes from Swahili, meaning “journey” or “expedition.” In Africa, a safari is more than just a trip—it's an immersive adventure into the natural world. For centuries, explorers, traders, and indigenous peoples have used safaris to hunt, observe, and understand the wild animals that share their habitat.

Today, safaris are about conservation, education, and experiencing nature up close. They’re journeys into the heart of Africa’s great national parks and wildlife reserves, where the big animals still roam freely and life unfolds on a majestic scale.

The Big Five and Wildlife Diversity

No safari would be complete without the famous "Big Five"—lion, elephant, buffalo, leopard, and rhinoceros. These creatures, once hunted by hunters and now protected for their beauty and ecological importance, symbolize the thrill of the wilderness.

But beyond the Big Five, Africa is a sanctuary for countless species:

- **Giraffes**, with their towering necks and gentle gaze
- **Hippopotamuses**, lounging in river waters
- **Zebras** packing the plains with black-and-white stripes
- **Cheetahs**, the fastest land animals with sleek, aerodynamic bodies
- **Hyenas**, curious scavengers with complex social structures
- **Birds**, from vibrant kingfishers to towering ostriches

The diversity of wildlife varies from region to region, each offering a unique perspective on the continent's rich ecosystems.

Iconic Safari Destinations

- **Serengeti National Park (Tanzania):** The legendary plains where the annual wildebeest migration takes place—millions of animals moving in an incredible display of survival and endurance.
- **Masai Mara (Kenya):** Part of the Serengeti ecosystem, known for abundant wildlife and the chance to witness the Great Migration.
- **Kruger National Park (South Africa):** One of Africa's largest reserves, with a wide variety of animals and luxury safari lodges.
- **Etosha National Park (Namibia):** Famous for its salt pans and waterholes that attract hordes of animals during the dry season.
- **Chobe National Park (Botswana):** Known for its massive elephant herds and river safaris.

Safari Experiences

Modern safaris range from guided game drives and walking safaris to hot air balloon rides over the plains. Many lodges offer eco-friendly accommodations, blending luxury with conservation. As you observe animals in their natural habitat, you gain a profound appreciation for the delicate balance of life in the wild.

The Sahara Desert: The Timeless Sea of Sand

The Great Desert's Origins and Mystique

Stretching over 3.6 million square miles, the Sahara is the largest hot desert in the world. Its name, derived from the Arabic word "ṣaḥrā’" meaning “desert,” captures the endless expanse of golden dunes, rocky plateaus, and sparse vegetation.

The Sahara’s history stretches back millions of years—the sands hold stories of ancient lakes, lost civilizations, and shifting climates. Once a lush green landscape teeming with life, it transformed into the arid desert we see today due to climatic changes.

Unique Geography and Climate

The Sahara features:

- **Vast Dunes:** Towering sand dunes like the Erg Chebbi in Morocco and the Grand Dune of Tato in Niger, some reaching heights over 500 feet.
- **Plateaus and Rock Formations:** The Tassili n'Ajjer in Algeria is famous for prehistoric rock paintings.
- **Oases:** Patches of life-sustaining water, like the oases of Ghadames and Siwa, vital for local communities.

The Safari Experience: From Dawn to Dusk

Embarking on a safari is more than just spotting animals; it’s an immersive journey through the rhythms of wilderness—an adventure that awakens all your senses and deepens your connection to nature.

Early Mornings: The Awakening of the Wild

The day begins before sunrise. The air is still cool, and there's a sense of quiet anticipation. Guided by experienced trackers and rangers, you set out into the wilderness as the first light of dawn spills across the horizon. The sky is painted in shades of gold, pink, and orange, creating a stunning backdrop for wildlife to start their daily routines.

At this magical hour, the bush comes alive with sound. The melodious calls of various bird species—ka-ka-ka of hornbills, the haunting hoot of owls, and the trumpeting of elephants—form a natural symphony that signals the dawn of a new day. During these early drives, you might spot a pride of lions lazily resting or catch sight of a herd of elephants making their way to water. The feeling of being so close to nature's most majestic creatures is humbling and awe-inspiring.

Daytime Adventures: The Heart of the Day

As the sun rises higher, the bush warms up, and many animals become more active. Predators such as lions and leopards often hunt during the cooler hours of the day—silent stalks and stealthy movements are a testament to their incredible hunting skills.

During the scorching midday hours, wildlife tends to seek shade and rest. This is an ideal time for safari guides to share stories about animal behaviour, ecosystems, and conservation efforts. Many lodges and camps offer relaxing interludes—perhaps a refreshing drink or a leisurely lunch—before heading out again in the late afternoon.

For explorers, this phase of the safari provides opportunities to observe animals in their natural habitat: watching a herd of elephants drink at a watering hole, a troop of baboons grooming each other, or a cheetah resting in the shade. The landscape—the sprawling plains, acacia trees, riverbeds, and rocky outcrops—comes alive with activity and sounds.

Evening and Night Safaris: The Bush Comes Alive Again

As the sun begins to set, the bush transforms once more. The sky turns into spectacular hues of crimson and violet, signalling the transition from day to night.

Evening safaris are a special treat. Guided by spotlights and torches, you enter the darkness of the night—a world of mystery and hidden life. Predators like lions, leopards, and hyenas come into their hunting prime, stalking prey silently through the shadows. Sometimes, you'll witness the glow of eyes watching from the darkness, or hear the distant roar of a lion.

Night safaris offer an exciting chance to observe nocturnal animals—owl species, bush babies, civets, and owls—whose behaviours are rarely seen during daylight. The guides use special equipment to track and identify animals, revealing the secret life of the African night.

Connecting with the Wilderness

Throughout the day, from dawn to dusk, a safari isn't merely about spotting animals; it's about experiencing their world. It's about feeling the cool breeze on your face, hearing the rustling of leaves, smelling the dust and wildlife scents, and watching the landscape change with the shifting light.

Every moment on safari—whether it's a close encounter, a quiet pause watching a herd, or listening to the sounds after sunset—fills your soul with a sense of wonder and respect for these incredible ecosystems.

Colors of Marrakech: Morocco's Magic

Introduction: A Land of Mystique and Majesty

Imagine a place where the ancient and modern collide—a land filled with rich colors, intoxicating smells, rhythmic music, and endless stories. Welcome to Morocco, a country that dances to its own tune, woven with history, culture, and a vibrant spirit that captivates every traveller's heart.

From the bustling souks of Marrakesh, the majestic sands of the Sahara, to the imperial palaces of Fez, and the coastal charm of Casablanca, Morocco is a mosaic of diverse landscapes and cultures. Every city, village, and mountain offers something magical, inviting explorers to get lost in a whirlwind of sensory delights and timeless beauty.

Marrakesh: The City of Lights and Colors

The Atmosphere of Marrakesh

Known as the "Red City" due to its striking ochre walls, Marrakesh is a kaleidoscope of sights, sounds, and smells. Its bustling markets (souks), towering mosques, and lively plazas create a vibrant tapestry of everyday life. The city's energetic atmosphere balances the tranquillity of its hidden gardens, grand palaces, and centuries-old traditions.

Walking through Jemaa el-Fna square, you are enveloped in a whirlwind of activity—street performers, snake charmers, storytellers, and food vendors all converge in a sensory festival. At sunset, the square transforms into a magical realm of lantern-lit stalls serving Moroccan mint tea, fragrant tagines, and sweet pastries.

The Souks and Markets

Marrakesh's souks are a labyrinth of narrow alleyways bursting with color and craftsmanship. Spices in vivid reds and yellows fill the air with aroma, while stalls display intricate textiles, beaded jewelry, leather slippers, and handcrafted lanterns. You can haggle with artisans over silver jewelry, buy a beautifully woven Berber rug, or simply marvel at the artistry of the woodcarving and metalwork.

Gardens and Palaces

- **Jardin Majorelle:** Once owned by Yves Saint Laurent, this lush, vibrant garden features shades of blue, exotic plants, and tranquil pools—an oasis amid the city's chaos.
- **Bahia Palace:** A stunning example of Moroccan architecture, with intricate tile work, lush courtyards, and ornate ceilings, reflecting the opulence of Moroccan history.
- **Saadian Tombs:** Rediscovered in 1917, these tombs are covered with elaborate mosaic tiles and offer insights into Morocco's imperial past.

The Medina's Tranquillity

Beyond the busy streets, Marrakesh hosts quiet riads (traditional guesthouses) with peaceful courtyards filled with orange trees, fountains, and aromatic herbs. Here, visitors can experience the serene side of Moroccan life, indulge in Hammams (traditional baths), or sip mint tea while watching the world go by.

Exploring Beyond Marrakesh: The Heart of Morocco

Casablanca: The Modern Marvel

Morocco's economic hub and largest city, Casablanca, offers a juxtaposition of tradition and modernity. Its famous **Hassan II Mosque**—one of the tallest religious structures in the world—is a testament to Moroccan craftsmanship and religious devotion. The city's skyline features sleek skyscrapers alongside historic art deco buildings.

Walking along the Corniche, visitors can enjoy beachfront cafes, shopping districts, and vibrant nightlife. Casablanca's blend of contemporary style with Moroccan soul makes it a dynamic stop for travelers seeking both history and modern comfort.

Fez: The Cultural and Spiritual Center

Known as Morocco's spiritual heart, Fez is home to one of the world's most authentic medinas—**Fes el-Bali**—a UNESCO World Heritage site. It's a maze of narrow, twisting streets, bustling markets, and ancient madrasas (Islamic schools).

Don't miss the **Al Quaraouiyine University**, founded in 859 CE—the oldest existing, continually operating degree-granting university in the world. The city's tanneries, with their vibrant dye pits, have been producing leather for centuries using traditional methods that are still fascinating to witness.

Chefchaouen: The Blue Pearl

Perched in the Rif Mountains, Chefchaouen is famous for its striking blue-painted streets and buildings. This small town exudes tranquillity, with narrow alleys, scenic mountain views, and artisanal shops selling woven textiles, ceramics, and local cheeses.

It's a photographer's paradise and a peaceful retreat from the busier cities.

Merzouga and the Sahara: The Golden Dunes

No trip to Morocco is complete without experiencing the awe-inspiring Sahara Desert. Nestled on the edge of the vast desert, the small town of **Merzouga** serves as the gateway to the towering sand dunes of Erg Chebbi—some of the most magnificent and iconic dunes in Africa, soaring over 150 meters high.

The Access Point to the Sahara

Merzouga offers an authentic gateway into the Sahara, where travelers can embark on unforgettable adventures—camel treks, hot air balloon rides, and overnight camping under the stars. The journey from

Merzouga into the dunes is a sensory experience: as the camels sway gently, the golden sands shimmer in the sunlight, and the silence of the desert wraps around you like a warm embrace.

Camel Trekking and Desert Camps

The classic way to explore the Sahara is on a camel. Guides lead you across rippling dunes, as the sun paints the landscape in fiery hues. Upon reaching a Bedouin-style desert camp, travelers are welcomed into cozy tents adorned with Moroccan textiles, lanterns, and carpets. Evening in the desert is magical—drinks are shared around a campfire while the sky fills with countless stars, far from any city lights.

Many camps organize traditional music and dance, allowing visitors to experience Moroccan culture firsthand. Waking up early to watch the sunrise over the dunes remains one of the most breathtaking moments, with endless landscapes turning shades of pink, orange, and gold.

The Mystique of the Desert

The Sahara is more than a barren wasteland; it is a symbol of endurance, mystery, and ancient cultures. Throughout history, it has been a vital trade route connecting sub-Saharan Africa with North Africa and beyond, famous for the camel caravans that carried gold, salt, and spices.

Today, the Sahara continues to fascinate travelers with its shifting sands and silent majesty. The Berber nomads, who have inhabited these lands for centuries, maintain traditional ways of life that connect them deeply to the desert environment.

Unique Landscapes and Hidden Treasures

Beyond the famous dunes, the Sahara hosts an array of natural wonders:

- **Oases** like **Tafilalet**, filled with date palms and lush greenery, providing vital water for local tribes and travelers.
- **Rock formations** such as the **Jebel Sagho**, once believed to be mystical sites and ancient settlement grounds.
- **Prehistoric Petroglyphs**: The Tassili n'Ajjer mountains in neighboring Algeria hold astonishing cave paintings and

carvings dating back thousands of years, depicting animals and human activities from prehistoric times.

The Cultural Heritage of the Desert

Bedouin tribes and nomads living in the Sahara maintain a rich heritage of storytelling, music, and traditional crafts. Their colorful tents, embroidered textiles, and exquisite jewelry reflect the artistry passed down through generations. Visitors often leave with a deeper appreciation for their resilience and adaptation to harsh desert life.

The Diverse Landscapes and Natural Beauty of Morocco

While Marrakech, Casablanca, Fez, Chefchaouen, and Merzouga introduce you to Morocco’s cultural identity, the country’s geography adds even more wonder:

- **The Atlas Mountains:** Stretching across Morocco, these rugged ranges offer breathtaking vistas, snow-capped peaks, and ancient kasbahs (fortresses) like Aït Benhaddou—a UNESCO World Heritage site featured in movies like *Gladiator* and *Game of Thrones*.
- **The Atlantic and Mediterranean Coasts:** Beautiful beaches like Essaouira, known for its laid-back vibe, fresh seafood, and windsurfing, contrast with the historic port city of Tangier—Morocco’s gateway to Europe.
- **Oases and River Valleys:** The lush Draa Valley and the fertile plains nourish traditional farming communities and date plantations, showcasing Morocco’s agricultural diversity.

Getting Immersed: Experiencing Moroccan Culture

Morocco isn't just a destination of sights—it's a cultural mosaic with traditions that engage all the senses:

- **Cuisine:** Moroccan food is an explosion of flavor—tagines slow-cooked with aromatic spices, couscous, fresh mint tea, and flaky pastries like baklava and msemen. Each dish tells a story of history and regional flavors.

- **Music and Dance:** Instruments like the *ouddoud* (a traditional string instrument), and *bendir*drums, fill the air with rhythmic tunes heard during festivals, weddings, and street performances.
- **Art and Craftsmanship:** From intricate tile work (zellige) to handwoven rugs, ceramics, and leather goods, Moroccan artisans create timeless pieces that beckon travelers to bring home a piece of the magic.

Conclusion: A Tapestry of Color, Culture, and Adventure

Morocco is a land of endless discovery—where ancient medinas hide bustling markets, timeless deserts stretch beyond the horizon, and majestic mountains guard centuries-old secrets. It is a country that invites travelers to immerse themselves in a kaleidoscope of sights, sounds, and flavors, each more captivating than the last.

From the vibrant pulse of Marrakech's lively streets to the serene blue alleys of Chefchaouen, from the grandeur of Casablanca's modern skyline to the silent beauty of the Sahara's dunes, Morocco offers a diverse palette of experiences. Its rich history, intertwined with Arab, Berber, African, and European influences, creates a cultural mosaic that is both ancient and vibrantly alive today.

Walking through its markets, you breathe in the aromatic spices and hear the melodies of street performers. Watching the sun set over the desert, you feel the timeless whisper of the sands, telling stories of nomads and explorers alike. And as you sip mint tea in a quiet riad or dance to traditional music around a campfire, you realize that Morocco's true magic lies in these moments of immersion—where tradition meets adventure and every corner reveals a new surprise.

In essence, Morocco is a living, breathing tapestry—a place that not only paints pictures in your mind but also leaves a deep imprint on your heart. It's a destination that stays with you long after you depart, urging you to return and continue exploring its endless wonders.

Wildlife Wonders: Serengeti and Beyond

Introduction: The Heartbeat of Africa's Wilderness

Imagine a vast expanse stretching as far as the eye can see, where the sky kisses endless plains of golden grass and the rhythm of life beats in every corner. Welcome to the Serengeti—a land where the wild reigns supreme, and nature's most spectacular stories unfold every single day. It is often called the "Serengeti Ecosystem," but truly, it is an entire universe—an orchestra of life, survival, and awe-inspiring beauty.

Beyond the Serengeti lie other incredible landscapes and parks—each a chapter in Africa's grand story of wildlife, adventure, and conservation. From the vast Maasai Mara of Kenya to the Okavango Delta of Botswana, and the Ngorongoro Crater in Tanzania, these pristine wilderness areas form a constellation of habitats where Africa's wild heart beats strong.

Together, they are the epitome of nature's resilience and splendour—places that draw explorers, conservationists, and dreamers, beckoning them with promises of unforgettable encounters. Here's a journey into these wild wonders that will leave you yearning to see, feel, and breathe their magic.

The Serengeti: A Theatre of Life and Death

The Great Migration: Nature's Epic Ballet

At the core of the Serengeti's fame is the unparalleled **Great Migration**—an awe-inspiring annual phenomenon that is one of the natural wonders of the world. Over two million wildebeest, zebras, and gazelles migrate across the plains in a perilous journey that spans hundreds of miles.

This migration isn't just about animals moving from point A to B; it's a high-stakes ballet of life and death. They cross crocodile-infested rivers, evade predators, and face unpredictable weather—all driven by instinct and the desire for food, water, and safety. Witnessing thousands of creatures rushing across the Mara River, with crocodiles lurking beneath and dust clouds rising behind them, is an adrenaline-fueled spectacle of survival and resilience.

The Big Five and More: A Rich Tapestry of Wildlife

While the world's focus often lands on the Big Five, the Serengeti hosts an astounding diversity of species:

- **Predators:** Lions, cheetahs, leopards, hyenas, and wild dogs—each mastering their domain. Lions pride themselves as the queens and kings of these plains, often resting under acacia trees after successful hunts.
- **Herbivores:** Giraffes with their elegant necks browsing tall trees, elephants wandering gracefully, and massive buffalo herds shaping the landscape.
- **Birds:** Over 500 species, from the striking Lilac-breasted Roller to the regal Secretary Bird, fill the skies with color and song.
- **Other Wildlife:** Hyraxes, jackals, baboons, crocodiles, and countless smaller creatures form a complex web of life that sustains the ecosystem.

The Landscape: A Painter's Dream

The Serengeti's rolling plains, dotted with acacia trees, rocky kopjes (outcrops), and seasonal rivers, create a mesmerizing backdrop for wildlife activity. The landscape is ever-changing—sometimes shimmering with the reflection of a rainstorm, sometimes shimmering in the setting sun—each moment capturing a different facet of the wilderness.

Beyond the Serengeti: Other Marvels of Africa

Maasai Mara, Kenya

Just across the border, the **Maasai Mara** shares most of the Serengeti's magic. It's renowned for breathtaking safaris, abundant wildlife, and the Maasai people's rich cultural heritage. The Mara's open grasslands and riverine forests host perhaps the most accessible and spectacular wildlife viewing experience, especially during the migration season.

Ngorongoro Crater: The Lost World

A UNESCO World Heritage site, the **Ngorongoro Crater** is an enormous volcanic caldera—a natural amphitheater teeming with game. It is estimated that over 25,000 animals inhabit this "Lost World," including black rhinos, lions, elephants, and flamingos. The crater's fertile floor acts like a natural wildlife sanctuary, where predators and prey coexist in breathtaking proximity.

Okavango Delta, Botswana: The Jewel of Waterlands

The **Okavango Delta** is a lush, sprawling inland delta, brimming with waterways, papyrus swamps, and islands. It offers a different kind of safari—a water-based adventure where elephants wade through channels, crocodiles bask on banks, and rare sitatunga antelopes drift through reeds. The delta's vibrant ecosystems support over 1,000 bird species, making it a birdwatcher's paradise.

The Heartbeat of the Wild: Ecological Interconnections

Beyond the breathtaking visual spectacles, Africa's wilderness is a finely tuned symphony of ecological interdependence. Every species, from the tiniest insects to the largest mammals, plays a vital role in maintaining balance. For instance, the acacia trees that dot the Serengeti are not just beautiful; they are essential to numerous herbivores, providing shelter and sustenance. In turn, the browsing giraffes help shape the canopy, ensuring the health of the ecosystem.

Predators help keep herbivore populations in check, preventing overgrazing that could devastate the grasslands. Birds and insects contribute to pollination and seed dispersal, ensuring plant life continues to thrive. Even the dust clouds kicked up by migrating herds serve to fertilize the soil, enriching the cycle of life.

This interconnectedness underscores why conservation efforts are so crucial—not just for individual species but for the entire web of life that sustains these ecosystems.

The Unseen and the Endangered: Conservation and Challenges

While the spectacle of wildlife can seem endless, the story behind it is one of resilience and ongoing struggle. Many species are under the threat of extinction, driven by poaching, habitat degradation, climate change, and human-wildlife conflict.

Rhinos, once abundant across Africa, have seen their numbers dwindle alarmingly due to illegal poaching for their horns. Effective anti-poaching patrols, community involvement, and international cooperation are vital to their survival.

Elephants, the gentle giants of the continent, face threats from poaching and habitat loss. However, extensive conservation programs, such as those in Amboseli National Park and the Chobe River region, have helped some herds recover, thanks to protective corridors and community engagement.

Big cat populations—lions and cheetahs—are shrinking due to competition with humans for land and resources, and increasing cases of disease. Many reserves now work to create wildlife corridors that connect fragmented habitats, allowing animals to migrate safely and maintain genetic diversity.

The Role of Tourists and Locals

Eco-tourism and responsible travel play instrumental roles in wildlife conservation. Visitors who choose sustainable safaris contribute funds towards park upkeep, community projects, and anti-poaching initiatives. Simultaneously, empowering local communities to benefit economically from conservation encourages their active participation in protecting their natural heritage.

Lesser-Known Marvels and Unique Adaptations

While the Big Five grab most headlines, Africa's wildlife is full of fascinating species and survival strategies that often go unnoticed:

- **Sitatunga Antelope:** An elusive swamp-dwelling antelope found in the Okavango and Congo Basin. Adapted to wet environments, they have splayed hooves to navigate marshy grounds and are masters of stealth—hard to spot unless you're lucky or highly skilled.
- **Secretary Bird:** A striking bird of prey, famous for its long legs and distinctive crest of feathers on its head. It hunts snakes and insects, striding confidently across grasslands.
- **Honey Badger:** Known for its fierce attitude and resilience, this small but formidable creature can fend off predators many times its size. Its ability to thrive in various environments, from deserts to forests, makes it a symbol of fierce independence.
- **Hornbill Birds:** With their large, curved beaks and vibrant plumage, hornbills are essential seed dispersers, helping maintain forest and woodland health in regions like the Congo and Uganda.

Unique Ecosystems and Microhabitats

Some of Africa's most captivating wildlife resides in specialized environments:

- **The Ngorongoro Crater's dense animal populations** thrive due to concentrated resources, making it one of the best places to observe predator-prey interactions up close.
- **The Kalahari Desert** hosts the elusive meerkats, resilient rear-guard animals that live in complex social groups, warning each other of danger with intricate alarm calls.

- **The Ethiopian Highlands** are home to the rare Ethiopian wolf, a species on the brink of extinction, resilient in the face of habitat encroachments.

The Role of Conservation Science and Local Communities

The future of Africa's wildlife hinges on innovative conservation science and the active involvement of local communities. Scientific research now employs satellite imagery, drone surveillance, and genetic studies to monitor animal movements, genetic health, and poaching hotspots.

Community-based conservation models have been successful in countries like Namibia, where land is jointly managed by governments and local tribes. These initiatives create a sense of ownership, pride, and responsibility among local people, leading to better protection of wildlife and habitats.

The Power of Education and Youth Engagement

Educating communities about the importance of biodiversity and fostering a new generation of conservation stewards is fundamental to ensuring the long-term survival of Africa's awe-inspiring wildlife. Knowledge empowers locals to see wildlife not merely as a resource to be exploited, but as a precious part of their cultural heritage and livelihood.

In many conservation success stories across Africa, youth education programs have played a pivotal role. Schools, community centers, and non-governmental organizations conduct awareness campaigns, nature clubs, and hands-on activities that instill a sense of pride and responsibility towards local ecosystems. Children learn about the intricate relationships among species and their habitats, understanding how their actions can either harm or help the natural world.

Youth as Advocates and Guardians

Young people, being the future custodians of Africa's wilderness, are increasingly involved in innovative conservation efforts. They participate in wildlife monitoring, anti-poaching patrols, and community projects that provide alternative livelihoods—such as eco-tourism, beekeeping, or sustainable farming—reducing dependency on activities that threaten wildlife.

For example, in Kenya's Maasai communities, youth groups have been instrumental in establishing community conservancies, where they actively manage and protect wildlife corridors, ensuring animals can migrate safely and their habitats are preserved. These initiatives not only boost local economies but also build a deep-rooted connection between the younger generation and their natural heritage.

The Impact of Education on Global Awareness

Beyond local communities, international awareness campaigns and educational programs foster a global appreciation for Africa's wildlife. Documentaries, social media, and virtual safaris bring the distant plains and elusive species into living rooms worldwide, inspiring millions to support conservation efforts—through donations, responsible travel, or advocacy.

The growing movement of eco-conscious travelers, especially millennials and Gen Z, is shifting the narrative from merely viewing safaris as entertainment to understanding their vital role in protecting biodiversity. Responsible tourism now emphasizes ethical wildlife encounters, community involvement, and the preservation of ecosystems, making education a catalyst for change.

In Summary

Education and youth engagement are powerful tools in safeguarding Africa's wild treasures. By sensitizing local communities, inspiring young conservationists, and raising global awareness, we forge a collective commitment to protecting these wonders for future generations. Because, ultimately, the future of Africa's wilderness depends not only on protected parks and reserves but also on the hearts and minds of those who will look after it tomorrow.

Historical Roots: Egypt and Ancient Civilizations

Introduction: The Cradle of Humanity's Greatest Legacies

There are few places on Earth that can rival the grandeur and mystery of Egypt—a land where history, myth, and archaeology converge to tell stories older than most civilizations. Known as the "Cradle of Civilization," Egypt has left an indelible mark on humanity through its groundbreaking innovations, magnificent monuments, and profound spiritual beliefs.

From the mighty Nile River nourishing the land to the towering pyramids that pierce the sky, Egypt's ancient legacy continues to fascinate, mystify, and inspire people across the globe. This is a story of kings and queens, gods and pharaohs, scribes and architects—the story of humanity's relentless pursuit of eternity.

The Nile: Life's Lifeline and the Birthplace of Egypt

The story of Egypt begins with the Nile River—its annual floods deposited fertile silt that transformed arid deserts into lush farmland. This life-giving waterway was more than just a physical resource; it was a divine force woven into Egyptian religion and mythology.

The Nile's predictable cycle enabled early Egyptians to develop complex irrigation systems, fostering one of the world's earliest civilizations around 3100 BCE. It served as a natural highway for trade, communication, and military conquest, creating a unifying backbone through millennia.

The Gift of the Nile and Early Settlements

Early settlements along the Nile, such as Horus and Nekhen, grew into powerful city-states. The unification of Upper and Lower Egypt under the first pharaoh, Narmer (or Menes), around 3100 BCE, marked the dawn of pharaonic civilisation.

The Age of Pharaohs: Building Eternity

The Formation of the Pharaoh Kingdom

Egypt's history is traditionally divided into three great dynastic periods, punctuated by intermediate eras of decline:

1. **The Old Kingdom (2686–2181 BCE):** The Age of the Pyramids
2. **The Middle Kingdom (2055–1650 BCE):** The Age of Stability and Artistic Flourishing
3. **The New Kingdom (1550–1070 BCE):** The Age of Empire and Mega-Construction

The Pyramids: Wonders of the World

The Old Kingdom is best remembered for the monumental pyramids—such as the Great Pyramid of Giza, built for Pharaoh Khufu. These architectural marvels are more than tombs; they are symbols of divine power and humanity's quest for immortality.

The construction techniques, including precise alignment with celestial bodies, vast limestone blocks, and complex labor organization, underscore the ingenuity of ancient Egypt. The Sphinx, guarding the pyramids' base, adds another layer of mystery—a colossal statue blending human intelligence and lion strength.

The Gods and Religious Beliefs

Ancient Egyptians believed in an eternal life governed by complex mythology and rituals. Gods like Ra (the sun god), Osiris (the god of the afterlife), Isis (the goddess of motherhood and magic), and Horus (the sky god) commanded reverence and shaped daily life.

Egyptian tombs and temples were adorned with hieroglyphic inscriptions—sacred symbols that recorded the deeds of pharaohs, spells for the afterlife, and astronomical knowledge.

Cultural Achievements and Innovations

Hieroglyphic Writing and Literature

The development of hieroglyphs around 3100 BCE marked a monumental leap in communication. This intricate writing system combined logograms, phonograms, and ideograms, capturing history, law, medicine, and poetry. The **Book of the Dead**, a collection of spells to guide souls through the afterlife, exemplifies the depth of Egyptian spiritual literature.

Art and Architecture

Egyptian art emphasized order, harmony, and symbolism. Wall paintings, sculptures, jewelry, and pottery reflected divine themes, royal power, and everyday life. The precise proportion and style established standards that persisted for thousands of years.

Science and Medicine

Egyptians excelled in medicine, with papyrus texts describing surgical techniques, anatomy, and treatments for various ailments. Astronomy played a critical role—aligning temples with solstices and lunar events, enabling them to create the 365-day calendar still used today.

The Decline and the Enduring Legacy

Conquests and Cultural Shifts

Egypt's grandeur waned during periods of internal strife, invasions, and foreign domination—Hyksos, Persians, Greeks under Alexander the Great, and eventually the Romans. Despite these upheavals, Egyptian culture persisted, adapting and influencing successive civilizations.

The Hyksos, a foreign Semitic people, invaded around 1650 BCE, introducing new technologies like horse-drawn chariots and bronze weaponry. Though they ruled Egypt for over a century, native Egyptian rulers eventually drove them out, instigating the Middle Kingdom, a time of renewed stability and artistic revival.

The Persians conquered Egypt in 525 BCE, incorporating it into their vast empire and leaving behind administrative innovations. Alexander the Great's invasion in 332 BCE marked the beginning of Hellenistic influence—hellenized Egyptian culture flourished, exemplified by the founding of the city of Alexandria by his general, Ptolemy.

The Ptolemaic Dynasty and the Alexandria Library

The Ptolemaic rulers blended Greek and Egyptian traditions, constructing magnificent temples, statues, and the legendary **Library of Alexandria**—the greatest center of learning in the ancient world. Scholars from all over the Mediterranean studied there, preserving countless texts on philosophy, science, astronomy, and literature. Though lost to time, the library symbolizes Egypt's role as a hub of knowledge and multicultural exchange.

The Roman Period and Decline

In 30 BCE, Egypt became a Roman province after the defeat of Cleopatra VII, symbolizing the end of the Pharaonic age. Under Roman rule, Egypt retained many of its traditions but gradually assimilated new influences—Christianity spread, and monumental temples transformed to Christian churches.

The decline was compounded by political instability, economic troubles, environmental changes, and invasions by Arab armies in the 7th century CE. The once-powerful Nile-based empire diminished into a region governed by foreign powers, yet Egypt's cultural core endured.

Egypt's Enduring Contributions to Humanity

Preservation of Knowledge and Cultural Identity

Despite centuries of upheaval, Egypt's contributions to world civilization remain monumental:

- **Language and Script:** Hieroglyphs, along with Demotic and Greek scripts, influenced the development of writing systems across the Mediterranean.
- **Art and Iconography:** Egyptian motifs—like the scarab beetle, the ankh symbol of life, and the lotus flower—became symbols of rebirth and eternity, influencing art for millennia.
- **Religion and Mythology:** Egyptian beliefs about the afterlife, divine kingship, and spiritual symbolism profoundly impacted later philosophies, including Christianity and Judaism, especially regarding concepts of resurrection and eternity.

Architectural and Engineering Marvels

Egypt's engineering feats—pyramids, temples, obelisks—remain awe-inspiring. They symbolize human potential, spiritual devotion, and scientific mastery. The pyramids' alignment with celestial bodies and their precise construction continue to baffle and inspire engineers and archaeologists alike.

In Modern Times: Ancient Egypt's Cultural Resurgence

Today, Egypt's legendary past attracts millions of tourists and researchers, fostering global appreciation. The discoveries of new tombs and artifacts still emerge, revealing more about life in the ancient Nile civilization.

Egyptian antiquities have become symbols of national pride and identity, inspiring art, literature, and education worldwide. Museums like Cairo's Egyptian Museum and the newly opened Grand Egyptian Museum showcase these treasures, igniting curiosity and reverence.

Conclusion: An Eternal Legacy

Egypt's story is not merely a chapter in history; it is a testament to humanity's enduring quest for knowledge, divine connection, and immortality. From the awe-inspiring pyramids and majestic temples to the scrolls of ancient wisdom, Egypt has gifted the world a legacy that transcends time.

The civilization that built pyramids for eternity, devised calendars, developed medicine and science, and crafted art of divine beauty continues to inspire us today. Its roots run deep into the very foundation of human achievement, reminding us that even in decline, the spirit of greatness can endure, evolve, and inspire countless generations to come.

In exploring Egypt's ancient past, we reconnect with our own roots—understanding that civilization is a continuous dance of innovation, resilience, and renewal—a timeless journey that makes Egypt's legacy immortal.

Journey Through Egypt: A Traveler's Guide to the Land of Mysteries

Imagine stepping into a land where history breathes through every stone, where the sands of time whisper secrets of ancient gods and kings. Egypt, with its mesmerizing pyramids, bustling markets, majestic temples, and timeless deserts, beckons explorers seeking to uncover the roots of civilization and experience a journey like no other.

If you're contemplating a trip to Egypt in its entirety, here's a curated guide—an itinerary that captures the essence of this incredible country, ensuring you don't miss its most iconic sites, hidden treasures, and cultural pulsations. Let's embark on a journey through Egypt, from the hustle of modern cities to the serene wonders of its ancient past.

Starting Point: Cairo – The Gateway to Egypt's Wonders

Your Egyptian adventure begins in **Cairo**, the pulsating capital that is a city of contrasts—where ancient artifacts stand side by side with modern skyscrapers. Cairo is the gateway to Egypt's history and cultural vibrancy.

Must-Visit Sites in Cairo:

- **The Egyptian Museum:** Home to thousands of artifacts, including the treasures of Tutankhamun, this museum is a treasure trove for history buffs. Don't miss the exquisite jewelry, statues, and mummies that tell stories from 5,000 years of history.

- **The Pyramids of Giza and the Sphinx:** No trip to Egypt is complete without visiting these iconic monuments. Stand in awe before the Great Pyramid—an architectural marvel that has mystified humanity for millennia. Explore the smaller pyramids and the enigmatic Sphinx, guarding secrets of ancient kings.
- **Coptic and Islamic Cairo:** Wander through historic neighborhoods, visit churches, mosques, and bustling markets. The Hanging Church and the Citadel of Saladin offer spiritual and architectural insights.

Practical Tips:

- Spend at least 2-3 days exploring Cairo.
- Take a guided tour or hire an Egyptologist for richer historical context.
- Beware of hustle in markets—haggle politely!

Luxor: The Open-Air Museum
From Cairo, take a short flight or an overnight train to **Luxor**, often called the world's greatest open-air museum.

Key Highlights:

- **The Valley of the Kings:** Hidden within the Theban Necropolis, it's the burial site of pharaohs like Tutankhamun, Ramses the Great, and Seti I. Marvel at intricately decorated tombs carved into the desert mountain.
- **Karnak Temple:** A sprawling complex dedicated to Amun-Ra, with colossal columns, obelisks, and sacred lake. It's a testament to the grandeur of ancient Egyptian religion.
- **Luxor Temple:** A stunning monument illuminated at night, where ancient ceremonies once took place.
- **Hatshepsut's Temple:** An architectural masterpiece nestled against the cliffs, honoring the female pharaoh.

Experience:

- Take a sunrise hot air balloon ride over Theban monuments for a breathtaking perspective.
- Wander through markets and sip tea in local cafes.

Aswan and Abu Simbel: Guardians of Nubian Heritage

From Luxor, travel south to **Aswan**, a city renowned for its tranquil Nile views and ancient monuments.

Must-See Attractions:

- **The Aswan High Dam:** An engineering marvel that controls the Nile's flow and provides electricity and irrigation.
- **Philae Temple:** Dedicated to Isis, this temple complex is set on an island, accessible by boat—a mystical site with beautiful river views.
- **Nubian Culture:** Visit colorful Nubian villages to experience vibrant traditions, crafts, and hospitality.

The Ultimate Highlight:

- **Abu Simbel Temples:** Carved into a cliffside by Ramses II, these colossal statues and temples are UNESCO World Heritage sites. The morning sun perfectly illuminates Ramses and his queens during specific times of the year—an awe-inspiring spectacle.

The Western Desert: Siwa Oasis and White Desert

Venture into Egypt's lesser-known northern deserts:

Siwa Oasis:

- A remote paradise with palm groves, mineral-rich springs, and ancient ruins.
- Explore the Oracle Temple of Amun, where Alexander the Great was declared a divine ruler.
- Experience Berber culture and traditions.

White Desert:

- A surreal landscape of chalk formations shaped by wind and time.
- Perfect for camping, stargazing, and discovering unique geological formations.

The Red Sea Coast: Relaxation and Marine Adventure

Finish your journey along Egypt's vibrant Red Sea coast, where crystal-clear waters and thriving coral reefs create a paradise for water lovers and relaxation seekers alike.

Sharm El-Sheikh and Hurghada

- **Snorkeling and Diving:** Among the top destinations globally, these resorts boast vibrant coral gardens, abundant marine life, and fascinating wrecks. Swim alongside schools of colorful fish, graceful manta rays, and even curious dolphins.
- **Sea Safaris and Glass-Bottom Boats:** For those less inclined to dive, these offer mesmerizing views of underwater worlds without getting wet.
- **Luxury Resorts and Spas:** Unwind in world-class hotels offering wellness treatments, private beaches, and spectacular views of the Red Sea.
- **Desert Excursions:** Explore the nearby Sinai Desert for quad biking, Bedouin camps, or stargazing under remarkably clear skies.

Marsa Alam and Dahab

- **Marsa Alam:** Known for its unspoiled reefs and peaceful ambiance, this area is perfect for eco-conscious travellers. Dive sites like Elphinstone Reef attract big pelagics, such as hammerhead sharks.
- **Dahab:** A laid-back alternative, famous for snorkelling at the Blue Hole, windsurfing, and relaxed cafes that line the beach.

Optional Add-On: Mount Sinai and Saint Catherine's Monastery
If you're craving a spiritual and physical challenge, consider visiting **Mount Sinai**—believed to be the mountain where Moses received the Ten Commandments. Climb at sunset for an unforgettable experience, and explore **Saint Catherine's Monastery**, one of the oldest working Christian monasteries in the world, filled with icons, manuscripts, and a peaceful ambiance.

Final Thoughts: An Egyptian Odyssey
This journey through Egypt is crafted to blend history, culture, adventure, and tranquillity into an unforgettable tapestry. Whether strolling amid the ancient stones of the Pyramids, drifting down the Nile on a traditional felucca, exploring timeless temples, or relaxing along the azure shores of the Red Sea, Egypt offers a spectrum of experiences that linger long after the journey ends.

Practical Tips for Your Trip:

- **Travel Logistics:** Domestic flights between Cairo, Luxor, Aswan, and coastal destinations save time. Trains and buses are available for budget travel.
- **Best Time to Visit:** October to April offers cooler, more comfortable weather—ideal for exploring archaeological sites and enjoying outdoor activities.
- **Cultural Respect:** Dress modestly, especially when visiting religious sites, and respect local customs.
- **Guided Tours:** Consider hiring licensed guides for historical sites—they enrich the experience with insights and anecdotes.
- **Responsible Tourism:** Support local artisans, stay in eco-friendly accommodations, and respect wildlife and heritage sites.

Why Egypt?

From the enigmatic face of the Sphinx to the bustling Islamic markets, the ancient relics to the serene waters of the Red Sea—Egypt is a living museum, a spiritual crossroads, and an adventure of a lifetime. It's a destination that feeds the soul with stories of human achievement and spiritual wonder, inviting travelers to walk in the footsteps of pharaohs and explorers alike.

Are you ready to unlock Egypt's ancient secrets and create your own timeless story?

Asia

India's Mystique – A Canvas of Timeless Footprints

Introduction: A Land Where Time and Spirit Intertwine

Imagine a land where every sunrise awakens a symphony of colors—where sacred rivers carve through ancient cities, and each monument whispers stories of gods, kings, and sages. Welcome to **India**, a colossal canvas painted with the brushstrokes of history, spirituality, and vibrant cultures. It is no exaggeration to call India the world's living museum—an intricate mosaic where the past and present coexist in harmonious vibrance.

India's story is etched into every stone, echoed in every prayer, and felt in every heartbeat of its people. It is a realm where the footprints of the oldest civilizations have left indelible marks—marks that have shaped the soul of humanity itself.

The Cradle of Civilizations: The Ancient Footprints

The Indus Valley: The Dawn of Urban Life

India's journey into history begins over 5,000 years ago with the **Indus Valley Civilization**—one of the world's earliest urban societies. Cities like **Mohenjo-daro** and **Harappa** were marvels of planning and engineering, featuring sophisticated drainage, grid-like streets, and impressive baths.

These cities reflected a civilization that valued cleanliness, trade, and social organization. Although their script remains undeciphered, artifacts and seals reveal a culture rich in artistry, spirituality, and commerce. The Indus Valley left behind a legacy of urban planning that predates many later civilizations.

The Vedic Age and the Birth of Spirituality

Following the decline of the Indus Valley, the Vedic period emerged around 1500 BCE, bringing forward the spiritual texts known as the **Vedas**—compositions of hymns, philosophies, and rituals that form the foundation of Hinduism.

During this era, sacred rivers like the Ganges and Yamuna gained divine status, and the establishment of the caste system shaped social hierarchy. The Vedic sages and their hymns laid the spiritual groundwork for India's enduring religious traditions.

The Age of Kingdoms and Empires

The Mauryan Empire (c. 322–185 BCE): The First Unified Empire

Under the rule of **Chandragupta Maurya** and his grandson **Ashoka**, India became a unified political entity. Ashoka's conversion to Buddhism and his edicts promoting non-violence, tolerance, and Dharma (righteousness) transformed the spiritual and political fabric of India.

His capital at **Patna** became a hub of Buddhist learning, and **Sarnath**, where Buddha delivered his first sermon, remains a symbol of spiritual awakening.

The Gupta Dynasty (c. 320–550 CE): The Golden Age of Culture

This era marked a renaissance in arts, sciences, mathematics, and literature. India produced monumental literary works like the **Mahabharata** and **Ramayana**, as well as advancements such as zero (mathematics), Ayurveda (medicine), and intricate temple architecture. Artistic masterpieces like the **Ajanta Caves** murals and **Kandariya**

Mahadev Temple showcase spiritual devotion through spectacular sculptures and carvings.

The Chola, Vijayanagara, and Medieval Kingdoms

Southern India's powerful dynasties, like the Cholas, built grand temples with intricate Dravidian architecture, engravings, and bronze sculptures—still revered today.

The medieval period saw the rise of Islamic sultanates, notably the Mughals—whose rule brought a fusion of Persian, Turkic, and Indian cultures. The **Taj Mahal**, built by Shah Jahan, epitomizes this synthesis—a symbol of love etched in marble, blending Islamic and Indian architectural virtues.

India's Spiritual and Cultural Footprints

The Sacred Rivers and Pilgrimage Sites

India's rivers are more than water—they are spiritual arteries. The **Ganges**, considered the most sacred, flows through cities like Varanasi, where millions come to purify their souls. Pilgrimages to **Kedarnath**, **Rishikesh**, and **Haridwar** are spiritual journeys connecting devotees with divine forces.

The Temples and Monasteries

From the towering spires of **Khajuraho** with their exquisite sculptures to the serene **Golden Temple** of Amritsar, India's architecture is a tribute to divine artistry. The **Ajanta** and **Ellora Caves** are cliff-carved monasteries filled with murals and sculptures depicting the lives of Buddha and Bodhisattvas.

Festivals and Traditions

India's festivals are an exuberant expression of its spiritual, cultural, and seasonal diversity. These celebrations, often rooted in ancient customs, are vibrant spectacles that bring communities together, showing the deep connection between people, nature, and the divine.

Diwali (Deepavali): Known as the Festival of Lights, Diwali marks the victory of good over evil and light over darkness. Homes are decorated with oil lamps, candles, and colorful rangoli designs. Fireworks illuminate the night sky, while families offer prayers to Lakshmi, the goddess of wealth, seeking prosperity and happiness.

Holi: The Festival of Colors celebrates the arrival of spring and love. People throw bright powders and water, dance to lively music, and share sweets. The exuberance of Holi symbolizes renewal, unity, and the victory of devotion over prejudice.

Durga Puja: Celebrated predominantly in Bengal, this festival honors the goddess Durga's victory over the buffalo demon Mahishasura. Elaborate pandals (temporary structures) house intricately carved idols, accompanied by music, dance, and rituals that last for days.

Raksha Bandhan: A celebration of sisterly bonds, where sisters tie a protective thread around brothers' wrists, symbolizing love and protection. Brothers, in return, give gifts and promise to safeguard their sisters.

Onam, Pongal, Navratri, Ganesh Chaturthi: Numerous regional festivals celebrate harvests, deities, legends, and mythological stories, each with distinctive rituals, music, dance, and cuisine.

Wedding Traditions: Indian weddings are grand affairs combining music, dance, elaborate rituals, and vibrant attire. Each region boasts unique customs—like the Punjabi *Baraat*, Tamil *Kalyanam*, or Bengali *Saat Paak*—woven into a tapestry of cultural identity.

Culinary Heritage: Festivals are also marked by specific foods—sweet mouthfuls like ladoo, barfi, and jalebi, or savory delicacies like biryani, dosas, and chaat. Sharing meals during festivals reinforces community bonds.

Traditional Arts and Crafts: Music (classical, folk, Bollywood), dance (bharatnatyam, kathak, odissi), clothing (saris, dhotis, sherwanis), and handicrafts (textiles, jewelry, pottery, woodwork) are integral parts of India's identity, passed down through generations.

The Spiritual Mosaic: A Living Heritage

India's mystical aura is rooted in its spiritual diversity. It is the birthplace of Hinduism, Buddhism, Jainism, and Sikhism—faiths that have shaped philosophical thought and daily life.

The spiritual landscape includes serene monasteries in Ladakh, bustling temples in Kashi (Varanasi), serene Buddhist stupas in Sikkim, and gurudwaras echoing with hymns. Pilgrims journey for salvation, enlightenment, or simple devotion—a testament to India's profound spiritual vibrancy.

India's Cultural Footprint on the World

Indian art, philosophy, cuisine, and spiritual practices have profoundly influenced regions across Southeast Asia, Central Asia, and beyond. Concepts like yoga and Ayurveda, now embraced worldwide, originate in India's ancient holistic worldview.

The richness of India's cultural and spiritual footprint continues to inspire artists, scholars, and travelers globally, making it a living, breathing testament to millennia of human creativity, faith, and resilience.

In Conclusion: Embarking on Your Indian Odyssey

From its ancient footprints carved in stone to dynamic festivals that light up the modern landscape, India remains an enchanting land where history is alive in every corner. Travelers who walk its sacred temples, dance in its colorful festivals, and indulge in its diverse cuisine carry home stories etched with the magic of an eternal civilization.

India invites you not just to observe its heritage but to immerse yourself in its vibrant, living tradition—a journey of discovery that promises awakening, wonder, and transformation.

An Enchanting 15-Day Odyssey Through India's Heart, Heritage, and Soul

Welcome, seeker of marvels, to a land where every dawn whispers stories of eternity, every city echoes the footsteps of gods and kings, and every moment offers a portal into the divine. India is not merely

a destination; it is an experience—a symphony of colors, aromas, textures, and timeless traditions that stir the soul and ignite the spirit.

Embark on this extraordinary journey—a thoughtfully curated voyage through India's most iconic, most mystical, and most soul-stirring destinations. This is your path to unravel the grand tapestry of India's past, present, and future, woven with threads of ancient wisdom, vibrant festivals, architectural marvels, and the warm embrace of its diverse cultures.

Days 1-3: Delhi — The Heartbeat of India's Legacy

Begin your sojourn in **Delhi**, the pulsating capital where history breathes through monuments and the streets vibrate with hustle and spirit. Witness the majestic **Qutub Minar**, marvel at the grandeur of **Humayun's Tomb**, and lose yourself in the bustling chaos of **Chandni Chowk**, a riot of spices, silk, and stories. At sunset, stand before the formidable **India Gate**, a solemn reminder of sacrifice, and soak in the regal charm of **Rashtrapati Bhavan** and **Lodhi Gardens**—verdant treasures where history whispers softly.

Must-do: Take a rickshaw ride through Old Delhi's labyrinthine lanes, taste street-side parathas, and pay homage at the serene **Lotus Temple**—a symbol of unity in diversity.

Days 4-6: Agra & Fatehpur Sikri — The Marvels of Mughal Grandeur

Journey to **Agra**, the city of eternal love. Gaze upon the ethereal glow of the **Taj Mahal**, a celestial monument of passion and poetry carved in white marble, standing as a testament to love that defies time. Explore the formidable **Agra Fort**, a formidable citadel that overlooks the Yamuna River, echoing tales of power and splendor.

Venture next into **Fatehpur Sikri**, the beautifully preserved remains of Emperor Akbar's grand city, with its intricately carved palaces and courtyards imbued with spiritual mysticism.

Must-do: Witness dawn's first light over the Taj Mahal, a spectacle of hues and harmony, and indulge in Mughlai delicacies that tantalize the senses.

Days 7-9: Jaipur — The Pink City of Palaces and Patios
Travel into Rajasthan's jewel—the **Pink City**, **Jaipur**, where regal forts, sprawling palaces, and bustling bazaars narrate stories of Rajput valor and royal opulence. Wander through the **Amber Fort**, ride an elephant up to its ramparts, and admire the intricate mirror work inside **Hawa Mahal**, the "Palace of Winds." Stroll through the lively **Johari Bazaar**, bursting with textiles, jewelry, and folk crafts.

Must-do: Experience a royal dinner under the stars at a heritage haveli, and catch the sunset over **Jal Mahal**, a palace floating serenely in Man Sagar Lake.

Days 10-12: Varanasi — The Spiritual Heart of India
Venture to **Varanasi**, the city where spirituality and eternity intertwine amid the sacred ghats along the Ganges River. Witness mesmerizing sunrise boat rides that reveal the city's soul—devotees bathing in holy waters, priests performing ancient rites, and pilgrims offering prayers that echo through time.

Visit the sacred **Kashi Vishwanath Temple** and sit in silent contemplation amidst timeless rituals. Experience the profound energy of the **Ganga Aarti** at Dashashwamedh Ghat, where chants, cymbals, and flickering lamps create a divine spectacle.

Must-do: Attend sunrise and sunset ceremonies, and immerse yourself in the spiritual ambiance—an experience that transcends words.

Days 13-15: Khajuraho & Orchha — The Temples of Desire and Devotion
Journey to the mystical land of Khajuraho, where centuries-old temples stand as silent testaments to the grandeur of Indian artistry and spirituality. These UNESCO World Heritage sites are not merely monuments—they are lyrical expressions of love, life, and divine ecstasy woven into intricate stone carvings that beguile the senses.

Khajuraho's temples, built between 950 and 1050 CE by the Chandela dynasty, explode in a riot of sculptures—each telling stories of gods and mortals, celestial dancers, and mystical animals. As you wander through these ornate corridors and courtyards, you

are transported into a universe where flesh and spirit dance in harmony, celebrating human joy and divine harmony in a tapestry of sensuality and spirituality.

Must-do: Stand in silent awe as the sun filters through the richly carved exteriors, casting intricate shadows—feel the pulse of history beating beneath your feet. Capture the iconic **Kamasutra** sculptures—silent whisperers of love's divine expression carved in stone.

From the divine sculptures of Khajuraho, venture to the tranquil town of Orchha, nestled in the heart of Madhya Pradesh. The city appears as a regal fairy-tale, with ancient palaces, grand temples, and chhatris (cenotaphs) that seem to rise from the lush Banarasi River banks—each whispering stories of kings and courtiers long gone but never forgotten.

Orchha's royal fort complex, with its labyrinthine courtyards and exquisite cenotaphs dedicated to Mughal and Bundela rulers, offers a surreal glimpse into India's regal past. The Raja Ram Temple, with its towering spires and intricate facade, stands as a beacon of faith and artistic mastery. As the evening falls, the river shimmers with reflected twilight, and the air is filled with the lingering spirit of bygone grandeur.

Must-do: Take a boat ride on the Betwa River at sunset, witnessing the silhouettes of palaces and temples illuminated by a soft golden glow. Capture the essence of regal tranquility that has inspired poets and painters throughout centuries.

Final Touch of Majesty

This enchanting stretch of your India journey—where sensual artistry meets spiritual ascent—reminds us that human passions and divine devotion are intertwined threads in the grand fabric of Indian culture. Khajuraho and Orchha are more than mere stops; they are portals to understanding the complex, sacred, and sensuous soul of India—a land that venerates love and spirituality as eternal companions.

Embrace these sacred spaces, and allow their history, art, and mysticism to seep into your senses. Let them inspire moments of reflection and joy, of longing and awe, as you continue your voyage through this mesmerizing country.

And Yet, India's Tapestry Is Ever-Expanding

As the sun rises and sets over this luminous land, one cannot help but feel a gentle ache—a longing to explore more, to immerse deeper into the endless mosaic of India's soul. For in these 15 days, you will taste its nectar, breathe its essence, and witness flashes of its infinite beauty. But know this, with a heart full of wonder and eyes brimming with dreams: India is a universe unto itself—a sprawling, vibrant canvas that defies complete capture in mere days.

India's hues are too rich, its stories too profound, its people too warm, and its traditions too deep-rooted for a single journey. It is a symphony that plays on endlessly, inviting you to listen more closely and discover your own harmony within its layers. The bustling streets of Delhi, the regal silence of Varanasi, the poetic symmetries of Khajuraho, the spiritual heights of the Himalayas—each landscape, each temple, each smile adds another thread to the grand fabric of your experience.

So let your soul be comforted by the knowledge that this is only a beginning. The colors of India—its festivals, its markets, its spiritual sanctuaries, its rustic villages, and majestic hills—are a ceaseless river of life. An invitation to return, again and again, to lose and find oneself anew in its timeless embrace.

Because truly, India's beauty is an eternal story—written across the skies, etched in stone, woven into the heart. And every visitor becomes a part of its grand, ongoing masterpiece—a song sung softly, yet ceaselessly, through the ages.

Thailand's Tranquility: A Land of Temples and Traditions

Step into Thailand, a land where the sacred whispers softly in every corner—where ancient temples rise gracefully amidst lush greenery, and the gentle rhythm of life soothes the soul. Here, spirituality and serenity blend seamlessly, forming a sanctuary of calm and inner peace that beckons the weary heart to pause, breathe, and reflect.

Thailand is a place where tradition is not merely preserved but celebrated with reverence, where each temple stands as a symbol of devotion, and every festival is an expression of deep-rooted faith and joy. From the shimmering gold spires of Bangkok's glittering Buddhist monasteries to the quiet, sacred groves of Chiang Mai, the country's spiritual landscape is a breathtaking tapestry of history, art, and spirituality.

Temples of Tranquility: Guardians of the Spirit

Thailand's temples, or "wats," are more than architectural masterpieces—they are living streets of meditation and divine connection. Their ornate rooftops, glittering with gold leaf, and intricate carvings tell stories of enlightenment, compassion, and transcendence.

- **Wat Arun**, nestled along the Chao Phraya River, glows like a jewel at sunset, its spires reaching skyward—an icon of renewal and hope.
- **Wat Phra Kaew** in Bangkok houses the revered Emerald Buddha, an embodiment of spiritual grace and royal dignity, watched over by centuries of monks and pilgrims.
- **Wat Doi Suthep** in Chiang Mai perches high on a mountain, providing panoramic views of the lush landscape while offering silent refuge for seekers of serenity.

- **The temples of Ayutthaya**, UNESCO World Heritage sites, reveal the grandeur of an ancient kingdom, with towering ruins that whisper tales of a glorious past.

Must-do: Engage in silent meditation, participate in morning alms-giving, or simply sit in quiet contemplation within the sanctuaries—each moment an invitation to reconnect with your inner selves.

The Spirit of Tradition: Festivals, Art, and Daily Rituals

Thailand's culture glows with a luminous array of traditions that have endured through the ages:

- **Festivals** like **Songkran** (the water festival) erupt in a cascade of water battles, symbolizing cleansing and renewal, celebrated with over-the-top gaiety and kindness.
- **Loy Krathong**, where luminous lanterns drift gently into the night sky, embody hope and wishes rising to the heavens.
- **Thai Dance and Music**, with graceful movements and enchanting melodies, tell stories of myth, love, and divine grace—performed during cultural festivals and in sacred temples.

Handicrafts and arts—elaborate textiles, intricate silver jewelry, vibrant silk scarves, and delicate ceramics—are expressions of the nation's artistic soul.

The culinary delights, from fragrant pad thai to spicy green curry, share stories of community, hospitality, and the sacred art of sharing a meal.

The Culture of Care: Unmatched Service and Hospitality

Thailand's reputation as the "Land of Smiles" is no idle phrase. Its gracious hospitality, sincere warmth, and impeccable service define every encounter—from serene boutique hotels nestled in emerald hills to luxurious spa retreats that melt your worries away.

Hospitality here is an art—every gesture genuine, every experience crafted to soothe your spirit and enrich your journey. Thai hosts greet with open arms, their kindness reflecting the deep-rooted cultural virtues of *"Nam Jai"*—a selfless generosity that embodies the Thai identity.

Luxurious resorts, eco- retreats, and boutique hotels seamlessly blend modern comfort with traditional elegance, offering tranquil sanctuaries that synchronize with the country's peaceful essence.

Must-do: Indulge in a traditional Thai massage, participate in a quiet meditation session, or dine al fresco in a candlelit garden—each a step closer to experiencing genuine Thai grace.

The Enduring Charm

Thailand's temples and traditions are more than relics—they are living expressions of a serene philosophy that values harmony, mindfulness, and compassion. It's a country that invites you to slow down, embrace tranquillity, and immerse yourself in a rich heritage where every moment offers a sacred pause.

In Thailand, peace is not just a mental state; it's a way of life. It's a promise that amid the chaos of the modern world, a tranquil sanctuary awaits—ready to nurture your heart and renew your spirit.

Must-Visit Places in Thailand: A Tapestry of Wonders & Hidden Paradises

Thailand, the Land of Smiles, is a dazzling tapestry woven with vibrant cities, tranquil temples, lush jungles, and some of the most beautiful islands in the world. Each destination whispers its own story—stories of ancient kingdoms, spiritual awakening, and serene natural beauty. Whether you crave the lively buzz of Bangkok, the cultural richness of Chiang Mai, or the tranquil embrace of remote islands, Thailand offers something for every soul seeking wonder and renewal.

Iconic Destinations: The Classics That Define Thailand

Bangkok: The Urban Heartbeat

- **Grand Palace & Wat Phra Kaew:** Marvel at the opulent architecture and the Emerald Buddha—Thailand's sacred jewel.
- **Wat Arun:** The Temple of Dawn, spectacular at sunset with its towering spires.
- **Chatuchak Market:** A sprawling maze of stalls offering everything from vintage collectibles to street food.
- **Chao Phraya River:** Cruise along the river, soaking in cityscapes blending tradition and modernity.

Chiang Mai: The Cultural Nexus

- **Doi Suthep Temple:** Perched atop a mountain, offering panoramic views and spiritual serenity.

- **Old City Temples:** Wat Chedi Luang and Wat Phra Singh are masterpieces of Lanna architecture.
- **Night Bazaar:** A vibrant hub of crafts, street food, and lively performances.
- **Elephant Nature Park:** An ethical sanctuary where you can interact with gentle giants.

Sukhothai: The Cradle of Thai Civilization

- The ancient city with UNESCO-listed ruins of Thailand's first capital—no visit is complete without wandering among the restored temples and statues of Buddha dawn.

The Lush Islands and Coastal Escapes
Thailand's islands are legendary—each with distinctive charm, from bustling beaches to remote retreats. Below is the spectrum from the popular to the hidden gems that promise unforgettable experiences:

The Famous and Cherished

- **Phuket:** Thailand's largest island, famous for its vibrant nightlife, beautiful beaches like Patong, and luxury resorts.
- **Ko Phi Phi:** The iconic islands known for stunning limestone cliffs, crystal waters, and the movie-set scenery of **"The Beach"**.
- **Ko Samui:** A tropical paradise offering luxury resorts, waterfalls, and lively night markets.
- **Ko Lanta:** A quieter island with pristine beaches, coral reefs, and a laid-back vibe.

The Less Visited, Unique Paradises

- **Koh Yao Islands:** Nestled between Phuket and Krabi, these islands are perfect for tranquility, authentic fishing villages, and stunning views with fewer tourists.
- **Koh Mak:** A tiny, peaceful island with long, uncrowded beaches and excellent snorkeling—ideal for those craving serenity.

- **Koh Tao:** Famous for superb diving and snorkeling, yet less commercial than Koh Samui or Phuket—offering vibrant marine life in unspoiled surroundings.
- **Koh Kood:** A true hidden gem boasting waterfalls and unspoiled beaches, away from the crowds, where nature unfolds in its purest form.
- **Koh Phayam:** With its untouched beaches, dense jungles, and rustic charm, this island is a jewel for eco-travelers seeking privacy and pristine beauty.

Off-the-Beaten-Path Islands for the Discerning Traveler

For those seeking a voyage into the extraordinary, these lesser-known islands promise a once-in-a-lifetime experience—diving into Thailand's raw, untouched beauty.

- **Koh Lipe:** Often called the "Maldives of Thailand," with turquoise waters, white sands, and exceptional coral reefs—yet remains a tranquil retreat.
- **Ko Hin Daeng & Ko Muang:** Remote islands renowned for world-class diving experiences, teeming with vibrant marine ecosystems.
- **Koh Tachai:** Part of the Similan Islands, famed for pristine beaches and rich underwater life, ideal for diving and snorkeling away from crowds.
- **Ko Rawi:** A serene and unspoiled island with coral reefs, mangroves, and a peaceful atmosphere—perfect for eco-conscious explorers.

The Essence of Travel in Thailand

While the well-trodden beaches and famous temples captivate millions, it is the quiet, hidden islands and pristine villages that etch the most memorable impressions on the soul. These lesser-visited spots offer authentic encounters—meeting local fishermen, experiencing untouched reefs, and basking in unspoiled sunsets that linger long in memory.

Whether you desire the buzz of vibrant markets and illuminated palaces or the whisper of waves against quiet sands—Thailand's vast canvas invites you to write your own story, vivid and unforgettable.

Cosmopolitan Cities: Tokyo's Pulse, the Vibrant Heartbeat of Asia's Future

In the heart of Asia, where tradition and innovation dance in an endless embrace, lies Tokyo—the pulsating metropolis that embodies the spirit of a nation at the forefront of progress while deeply rooted in its rich cultural tapestry. This city is a living, breathing phenomenon—a shimmering mosaic of ancient shrines, neon-lit streets, cutting-edge technology, and unwavering discipline.

Welcome to Tokyo, a city where every moment hums with purpose, passion, and a promise of discovery—an urban symphony played effortlessly on the strings of time, tradition, and futuristic possibility.

The Cultural Tapestry: Where Tradition Meets Tomorrow

Tokyo is a city of contrasts—a realm where centuries-old temples stand quietly amidst soaring skyscrapers, and centuries-old customs intertwine seamlessly with technological marvels.

- **Historic Gems:** Visit the serene **Senso-ji Temple** in Asakusa, Tokyo's oldest temple, its vibrant gate and incense-filled air evoking the city's spiritual core. Wander through traditional **kimono shops** and taste street foods at Nakamise-dori.
- **Modern Icons:** Marvel at the massive **Tokyo Tower** or the **Tokyo Skytree**, offering panoramic views that stretch across the skyline, blending beauty with technical mastery.
- **Artistic Expressions:** Explore sleek art galleries, futuristic design districts like **Omotesando**, and the quirky, colorful streets of **Harajuku**, where fashion and self-expression reign supreme.

Must-do: At night, attend a traditional **kabuki show** or experience a tea ceremony—a window into the city's reverence for art, patience, and poetic beauty.

Culinary Odyssey: A Feast of Flavors

Tokyo's culinary scene is a shimmering galaxy of flavors, from world-renowned sushi bars to cozy ramen shops and avant-garde cafes showcasing innovative gastronomy.

- Dine at a **sushi conveyor belt** or a **Michelin-starred kaiseki** restaurant—each offering artistry in taste and presentation.
- Indulge in **street food:** Takoyaki (octopus balls), tempura, yakitori (grilled skewers)—culinary traditions handed down through generations.
- Explore **depachika** (department store food halls)—a feast for the senses with hundreds of delicacies waiting to be sampled.
- Don't miss the **matcha** desserts and wagashi (Japanese sweets), crafted with delicate precision and serving as edible poetry.

Must-do: Participate in a Japanese cooking class, learning the secrets of perfect sushi or tempura, immersing yourself in Japan's meticulous approach to craft and flavor.

Impeccable Service and Timeliness: The Japanese Way

One of Japan's most renowned qualities is its relentless commitment to excellence and punctuality. In Tokyo's service culture, every gesture reflects a dedication to perfection—a quiet discipline that permeates daily life.

- **Unwavering punctuality:** Trains arrive and depart with astonishing accuracy—within seconds of their scheduled times. Your train, bus, and flight experiences will almost always be seamless, reliable, and stress-free.

- **Politeness and respect:** From smiling staff in shops to attentive hotel service, the courteous demeanour of the Japanese creates a welcoming, calming atmosphere.
- **Attention to detail:** Whether it's the pristine cleanliness of the streets, the meticulous presentation of meals, or the thoughtful packaging of goods, Tokyo's service industry elevates everyday acts into a form of art.

Must-do: Respect the polite bow—an act that encapsulates Japan's core value of humility, humility that transforms simple interactions into heartfelt exchanges.

The Travel Potential: A City of Endless Discovery

Tokyo is a city that offers endless possibilities for exploration and adventure.

- **Neon-lit districts:** Discover the electric energy of **Shibuya Crossing**, the busiest pedestrian intersection in the world, and explore its countless shops, cafes, and entertainment venues.
- **Shopping:** Indulge in high fashion at **Ginza**, quirky souvenirs in **Akihabara** (the paradise for anime and electronics fans), or vintage finds in **Shimokitazawa**.
- **Nature amidst the city:** Escape to **Ueno Park** or the **Imperial Palace Gardens** for moments of tranquility amid urban life.
- **Day trips:** Venture to **Mount Fuji** with its iconic snow-capped summit, or visit historic towns like **Kamakura** with its giant Buddha statue and peaceful temples.

Must-do: Experience **Odaiba**, a futuristic entertainment district on an artificial island, with marvels like the **TeamLab Borderless** digital art museum or relaxing on a seaside promenade gazing at Tokyo's skyline.

In Summary: The City of Dreams and Discipline

Tokyo stands as a luminous testament to what relentless innovation, unwavering discipline, and deep-rooted tradition can create—an awe-inspiring metropolis where every moment invites discovery and every corner whispers stories of progress and preservation. It is a city that seamlessly marries the ancient with the ultramodern, where lantern-lit shrines coexist with neon-lit skyscrapers, and where the humble act of bowing embodies humility and respect in a culture defined by meticulous care.

Tokyo's pulse beats with a quiet rhythm—one that echoes in the punctual cadence of its trains, blooms in the artistry of its cuisine, and vibrates in the energy of its bustling streets. It is a city that awakens the senses, nurtures the soul, and inspires dreams—where the future is being written in the ink of tradition and innovation.

For the traveler seeking a place that challenges perceptions and elevates spirits, Tokyo offers an endless banquet—each experience richer than the last, each dawn a promise of new wonders. It is, without doubt, a city that leaves an indelible mark—a dazzling jewel in the crown of Asia's vibrant mosaic.

The Cities to Discover: Beyond Tokyo's Skyline

While Tokyo dazzles with its blend of old-world charm and future-forward design, Japan's other cities beckon with their own stories, flavors, and landscapes:

Osaka: The Kitchen of Japan

Famous for its hearty street food, lively atmosphere, and warm friendliness, Osaka is the nation's culinary capital. Stroll through **Dotonbori**, a vibrant entertainment district illuminated by neon signs and offering specialties like takoyaki (octopus balls) and okonomiyaki (savory pancake). Visit **Osaka Castle** for a glimpse into samurai history, and explore the universe of Osaka Aquarium Kaiyukan—one of the largest and most impressive aquariums in the world.

Kyoto: The Heart of Tradition

Step into a world where centuries-old temples, serene tea houses, and historic streets evoke a bygone era. Visit the majestic **Kinkaku-ji** (Golden Pavilion), wander through the enchanting **Arashiyama Bamboo Grove**, and participate in a traditional tea ceremony. Kyoto's **Gion District** offers glimpses of geishas gliding along lantern-lit streets—living symbols of Japan's refined heritage.

Nagoya: The Industrial and Cultural Crossroads

A hub of innovation and tradition, Nagoya features the **Nagoya Castle**, Nissan's automotive marvels, and exquisite local cuisine—especially hitsumabushi (grilled eel). It's a city of contrasts, blending modernity with history.

Nagasaki: The City of Peace

Resilient and profound, Nagasaki's history as a trading port and its poignant role in WWII have shaped its peaceful yet powerful character. Visit the **Peace Park**, the **Atomic Bomb Museum**, and take a cable car up **Mount Inasa** for a breathtaking panoramic view of the city's beautifully lit nightscape.

Hiroshima: The City of Hope

From the peace parks to its vibrant street life, Hiroshima symbolizes resilience. The **Hiroshima Peace Memorial** (Genbaku Dome) and **Miyajima Island's floating torii gate** are essential stops.

The Magic of the Shinkansen and the Japanese Boarding Experience

Traveling in Japan is an experience of grace and punctuality. The **Shinkansen**, Japan's elegant bullet trains, are a testament to precision engineering and world-class service. Arriving at the station feels like stepping into a temple—quiet, orderly, and welcoming. Each station is a marvel of cleanliness and efficiency, meticulously designed to ensure comfort and ease for travelers.

Boarding the Shinkansen is an art form in itself—polished, punctual, and precise. Announcements are made softly in multiple languages, and staff members bow deeply as they guide you to your seat. The seating is comfortable, with large windows offering panoramic views of Japan's diverse landscapes—ranging from lush countryside and misty mountains to sprawling urban skylines.

As the train departs, the world outside silently shifts, passing by at breathtaking speed yet maintaining an almost meditative stillness within. The serene hum of the train, coupled with the impeccable service—from crisp bento boxes and steaming green tea to attentive staff—creates a journey as calming as it is exhilarating.

Seamless Connectivity and Reliability

The Shinkansen network links Tokyo with Osaka, Kyoto, Nagoya, Hiroshima, Fukuoka, and beyond, offering travelers the freedom to explore multiple regions with utmost ease. With **ever-accurate schedules**—trains arrive and depart within seconds of their listed times—your travel plans are guaranteed to flow smoothly.

Luggage forwarding services are another feather in Japan's cap. Forgot about heavy bags or cumbersome suitcases? No problem. With reliable **takuhaibin** services, your luggage is swiftly and safely forwarded from your hotel to your next destination or airport overnight, ushering in a new level of travel comfort. This thoughtful service allows you to journey effortlessly, pausing only to soak in the sights or savor a quick snack along the way.

A Journey Beyond Transportation: An Art of Moving

In Japan, **mobility is an experience of harmony and artistry**. The stations feature beautifully designed waiting areas, comfortable lounges, and plenty of local delicacies—each station a destination in itself. The entire transit process, from ticket purchase to boarding, exemplifies a culture that values punctuality, mindfulness, and attention to detail.

And it's not merely the trains. Japan's extensive network of **local subways, buses, and ferries** provide seamless access to historic landmarks, bustling markets, and serene temples. Inside these systems, cleanliness is immaculate, staff members are consistently courteous, and schedules are tightly adhered to—delighting the traveler with a sense of order and reliability.

The Japanese Travel Philosophy: An Unseen Journey
Traveling in Japan is more than moving point-to-point; it's an experience of **mindfulness**—a dance of discipline and grace. Whether you are ascending the steps to a historic shrine, savoring a matcha latte at a café in Ginza, or bowing politely to the maître d' at a hidden ryokan, every gesture, every moment, is imbued with respect and reverence.

This is the philosophy that underpins Japan's seamless travel culture—a quiet harmony that transforms a simple journey into a memorable event. It invites travelers to embrace patience, gratitude, and a deep appreciation for both the moment and the marvels around them.

Conclusion: An Invitation to Explore Japan's Heartbeat

In Japan, your journey is never just physical; it's an immersive voyage into a world where technology, tradition, and service coalesce into an art form. The Shinkansen embodies the country's relentless pursuit of perfection and grace—an agile, elegant symbol of Japan's ability to move forward while honouring its past.

Embark on a voyage that marries speed with serenity, innovation with tradition, and efficiency with heartfelt hospitality.™ In Japan, every journey is an ode to the meticulous beauty of life—a symphony composed in steel, service, and silent wonder.

Cultural Kaleidoscope: Indonesia's Archipelago

Imagine a world where thousands of islands, each with its own story, dances in a symphony of colors, sounds, and traditions. Welcome to Indonesia—a mesmerizing archipelago that is, in essence, a living kaleidoscope of culture, nature, spirituality, and history.

Stretching across the equator and spanning over 17,000 islands, Indonesia is a treasure trove of diversity—an intricate mosaic of tribes, languages, cuisines, dances, and rituals. It is a land where ancient traditions coexist with modern innovations, where the mountains echo with the chants of harmonious living, and the oceans whisper age-old tales of discovery.

This is a country that awakens all your senses and beckons your curiosity—inviting you to explore its vibrant tapestry woven with threads of history, spirituality, art, and nature's boundless beauty.

The Cultural Tapestry: A Living Kaleidoscope

A Melting Pot of Ethnicities and Languages

Indonesia is home to over 300 distinct ethnic groups, each with its own language, costume, and customs. The Javanese, Balinese, Sundanese, Batak, Acehnese, and many others create a colorful mosaic of civilizations that have thrived for centuries.

In Bali, Hindu traditions, intricate dances, and temple ceremonies flourish amidst lush rice terraces. In the Toraja highlands of Sulawesi, elaborate funeral rites, wooden carvings, and cliffside tombs tell stories of life, death, and ancestral reverence.

Festivals of Wonder and Spirit

The Indonesian calendar is bursting with festivals that reflect deep spiritual, cultural, and artistic expressions:

- **Nyepi (Balinese Day of Silence):** A day of fasting, meditation, and reflection, where the island of Bali virtually shuts down—an act of spiritual renewal.
- **Waisak:** Celebrating the birth, enlightenment, and death of Buddha, observed with colorful processions and prayer.
- **Bali Arts Festival:** An exuberant display of dance, music, crafts, and theater—showcasing the island's rich artistic heritage.
- **Toraja Funeral Festivals:** A spectacle of elaborate rituals, buffalo offerings, and cliffside ceremonies honoring ancestors.

Art, Dance, and Craftsmanship

From the intricately woven ikat textiles and beadwork of Sumba to the dramatic shadow puppetry (Wayang Kulit) of Java, Indonesian arts are alive with stories and symbolism. Traditional dances—like the mesmerizing **Kecak** trance dance of Bali or the elegant **Tari Pendet**—are expressions of devotion, history, and community.

Hand-carved masks, silk scarves, ceramics, and woodwork reflect a mastery handed down across generations—each piece a mirror of cultural identity and spiritual harmony.

Nature's Palette: Land, Sea, and Sky

Indonesia's natural wonders are as diverse as its culture. Towering volcanoes like **Mount Rinjani** and **Krakatoa** remind us of the earth's fiery power, while the lush rainforests and coral reefs teem with unique wildlife.

- **Komodo National Park:** Home to the legendary Komodo dragons—giant lizards that have roamed the earth for millions of years.

- **Bali's beaches:** From the surfer's paradise at Uluwatu to the tranquil shores of Amed—each beach is an invitation to relax and reconnect with nature.
- **Borneo's orangutans:** One of the last refuges for endangered orangutans, offering chances to witness these intelligent creatures in their semi-wild habitat.

The Culinary Kaleidoscope

Indonesian cuisine is an intoxicating mix of spices, herbs, and flavors—each island and region offering a unique taste of its heritage.

- Savor **Nasi Goreng** (fried rice), **Sate** skewers, and **Rendang** (spicy beef stew), each dish laden with history and warmth.
- Indulge in **Bakso** (meatball soup), **Gado-Gado** (vegetable salad with peanut sauce), or exotic fruits like mangosteen and durian.
- Experience street food markets alive with aroma and life—an essential part of the Indonesian experience.

A Journey into the Heart of the Archipelago

Indonesia is a vast, living mosaic—each island a vibrant tile in a sprawling masterpiece. To truly understand this country's soul, one must wander beyond the well-trodden paths, venture into remote villages, participate in sacred rituals, taste indigenous flavors, and listen to stories whispered by elders.

Because in Indonesia, every moment is a kaleidoscope—a fragment of eternity, shimmering with history, spirituality, and a shared longing for harmony amid diversity.

The Enchanting Depths of Indonesia: Beyond the Kaleidoscope

Indonesia isn't merely a country; it's a living, breathing mosaic—an intricate dance of islands, each whispering a different melody, each echoing a distinct story. The true magic of this archipelago lies not only in its visual splendor but in its unending capacity to surprise, humble, and inspire those willing to venture beyond the surface.

The Sacred and the Simple: Mystical Landmarks and Everyday Rituals

While Indonesia is famed for grand temples, ancient rituals, and vibrant festivals, it is also embodying the quiet poetry of daily life:

- **Javanese and Balinese rice terraces**—terraced landscapes of marble-like green that ripple across hillsides, where local farmers tend to crops with reverence as sacred as their ancient rituals. Walking through these terraces offers a profound sense of harmony—an organic connection to the land that sustains life itself.
- **The quiet spirituality in small villages:** In remote areas of Nusa Tenggara or Papua, elders preserve age-old customs, where daily prayers, offerings, and communal meals are woven into the fabric of life, maintaining a resilient link to the ancestral world.
- **Traditional crafts:** Batik weaving, silver-smithing in Celuk, or papermaking from sago leaves are living art forms—each piece telling a story of environmental harmony and cultural resilience.

Marine Splendors and Underwater Wonderland

Indonesia's underwater realm remains one of its greatest treasures, yet many travelers only glimpse its surface. Beneath the waters are vibrant kingdoms teeming with life:

- **Raja Ampat,** the "Four Kingdoms," is often considered the epicenter of global marine biodiversity. Its kaleidoscopic coral reefs and crystal-clear waters host more species of coral and fish than anywhere else on Earth—an unspoiled sanctuary for divers and snorkelers seeking otherworldly encounters.
- **Bunaken Marine Park:** A haven of colorful reef life off North Sulawesi, where turtles, manta rays, and reef sharks glide effortlessly amid corals in kaleidoscopic hues.
- **Cenderawasih Bay:** Home to the elusive whale sharks, this "Bird's Head Peninsula" offers a rare chance to swim alongside gentle giants in their natural habitat.

These underwater worlds are whispers of time—fragile, vibrant, and begging for preservation.

Mountains and Valleys: The Roots of Indonesian Identity

Beyond the islands and seas, Indonesia's volcanic landscapes and highlands cradle some of the world's most profound stories of resilience and spirituality:

- **The Bromo-Tengger-Semeru volcanoes:** A surreal lunar landscape where locals perform sunrise offerings atop the smoky caldera—an active reminder of nature's fierce beauty and spiritual humility.
- **The highlands of Sumatra and Bali:** Terraced farms produce not only rice but also aromatic spices such as clove, cinnamon, and pepper, harvested in harmony with centuries-old rituals.
- **Papua, the "Third Stone from the Sun,"** is a land of indigenous tribes, where ancestral traditions remain unbroken. Dance rituals around fires and face-painting ceremonies connect the present with mythic origins.

The Call of the Wild: Endangered Guardians and Their Stories

Indonesia's rich biodiversity is also a narrative of fragility. Endangered species like the orangutans of Borneo and Sumatra, the Javan rhino, and the Sumatran tiger tell stories of survival against great odds:

- **Orangutan rescue and rehabilitation centers** in Kalimantan and Aceh are not only about conservation—they are beacons of a harmonious relationship between humans and nature.
- **The amazingly elusive Hornbills** and the dancing, iridescently plumaged **Bird-of-Paradise**—each a symbol of Indonesia's avian kingdom—remind us that every creature, no matter how small, is integral to the ecosystem's symphony.

Gastronomic Journeys: Flavors of the Archipelago

Diving into Indonesia's cuisine is akin to exploring a universe of flavors:

- Savor **Rijsttafel** (rice table), a Dutch-Indonesian culinary legacy that offers dozens of tiny dishes—spicy sambals, satays, and sweet sambal paste—that tell tales of trade routes and cultural exchanges.

- Taste **Bali's Lawar**, a traditional vegetable and meat salad infused with rich coconut and spices, or **Papeda**, sago porridge eaten with rich, tangy fish broth in Eastern Indonesia.
- Street stalls serve **Gado-Gado**—a colorful vegetable salad with peanut sauce—or **Es Campur**, a frozen dessert of crushed fruits and jellies in sweet syrup—each a window into local life and hospitality

Europe

A Mosaic of Time and Culture

Imagine a continent where the echoes of empire and artistry resonate through every cobblestone street, every majestic monument, and every whispers of ancient stories. Welcome to Europe—a living tapestry woven from centuries of history, innovation, and cultural renaissance.

Europe is a majestic mosaic of over 50 countries, each a unique window into the soul of human achievement—countries that have shaped empires, crafted masterpieces, and laid the foundations of modern civilization. From the regal palaces of Madrid, Paris, and Vienna to the cobblestone alleys of Rome, the wind-swept coastlines of Greece, the picturesque fjords of Scandinavia, and the lush vineyards of Bordeaux—every corner of Europe offers a new chapter in the epic saga of human ingenuity.

This continent's history is a kaleidoscope—where mighty Roman legacies, medieval castles, Renaissance art, Enlightenment philosophies, and revolutionary ideals collide and coexist, creating a complex yet harmonious symphony that continues to inspire and redefine the future.

The heart of Europe, the Schengen Area, unites 26 countries with open borders and a shared commitment to freedom of movement, allowing travelers seamless passage from the beaches of the Mediterranean to the snowy peaks of the Alps, from bustling cities to tranquil villages. In this enchanting realm, a journey is not merely about crossing borders—it's about crossing epochs—where ancient ruins, Gothic cathedrals, Baroque palaces, and sleek modern skylines narrate the marathon of human history.

Europe's magic lies in its diversity: a tapestry embroidered with languages, cuisines, art, music, and traditions—each harmonizing into a timeless ode to human aspiration and resilience. Its allure is unpredictable and eternal; it beckons explorers to lose themselves in its stories, to find themselves anew amid its ever-changing hues.

Europe is not just a continent—it's a living museum, a vibrant festival, a timeless creator of wonders. It whispers the tales of our collective past and invites us to dream boldly about our shared future—part of a grand, eternal dance of history and hope.

Historical Tapestry Italy's Renaissance

Imagine a land where art dances across the streets, where philosophy and innovation spark a cultural explosion, and where history is etched into every stone—a land that redefined civilization itself. Welcome to Italy, the cradle of the Renaissance—a glorious epoch that transformed the ordinary into the extraordinary, forging masterpieces that continue to captivate the world centuries later.

Italy, a boot-shaped jewel in the heart of Europe, is more than just a picturesque landscape of rolling hills, dramatic coastlines, and charming villages. It is a living, breathing museum, brimming with stories of genius and grandeur, of creativity and rebellion, all woven together in a vibrant tapestry that still adorns our cultural fabric.

The Birth of a New Dawn: The Renaissance

The Renaissance (meaning *rebirth* in French)—a seismic cultural shift that began in Florence in the 14th century—was a glorious awakening that pulled humanity from the shadows of medieval dogma, igniting an explosion of art, science, philosophy, and innovation. It was a time when thinkers like **Leonardo da Vinci** sketched flying machines and mysterious Mona Lisas, and **Michelangelo** sculpted the divine in the marble prisons of his mind.

It's almost as if Italy's soul suddenly decided to throw a magnificent party—one that would last for centuries, with artistic masterpieces, scientific breakthroughs, and revolutionary ideas serving as its glittering decorations.

Italy's Artistic Treasure Trove

Step into Italy today, and you're walking through an open-air gallery—each city a chapter of artistic brilliance:

- **Florence:** The birthplace of the Renaissance. Its **Duomo** dares to challenge the sky with Brunelleschi's daring dome, while the **Uffizi Gallery** holds Botticelli's 'Birth of Venus'—a work so beautiful it almost makes you forget to breathe.
- **Rome:** The eternal city, where the **Pantheon** stands as a witness to Roman engineering, and the **Vatican Museums** house Michelangelo's **Sistine Chapel** ceiling—a divine masterpiece that might just make even the most hardened skeptics believe in miracles.
- **Venice:** The city of water and wonder, with delicate glass artistry and canals that seem to float on the dreams of explorers past.

The Power of the Renaissance Spirit

This wasn't merely an art revival—it was a revolution that challenged old ways of thinking:

- **Science and Innovation:** Thinkers like **Galileo** looked at the stars and said, "Hey, I think I see a new way of viewing the universe"—and the Church, politely, responded with a share of celestial skepticism.
- **Philosophy and Humanism:** The focus shifted from divine omnipotence to human potential—embodying the idea that *we* can shape our destiny, armed with curiosity and courage rather than fear.

The Great Masters: From Michelangelo to Leonardo

The Renaissance's luminous jewel was its unparalleled geniuses—artists whose works continue to define Western art:

- **Michelangelo Buonarroti**, the sculptor of **David**, the creator of the **Sistine Chapel ceiling**, and the architect of **St. Peter's Basilica**, combined divine inspiration with infinite patience. His art is a testament to the belief that the divine dwells within the human form.

- **Leonardo da Vinci**, the quintessential Renaissance man, blended art with engineering and science. The **Mona Lisa**'s mysterious smile, the **Vitruvian Man**'s perfect proportions—these are not just paintings; they are symbols of a new way of seeing the world, emphasizing observation and curiosity.

The Art of the Renaissance: A Cultural Revolution

Renaissance art broke boundaries with **linear perspective**, **chiaroscuro** (play of light and shadow), and **anatomical accuracy**—all techniques that transformed two-dimensional images into portals to another realm. These masterpieces weren't just decorations; they challenged notions of beauty, mankind's place in the universe, and the divine spark within.

The Renaissance's Lasting Impact

Italy's artistic and intellectual revolution didn't just end in breath-taking paintings and sculptures. It laid the groundwork for modern science, politics, and even our understanding of human rights—a true case of "what happens in Florence, doesn't stay in Florence."

Today, walking through Italy's cities feels like flipping through a living history book—each piazza, each basilica, each ancient ruin is a page that beckons you to uncover secrets of a world that once changed everything.

In Conclusion

Italy's Renaissance is a testament to the human spirit's ability to reinvent itself through art, science, and bold ideas. It's a celebration of creativity and curiosity—a period when genius was summoned to challenge conventions and shape the future.

Today, Italy stands as a luminous reminder that the greatest treasures are not just in galleries and monuments but in the awakened, inspired minds of those who dare to dream—even if those dreams involve flying machines, divine art, or simply perfecting the art of a perfectly cooked pizza.

Italy's Renaissance is not just history; it's an ongoing inspiration—a timeless invitation to imagine, to create, and to believe in the transformative power of human ingenuity.

1. **Unmissable Cities and Towns Beyond the Main Highlights**
   - **Pisa:** Dive into the charm of the Leaning Tower and explore the beautiful Piazza dei Miracoli, combined with lesser-known squares and local eateries that capture Italy's authentic spirit.
   - **Siena:** Discover its medieval altarpieces, narrow winding streets, and the stunning Piazza del Campo where the historic Palio horse race still takes place.
   - **Lucca:** Walk or cycle along the perfectly preserved Renaissance city walls and relax in its quiet, enchanting streets filled with artisan boutiques and cafes.
2. **Hidden Artistic Gems and Renaissance Artworks**
   - **Brera Gallery in Milan:** A lesser-crowded sanctuary of Italian Renaissance art.
   - **Ferrara:** A Renaissance city boasting grand palaces, frescoed castles, and less-touristed medieval streets.
   - **Padua's Basilica di Sant'Antonio:** A masterpiece of religious art and architecture, with exquisite frescoes and sculptures.
3. **Unique Architectural and Cultural Experiences**
   - **Florence's Oltrarno District:** Dive into artisan workshops, studios of goldsmiths, leather artisans, and traditional craftsmen.
   - **Venice's Lido:** Experience the glamour of the historic Venice Film Festival and explore the quieter, less touristy islands like Torcello and Burano, famous for colorful houses and lace work.
   - **Rome's Villa Borghese Gardens:** Walk in serenity amidst Renaissance sculptures, fountains, and art installations.

4. **Local Festivals and Traditions**
   - **Palio di Siena:** Watch this ancient horse race held twice a year, a vivid display of medieval pageantry and passionate community pride.
   - **Florentine Craftsmanship Festivals:** Enjoy live demonstrations of gilding, leatherworking, and fresco painting, where artisans keep Renaissance techniques alive.
   - **Venice Carnival:** Experience masks, costumes, and masked balls that revive Renaissance masquerade traditions.

5. **Gastronomic Delights and Culinary Experiences**
   - Engage in cooking classes, learning to make traditional *pici* pasta in Tuscany or *merenda* in Emilia-Romagna.
   - Sample local wines from Chianti or Brunello di Montalcino, or enjoy fresh seafood along the Ligurian coast in Liguria.
   - Dine in trattorias where recipes have been passed down through generations—comforting dishes that embody Italy's culinary heritage.

6. **Experiential Travel: Walks, Workshops, and Offbeat Tours**
   - **Walking Tours in Florence and Rome:** Curated experiences that reveal lesser-known Renaissance sites, hidden chapels, and art studios.
   - **Fresco and Sculpture Workshops:** Participate in art classes inspired by the masters, held in historic workshops.
   - **Religious Pilgrimages:** Visit sacred sites like Assisi, home to St. Francis, with its Renaissance churches and tranquil atmosphere.

7. **Natural and Scenic Splendors**
   - **Lake Como:** A serene retreat with villas and gardens once frequented by Renaissance nobility and now a tranquil luxury destination.

- **Amalfi Coast:** The breathtaking cliffs, lemon groves, and colorful towns like Positano and Ravello, where nature's beauty complements Italy's artistic grandeur.
- **Dolomites:** Majestic mountain ranges providing outdoor adventures and stunning vistas—an inspiring contrast to Italy's Renaissance art.

In essence, beyond the history and art, what makes Italy an ongoing Renaissance is its living, breathing culture—artisans still crafting by hand, chefs honoring centuries-old recipes, festivals celebrating community and tradition, and landscapes that have inspired countless masters. The most compelling itinerary leaves no stone unturned, inviting travellers into a vibrant, multi-layered experience—where every city, island, and mountain whispers stories of a glorious past and a lively present.

Majestic Castles and Fjords: Norway & Scotland

Imagine a land where fairy-tale castles rise amidst sweeping highlands, where rugged mountains meet fjords so dramatic they seem carved by myth and magic. Welcome to Norway and Scotland—two extraordinary nations where history breathes through stone walls, and natural landscapes tell stories of ancient kingdoms and wild adventure.

In these lands, centuries of history, indomitable spirit, and breathtaking scenery intertwine to create a landscape that's both steeped in legend and alive with modern vitality.

Norway: The Land of Fjords, Folk Tales, and Frozen Marvels

Nestled in Scandinavia, Norway is often called the gateway to the Arctic, but its true treasures extend far beyond icy horizons. Known for its towering fjords, cascading waterfalls, and vibrant cultural history, Norway is a land where nature is both awe-inspiring and humbling.

The Castles and Historic Sites

- **Akershus Fortress (Oslo):** Built in the 13th century, this medieval castle offers sweeping views over Oslofjord and is a symbol of Norway's resilience and royal heritage.
- **Trondheim's Nidaros Cathedral:** A masterpiece of Gothic architecture, this historic cathedral dates back to the 11th century and has been a pilgrimage site for centuries.

- **Kongsvinger Fortress:** A fortress standing guard over Norway's eastern border, surrounded by dense forests and history of conflict and peace.
- **Borgund Stave Church:** An astonishing example of medieval wooden craftsmanship—one of the best-preserved stave churches in the world, whispering stories of Norway's pagan origins and Christian conversion.

Natural Wonders and Activities

- **Fjord Cruises:** Glide through the UNESCO-listed Geirangerfjord or Nærøyfjord—world-famous for their towering cliffs, cascading waterfalls, and mirror-like waters.
- **Lofoten Islands:** Dramatic mountain peaks meet pristine beaches and quaint fishing villages. Ideal for hiking, kayaking, and witnessing the Northern Lights.
- **Northern Lights:** Witness the cosmic dance of the Aurora Borealis, a celestial spectacle that transforms the night sky into a swirling canvas of green and violet.

A Tapestry of Culture and History

Norwegian culture is a resilient blend of Vikings, Sami heritages, and modern innovation. Traditional music, folk art, and storytelling remain vital, and the nation's reverence for nature is deeply woven into its identity.

Scotland: The Land of Myth, Monasteries, and Majestic Highlands

Across the North Sea lies Scotland—a realm where ancient castles stand proud atop craggy hills, where lochs mirror the sky, and legends of giants and warriors echo through its barren moors.

The Castles and Historic Fortresses

- **Edinburgh Castle:** Perched atop Castle Rock, this iconic fortress dominates Scotland's capital and offers a glimpse into royal history, wars, and royal ceremonies spanning centuries.
- **Stirling Castle:** A strategic stronghold in medieval Scotland, it saw battles, kings, and queens—its ramparts whispering tales of independence and heroism.
- **Eilean Donan Castle:** Nestled on a small island at the head of Loch Duich, this fairy-tale castle is one of Scotland's most photographed sites, blending history and legend amidst dramatic scenery.
- **Urquhart Castle (Loch Ness):** Overlooking the famous loch, it's entwined with stories of monsters and mysteries—perfect for those who believe in the magic of legend.

Cultural Heritage and Adventures

- **Whisky Tours:** Scotland is the birthplace of Scotch whisky. Explore distilleries in Speyside or Islay, and toast to centuries-old traditions of craftsmanship.
- **Highland Games and Festivals:** Experience traditional Scottish music, dance, and athletic feats—an authentic celebration of Scottish pride.
- **Loch Ness and the Highlands:** Wander through moors and mountains, seek the legendary monster, or hike trails that reveal stunning vistas and ancient ruins.

Historical Triumphs and Legends

Scotland's deep-rooted history of clan rivalries, battles for independence, and cultural resilience shine through in its castles, museums, and battlefield sites like Culloden. The nation's folklore—featuring leaders like William Wallace and Robert the Bruce—continues to inspire stories of courage and defiance.

Why Visit Norway & Scotland?

Both countries are a testament to nature's raw power and mankind's enduring legacy. Whether you're sailing through fjords that seem to touch the sky, wandering ancient Nordic ruins, or exploring distant castles shadowed by legends, these lands beckon explorers with promises of history, adventure, and myth.

Enchanted Journeys: A 15-18 Day Odyssey Through Norway & Scotland

Embark on a voyage where majestic fjords carve a celestial canvas of icy blue splendor, and ancient castles whisper tales of valor and legend. This is a journey that threads together Norway's icy grandeur with Scotland's rugged beauty—where every step becomes a chapter in an epic tale of natural wonder and historic grandeur.

Let your spirit soar as you traverse two of Europe's most evocative landscapes—each a living testament to the enduring poetical muse of Mother Nature and the sagas of ancient kings and clans.

Days 1-4: Oslo & the Fjords of Norway — The Nordic Heartbeat

Start in Oslo—The Contemporary Crown of Scandinavia

Begin your voyage in **Oslo**, Norway's dynamic capital, where modernity meets heritage against a backdrop of stunning fjords and lush green hills.

- **Vigeland Sculpture Park:** Walk among life-sized sculptures that celebrate life, love, and the human condition.
- **Oslo Opera House:** A sculptural masterpiece where architecture seems to float on the fjord, promising cultural grandeur and breathtaking views.
- **Akershus Fortress:** A medieval castle that whispers tales of Nordic resilience through centuries of war and peace.

Auntie Nature's Masterpiece: Fjord Cruising

From Oslo, travel to **Bergen**, via scenic train or a coastal cruise, to immerse yourself in Norway's iconic fjords. The journey itself is a breathtaking tableau—luminous mountains, shimmering lakes, and distant waterfalls.

- **Geirangerfjord or Nærøyfjord:** These UNESCO-listed natural wonders are like giant, glassy masterpieces crafted by glaciers—towering cliffs, cascading waterfalls, and mirror-like waters beckon explorers to drift into serenity.

Bergen & the Fjord Village Charm

- **Bryggen Wharf:** The historic Hanseatic wharf, with its colorful wooden houses and narrow alleys, evokes a fairy-tale setting.
- **Mount Fløyen:** Take the funicular for sweeping city views and misty mountain air.

Must-do: A kayaking trip or a scenic drive along the Atlantic Road—one of the most spectacular coastal roads in the world.

Days 5-7: The Arctic Spectacle & Scenic Norway

Tromsø & the Northern Lights

Fly northward to **Tromsø**, the gateway to the Arctic.

- **Aurora Borealis:** Witness nature's celestial ballet—dancing emerald curtains that weave through the icy night sky.
- **Arctic Wildlife Tours:** Look out for reindeer herds, majestic whales, and Arctic foxes, in a land where nature's raw power is on full display.
- **Dog Sledding & Snowshoeing:** Cross snowy landscapes in hushed silence, guided by the spirit of the musk ox.

Days 8-10: Journey to Scotland — From Fjords to Highland Glens

From Norway to Edinburgh—Bridging Two Mystical Worlds

Fly from Tromsø (or Oslo) to **Edinburgh**, Scotland's jewel of history and legend.

Edinburgh's Historic Majesty

- **Edinburgh Castle:** Crowned atop Castle Rock, this fortress embodies Scotland's turbulent past and regal grandeur.
- **Royal Mile:** Wandering through the cobblestone streets experiencing vibrant markets, ancient taverns, and stories whispered by the wind.
- **Arthur's Seat:** Climb this dormant volcano for panoramic views of the city, and soak in the magic of the Scottish Highlands from afar.

Days 11-13: The Highlands & Lochs of Scotland

Venture into Scotland's soul—its mystical lochs, rugged mountains, and castles.

- **Loch Ness & Urquhart Castle:** Search for Nessie, the legendary monster, amid a tranquil lake that echoes with myth.
- **Glencoe Valley:** Witness the dramatic mountains and glistening waterfalls—nature's own cathedral of awe.
- **Isle of Skye:** A jewel of untouched beauty—cliffs, fairy pools, and villages frozen in time, whispering tales of ancient clans and mythic beings.
- **Eilean Donan Castle:** A fairy-tale fortress hugging the loch's edge, a perfect symbol of Scottish resilience.

Days 14-16: Cultural Riches & Historic Depths

Stirling Castle & Wallace Monument: As you walk amidst the grandeur of Stirling Castle, perched high above the fertile plains, you tread upon grounds soaked in tales of heroism, rebellion, and the fight for independence. The Wallace Monument, an imposing spire dedicated to William Wallace—the legendary Scottish hero—stands as a testament to valor and resilience etched into the rugged Scottish landscape. Here, legend and history entwine, inspiring every visitor to ponder the enduring spirit of liberty.

Edinburgh & Stirling Museums: Dive into Scotland's soul through its museums and historic sites. Discover the stories of clans fighting for survival, kings and queens shaping nations, and filmmakers capturing its mythic landscape. The National Museum of Scotland, the Museum of Edinburgh, and the Museum of Stirling weave tales of traditions, battles, and the enduring pride of a land where history is alive in every stone and story.

Whisky Tours: No Scottish journey would be complete without savoring its liquid gold. Visit renowned distilleries nestled in lush valleys and rugged highlands—where expert artisans craft whisky with centuries-old techniques. Experience the tradition, taste the heritage, and raise a toast to the landscape that inspired centuries of storytelling, music, and mythical legends.

Days 17-18: Final Flourishes & Farewell

A Journey of Endless Discovery: As your grand voyage draws to a close, take a moment to reflect on the symphony of landscapes and stories you've encountered. From the icy fjords of Norway to the legendary castles and misty lochs of Scotland, you have traveled through the very heartbeats of two extraordinary worlds—each echoing with myth, history, and the indomitable human spirit.

Parting Gifts: Carry with you the memories of the Northern Lights dancing across the icy Norwegian sky, the serene beauty of the fjords, the castles whispering tales of old, and the rugged grandeur of Scotland's highlands. May your journey inspire you to seek new horizons, embrace the unknown, and always cherish the timeless muse of exploration.

In conclusion:

This 18-day odyssey through Norway and Scotland is more than a journey; it's a stirring saga woven with wonder, history, and the majestic poetry of nature and human achievement. It's about discovering that legends are alive, that castles and fjords are the gateways to the soul, and that every step taken in these legendary lands is a step into your own epic story.

Art, Coffee, and Canals: France and Venice

Charmed by Cafés and Canals: France & Venice—A Love Letter in Two Acts

In the grand theatre of Europe, two cities perform in silent harmony, each whispering stories of romance, revolution, artistry, and water. They are the yin and yang of the continent—one a masterpiece of refinement and rebellion, the other a lagoon of dreams and murmurs—each undeniably essential, each uniquely irresistible.

Welcome to a voyage that transcends history and becomes a dance of senses—an exploration of France's chic allure and Venice's watery poetry, where every sip, every gaze, every ripple embodies love, life, and the art of living well.

France: The Symphony of Sartorial Elegance & Subversive Spirit

Imagine a country where cherry blossoms bloom alongside revolutionary ideas—where haute couture is as natural as the Parisian air, and joie de vivre is an unspoken national motto. France isn't just a destination; it's an attitude—a curated collection of moments that make time pause, breathe, and admire.

Paris: The City of Light, Love, and Little Surprises

- **Cafés on the Boulevard:** Picture yourself sipping delicate espresso in a sidewalk café, watching the world drift by—artists sketching, lovers whispering, philosophers pondering. Parisian cafés are not just places to drink coffee; they're the wombs of ideas, where Baudelaire, Picasso, and Sartre might have once exchanged a glance or a thought.

- **Montmartre & Sacré-Cœur:** Climb the artistic mountain of Montmartre, where painters like Monet once sought inspiration. Gaze upon the city from the basilica and realize that every cityscape is a canvas.
- **The Louvre & Musée d'Orsay:** Art isn't mere decoration here; it's an ongoing love affair. Walk through halls filled with Renaissance reveries, Impressionist dreams, and sculptures whispering stories of the divine and the mortal.
- **Hidden alleys & secret gardens:** Discover tiny courtyards and bookshops where time has slowed, secrets have been kept, and love letters remain unread.

Humor break: And yes, it's true—if you get lost in Paris, just confirm you're *not* on a film set. Because everything looks scripted, and nobody is in a rush because they're too busy living art.

Provence & Beyond: The Spirit of La Belle Vie

- **Lavender fields:** A visual feast where purple clouds drift endlessly, whispering old Provençal tales.
- **Château & vineyards:** Indulge in wine tastings where history, terroir, and tradition toast to life's finest moments.
- **Medieval villages:** Step into stories from a time when kings and peasants shared the same land—each stone a testament to resilience, romance, and rebellion.

Twist: France's true charm isn't just in its art or its cuisine—it's in the way it seduces you into believing that life is about savoring each sip, each sunset, each stolen moment.

Venice: The Canals, the Murmurs, and the Eternal Romance

Venice isn't just a city; it's a living poem—an intricate melody composed of water, stone, and the whispers of lovers and poets. It's a place where mornings begin with gondolas gliding like dreams across shimmering lagoons, and nights are painted with stars and the glow of a thousand lanterns reflecting on gentle currents.

The Water City & Its Secrets

- **Gondola Rides:** Glide silently through the labyrinth of canals, where every turn reveals an unseen palace, a secret garden, or a bridge whispered about in countless love stories.
- **St. Mark's Square & Basilica:** The beating heart of Venice, where history and devotion swirl amid the clatter of pigeons and the serenades of wandering minstrels.
- **Dorsoduro & Accademia Galleries:** Less crowded than St. Mark's, these neighborhoods nurture the city's artistic soul—a serene space to soak in Titian, Tintoretto, and Veronese masterpieces.
- **Hidden Corners:** Discover quiet courtyards, artisan shops, and whispering alleys—places where Venice keeps her secrets.

Humor alert: Remember, Venetian streets are meant for legend—if you get lost, simply embrace it. For in Venice, losing your way is the best way to find the city's hidden love stories and secret passages.

France & Venice: Two Eternal Love Stories

France and Venice—each a lover's secret, each a dream woven in water and stone. The charm of France's cafes, vineyards, and châteaux is matched only by Venice's canals, floating piazzas, and whispered legends. Together, they form a symphony of romance, history, and artistry—each city an unending ode to the art of living and loving.

In France, enjoy long afternoons lost in cafés, where the air is thick with croissants, coffee, and the scent of revolution—an enduring spirit that has shaped modern civilization. Traverse vineyards that stretch into eternity, explore medieval castles guarding secrets, and let the refined elegance of Parisian streets awaken your inner poet.

In Venice, let the city's gentle waters and historic whispers write poetry on your soul. Glide through a dreamscape of water and stone, uncover hidden corners, and lose yourself in a city that has, for centuries, proved that even in eternal change, love and beauty remain constant.

The grand adventure of France and Venice isn't just about seeing—it's about experiencing. It's about feeling the heartbeat of art, whispering in the wind; tasting the soul of a cuisine perfected over centuries; and soaking in the poetry of water and stone that define these two eternal love stories.

So, pack your curiosity, embrace the unknown, and let the magic of water, wine, art, and whispers guide you through this symphony of romance—a journey crafted not just to see, but to be seen in the mirror of centuries-old dreams.

Discovering France: Beyond the Beaten Path

While Paris and Saint-Germain are undeniably the heartbeats of French culture—luminescent boulevards, historic landmarks, and irresistible cafés—France's true soul lives in its enchanting lesser-known corners, waiting to surprise even the most seasoned traveler.

Imagine wandering through medieval villages perched atop rolling hills, where cobbled streets wind past fairy-tale châteaux and vineyards whisper stories of ancient winemakers. From the whimsical charm of **Colmar**, with its colorful half-timbered houses and fluttering butterflies in its gardens, to the rugged allure of **Rocamadour**, a cliffside pilgrimage site where history and spirituality intertwine amidst dramatic landscapes—each destination beckons with an invitation to explore untouched France.

Venture into the **Loire Valley**, the "Garden of France," where majestic castles like Château de Chambord and Château de Chenonceau rise gracefully from lush greenery—perfect for picnics, vineyard tours, and dreaming spires. Or lose yourself in the **Camargue**—a wild, saline marshland teeming with flamingos, wild white horses, and salt flats—an untouched paradise for birdwatching and scenic rides.

For a truly magical experience, hop over to **Fontainebleau**, a regal town adorned with one of France's most exquisite royal châteaux, nestled deep in ancient forests—brimming with art, history, and outdoor adventure. And let's not forget the artistic charm of **Honfleur**, whose port inspired painters like Monet, with cafes overlooking quaint harbors and streets alive with jazz and poetry.

And if you're craving a taste of the country's legendary cuisine, visit a small village in **Burgundy** or **Provence**, where organic farms, olive groves, and sunflower fields create a sensory symphony of flavors—cured meats, oils, wine, and lavender—each a reflection of centuries of tradition and soul.

In France, the beauty isn't just in the landmarks but in the quiet beauty of everyday life—an open-air market, a vineyard tour, a village festival. The country's magic is woven into its land, its people, and its stories—waiting patiently to reveal themselves to those with the curiosity to wander off the well-worn trail.

So, pack your sense of adventure and let France surprise you—beyond the Eiffel Tower and the Louvre, there's an entire universe of enchanting places, waiting to turn your journey into an unforgettable story of discovery.

The Essence of Eastern Europe: A Realm of Unseen Wonder

Diverse, dynamic, and delightfully unpredictable, Eastern Europe boasts a patchwork of nations—each with a soul of its own. Countries like Hungary, Czechia, Slovakia, Romania, Bulgaria, Poland, and the Balkans collectively offer a sprawling canvas of history, culture, and natural beauty.

Unlike the polished tourist routes of Western Europe, this region invites you to walk in the footsteps of kings and commoners, philosophers and poets, in places where the past breathes freely.

How to Cover All of Eastern Europe

Smart travel here is about embracing diversity—an immersive expedition through countries that have preserved their traditions amid rapid change. The key is a thoughtfully curated route—focusing on geographical proximity, cultural contrast, and iconic highlights:

- **Begin in Prague**, the fairy-tale capital of Czechia, with its Gothic spires, winding alleys, and colossal castles.
- **Head south to Vienna and Budapest**, cities that sing of empire, elegance, and resilience—each offering a symphony of art, architecture, and thermal baths.
- **Venture east into Romania**, to Transylvania's castles and the mysterious Carpathian forests.
- **Explore the Balkans**—Croatia's Adriatic coast, Slovenia's alpine charms, Serbia's lively Belgrade, and the waterfalls and lakes of Montenegro and Kosovo.

Travel tip: Utilize regional train passes and local flights—this region's infrastructure has improved but remains delightfully unhurried. The journey itself is part of the adventure, so savor the allure of rustic stations, scenic train routes, and charming countryside.

The Crown Jewels of the Hidden East: Must-Visit Towns and Cities

Prague, Czechia: The fairytale city where Gothic spires reach to touch the sky, and cobblestone streets shimmer with stories of defenestrations and divine architecture. The Charles Bridge, the Old Town Square, and the majestic Prague Castle are timeless icons of resilience and beauty.

Budapest, Hungary: The 'Pearl of the Danube,' with its dramatic Parliament, ancient thermal baths, and the romantic Fisherman's Bastion. A city that pulsates with history—once the heart of the Austro-Hungarian Empire and now a hub of cultural revival.

Ljubljana, Slovenia: A hidden gem of charming bridges, a baroque old town, and the mystical Ljubljana Castle overlooking a city that's both youthful and rooted in centuries-old traditions.

Kraków, Poland: The city of kings, with a beautifully preserved medieval Old Town, the haunting Auschwitz-Birkenau Museum nearby, and the vibrant Jewish quarter of Kazimierz—an ode to resilience, culture, and remembrance.

Cluj-Napoca & Sibiu, Romania: Urban hubs filled with Gothic and Renaissance architecture, nestled amidst the legendary Carpathian Mountains— gateways to Dracula's Transylvania and the land of folklore.

Mostar, Bosnia & Herzegovina: The iconic Ottoman-era bridge, the vibrant bazars, and the river that whispers tales of reconciliation and ancient trade routes.

Dubrovnik, Croatia: The "Pearl of the Adriatic," with its ancient city walls, navy-blue waters, and a history deeply intertwined with maritime prowess and resilience

The Ethereal Experience: What in the World to Do & See?

Castles & Palaces: From Bucharest's Palace of the Parliament—an unwieldy behemoth that's almost surreal in its scale—to Bran Castle in Romania that cast a shadow of legend and mystery, Eastern Europe's fortresses are gateways into tales of kings, queens, and mythic beasts. Imagine stepping into the very halls where century-old secrets echo through corridors, or the battlements where countless armies fought for pride and survival. These citadels are not just stones and bricks; they are the embodiment of resilience, revolution, and romantic legend.

Wine & Dine: Savor Balkan wines that carry the warmth of sun-drenched vineyards nestled in rugged mountains, paired with robust Serbian stews that warm the soul during wintry nights. Tantalize your taste buds with Slovenian cheeses, crafted with age-old techniques, or enjoy fresh river fish on a Croatian coast where salt air and sea breeze refresh the senses. Each meal tells a story—of ancient trade routes, cultural exchanges, and love for good, honest food.

Cultural Festivals: Dance to the infectious beats of Balkan folk music, where lively tamburas and accordions stir the very air, and watch street performances filled with color, costumes, and stories. In the town squares of Romania, Moldova, and Serbia, traditional dances swirl with the rhythms of drums and flutes, echoing the heartbeat of a region that has fought, loved, and endured through centuries of upheaval and renewal.

Markets & Artisans: Lose yourself in local bazaars, bursting with handcrafted jewelry, embroidered textiles, and pottery. These markets are living museums where artisans preserve centuries-old crafts, each piece a testament to cultural identity and artistic mastery. Pick up a hand-woven rug from Bulgaria, a carved wooden icon from the Balkans, or a delicate lace from Poland—each imbued with stories spun into every thread.

Hidden Trails & Nature's Embrace: Escape into the untouched wilderness of the Carpathians, the Julian Alps, or the Dinaric Mountains. Trek through wildflower-carpeted meadows, spot brown bears and lynxes in their shadowy retreats, and breathe in the pure, oxygen-rich air. These landscapes—so often overlooked—are the soul's sanctuary, offering peace and inspiration that stay long after your journey ends.

Historic Towns & Spiritual Sanctuaries: Wander the ancient streets of Sighişoara or Sibiu in Romania, where medieval towers and alleys whisper of old-world charm. In Sofia, Bulgaria, step into monasteries carved into mountainsides—places of reflection and resilience, where history and faith have coexisted harmoniously for centuries.

Why This Region?
The true magic of Eastern Europe lies not only in its sights but in its soul—the slow, poetic rhythm of life, the resilience of communities, and the timeless stories embedded within every stone and song. It beckons explorers hungry for authenticity, for stories that books cannot tell, and for landscapes that feel like dreams made real.

This region is a treasure chest hidden amidst Europe's giants—an unpolished jewel waiting for those brave enough to seek its sparkle, a place where legends are still alive, waiting to be discovered anew.

Eastern Europe's Hidden Gems: A 15-Day Immersive Journey

Day 1-2: Budapest, Hungary

- **Morning:** Arrive in Budapest, the "Pearl of the Danube." Check into a boutique hotel in the historic Castle District.
- **Afternoon:** Explore Buda Castle, the Fisherman's Bastion, and Matthias Church, enjoying panoramic views over the Danube.
- **Evening:** Relax at Széchenyi Thermal Bath, soaking in centuries-old thermal waters.
- **Must-do:** Take a nighttime cruise on the Danube to see Budapest's illuminated skyline—a fairy-tale floating in the night.

Day 3-4: Bratislava, Slovakia

- **Morning:** Travel to Slovakia's charming capital, just a 2-hour train ride.
- **Explore:** The Old Town with its colorful squares, Bratislava Castle perched above, and the quirky UFO Observation Deck for stunning vistas.

- **Cuisine:** Dine in traditional taverns serving hearty Slovak fare—goulash, bryndzové halušky, and local wines.
- **Hidden gem:** Walk along the old city walls, and discover quiet courtyards and artisan shops.

Day 5-6: Kraków, Poland

- **Morning:** Drive or take a train to Kraków, Poland's medieval jewel.
- **Explore:** The historic Main Market Square, Wawel Castle, and the haunting Auschwitz-Birkenau Memorial (optional but impactful).
- **Cultural Escape:** Lose yourself in the Jewish Quarter of Kazimierz, today a lively hub of cafes, galleries, and street art.
- **Must-do:** Attend a traditional Polish folk concert or visit the Cloth Hall for handcrafted souvenirs.

Day 7-8: Lviv, Ukraine

- **Morning:** Cross into Ukraine and arrive in Lviv, a city brimming with European charm.
- **Discover:** The UNESCO-listed Old Town with its ornate churches, cozy cafes, and bustling markets.
- **Cultural:** Experience the vibrant Lviv Opera House, and try local specialties like borscht and Lvivs' famous coffee.
- **Hidden gem:** Explore the secret courtyards of Viktors' Church or take a walk along the serene High Castle Hill for panoramic vistas.

Day 9-10: Transylvania, Romania

- **Morning:** Journey to the legendary land of Dracula, with a base in Sibiu or Brașov.
- **Explore:** The medieval-era **Bran Castle**, Plovdiv-like streets of Sibiu, and stunning natural scenery of the Carpathian Mountains.
- **Experience:** Stay in an authentic guesthouse, enjoy traditional Romanian dishes, and visit fortified churches—reminding you of legends that breathe life into every stone.

Day 11-12: Belgrade, Serbia

- **Morning:** Head to Serbia's capital—a city of resilience and rhythm.
- **Walk:** The bohemian Skadarlija street, Belgrade Fortress, and the Temple of Saint Sava.
- **Experience:** Dive into lively cafes with Balkan folk music, lively markets, and explore the vibrant riverbanks.
- **Hidden gem:** Discover the serene botanical gardens and quiet alleys where history seems to whisper softly.

Day 13-14: Kotor & Montenegro

- **Morning:** Travel to the fjord-like Bay of Kotor.
- **Explore:** The fortified old town with winding streets, the ancient Cathedral of Saint Tryphon, and breathtaking views from Lovćen National Park.
- **Experience:** Boat trips to nearby small islands, or relax by the turquoise waters, soaking in Balkan serenity.

Day 15: Return & Reflection in Dubrovnik, Croatia

- **Morning:** Arrive in Dubrovnik's ancient city walls—standing like a resilient museum of maritime history.
- **Walk:** Wander the fortress walls at sunrise, sip coffee overlooking the sea, and reflect on an extraordinary journey that wove through Europe's hidden heart.

This journey of discovery is about more than just sights; it's about immersing yourself in the untold stories of resilience, tradition, and unspoiled natural beauty lying just beneath the surface of Europe's popular routes. Each town, each landscape, each festival will leave behind ripples of inspiration—reminding you that some of the most profound treasures are hidden just out of sight.

North America

A Mosaic of History, Diversity, and Wonders

Imagine a continent where every horizon whispers stories of ancient civilizations, where modern cities pulse with innovation, and where natural landscapes stretch from icy Arctic peaks to sun-kissed Caribbean beaches. Welcome to North America—a sprawling mosaic of history, cultures, and landscapes that has shaped the world's imagination.

Stretching from the icy climes of Canada, across the United States, to the vibrant islands of the Caribbean and the rainforests of Central America, North America is a continent that offers something extraordinary for every traveler. It's a land where the echoes of indigenous peoples resonate through sacred sites, where explorers crossed uncharted territories, and where cities of tomorrow rise upon foundations laid centuries ago.

A Rich and Complex History

North America's story begins long before Europeans arrived—home to diverse Indigenous nations with rich cultures, spiritualities, and histories spanning thousands of years. From the majestic ruins of the Mayan city of Chichen Itza to the mound builders of the Mississippi Valley, this continent is a living testament to innovation and resilience.

European explorers, from Columbus to Hudson, charted new worlds, igniting waves of migration, conflict, and cultural exchange. The birth of the United States, the Canadian confederation, and the energy of Latin America shaped global politics, economies, and ideas—creating a tapestry of nations intertwined in evolving stories of freedom, struggle, and hope.

What Does North America Bring to the Table?

Unmatched Diversity: From the snowy peaks of the Rockies, the lush Amazonian rainforests, to the sun-drenched beaches of California and the Caribbean, North America's diversity is its greatest strength.

Innovative Spirit: Known for Silicon Valley, Hollywood, and skyscraper skylines, this continent is the birthplace of technological progress, entertainment, and groundbreaking ideas.

Natural Wonders: Witness Yellowstone's geysers erupting in wonder, hike across the Grand Canyon's dizzying depths, or snorkel in the crystal-clear waters of Belize—adventures that redefine awe.

Cultural Melting Pot: Experience festivals blending indigenous traditions with immigrant influences—Mexican Día de los Muertos, the jazz beats of New Orleans, or the multicultural kitchens of Toronto.

Why Visit North America?

North America is a continent of contrasts—where ancient ruins sit alongside space-age cities, where deserts meet rainforests, and where diverse languages, cuisines, and stories blend into a living mosaic. It's a place that challenges perceptions and expands horizons—an endless arena for discovery, adventure, and inspiration.

For the curious traveler, North America isn't just a destination—it's an ongoing journey into the heart of human resilience and innovation, set amidst landscapes that seem to touch the heavens and stories that echo through eternity. It's a continent that invites you to explore not only new places but new parts of yourself—reminding us all that the most remarkable adventures are still waiting to be written.

Vast Wilderness and Urban Marvels: USA & Canada

Imagine a land where the horizon stretches endlessly, where towering mountains scrape the sky, and sacred rivers whisper stories of ancient Earth. Welcome to the twin giants of North America—USA and Canada—where nature's grandeur is both an unspoiled sanctuary and an exhilarating adventure. This is a continent where the spirit of exploration ignites in every breath, and every landscape is a testament to the boundless beauty and infinite diversity of the natural world.

The Past: From Indigenous Legacies to Cosmic Courage

Long before the sprawling metropolises and skyscraper cities, this land was alive with the heartbeat of Indigenous nations—wisdom whispering through sacred forests, mountain peaks, and wide-open plains. From the mystic stories of the Iroquois, Sioux, and Cree to the majestic totems of the Coast Salish, their cultures are woven into the very fabric of this landscape.

With the age of explorers and settlers, this continent became a canvas of dreams—boundless territories that challenged pioneers to conquer, settle, and celebrate the awe of the wild unknown. From Lewis and Clark's daring expedition to the gold rushes that sparked rivers of hope, the history of North America is a tale of courage, resilience, and an unquenchable thirst for discovery.

The Wilderness of the USA & Canada: Nature's Unbridled Poem

This continent's greatest treasure lies in its unspoiled, sprawling wilderness—an unbroken symphony of ecosystems, peaks, and plains that stir the soul in every sense.

- **Yellowstone National Park:** The first national park in the world, where geysers erupt like celestial fountains and bison roam freely across rolling meadows—nature's own orchestration of power and grace.
- **Grand Canyon:** A colossal rift in the Earth, carved over millennia by the Colorado River. Standing atop its shimmering rims, you witness a vast canvas of layered rock whispering stories of Earth's ancient heartbeats.
- **Canadian Rockies & Banff:** Here, jagged mountains cloak emerald lakes in their shadows, while glaciers shimmer in the sunlight—an alpine masterpiece of pristine snow and curious wildlife.
- **Great Bear Rainforest:** Among the last wild frontiers, this temperate rainforest hums softly with life—home to rare white bears and ancient cedars, a haven of serenity untouched by time.
- **Alaska's Wilderness:** From the icy fjords of Kenai Peninsula to Denali—the highest peak in North America—you are invited into a world where the land and wildlife coalesce into a singular, breathtaking symphony.

Marvels of Motion & Stillness: Landmarks and Experiences

- **Niagara Falls:** A thunderous cascade of water and mist, embodying nature's raw, unstoppable energy.
- **Hudson Bay & Arctic Circle:** Witness polar bears, belugas, and aurora borealis—nature's luminous ballet that ignites the night sky.
- **Pacific Coast & Oregon's Coastline:** Spiraling cliffs and sandy coves invite surfers, hikers, and dreamers to linger forever in the embrace of the vast Pacific.

The Journey of Discovery

Beyond the awe-inspiring vistas, these lands invite you into a mosaic of exhilarating pursuits:

- **Hiking & Backpacking:** Traverse the Appalachian Trail or Rocky Mountain highlands—threads that connect sky, earth, and spirit.
- **Wildlife Safaris & Whale Watching:** Spot grizzly bears, bald eagles, or orcas—each encounter a profound reminder of nature's resilience.
- **Camping & Stargazing:** Lie under a canopy of stars, where the universe reveals its secrets in a silence broken only by the whispering winds.

Why the Wilderness Calls So Deeply

This vast wilderness isn't merely a scenic backdrop—it's an invitation to rediscover ourselves amid the untouched, unspoiled splendor of North America. It whispers of primal roots, of wild spirits that refuse to be tamed, and of a world that still reminds us—the most extraordinary marvels are found in places where the Earth's ancient soul still breathes freely.

In these lands of infinite skies and endless horizons, every dawn renews the promise of discovery, every sunset kindles the fire of adventure, and every breath is a testament to the eternal dance between humankind and nature's majestic, unspoiled symphony.

The Ultimate Immersive Guide to North America's Wilderness

1. Yellowstone National Park, USA

The Genesis of Wilderness

Step into the world's first national park, where geysers spurt forth like celestial fountains, and vast herds of bison roam free. Witness the iconic **Old Faithful**, and explore the otherworldly **Grand Prismatic Spring**, its vibrant colors a testament to Earth's fiery core. Hike among steaming fumaroles and spot elk, wolves, and bears in their ancient playground.

Must-try: Take a moonlit hike at Lamar Valley, where the call of wolves echoes through the wilderness—a symphony of primal life.

2. Banff & Jasper National Parks, Canada

Alpine Majesty & Glacier Wonders
Nestled in the heart of the Canadian Rockies, Banff offers emerald lakes like **Lake Louise** and soaring mountain peaks. Cross the glacier-fed **Athabasca Falls**, or bike along scenic trails through pine forests and wildflower meadows.

Must-try: Take a wildlife safari at dawn, when moose and bears emerge from their hidden refuges, or trek to **Sulphur Mountain** for panoramic views that touch the sky.

3. The Sierra Nevada & Yosemite, USA

Granite Giants & Towering Waterfalls
In California, Yosemite's colossal **El Capitan** and **Half Dome** challenge climbers and awe-struck hikers alike. Witness the thunderous **Yosemite Falls** cascading over 2,400 feet—nature's towering sculpture.

Must-try: Roam the Mist Trail to **Vernal Fall**—a refreshing shower and a view of the wild beauty that carved this mountain masterpiece.

4. The Great Smoky Mountains, USA

Mystic Mists & Forest Whispers
Venture into the misty depths of Tennessee and North Carolina, where ancient Appalachian forests whisper secrets of lost worlds. Explore the vibrant **Cades Cove**, teeming with deer, black bears, and wild turkeys.

Must-try: Take a sunrise walk along Clingmans Dome's observation tower, where the mist swirls around your feet, and the world feels ageless.

5. Denali National Park, Alaska

The Roof of North America
Discover Denali's towering summit, the highest in North America, cloaked in perpetual snow. Cross glacier-carved valleys and spot grizzly bears, caribou, and wolves in their rugged home.

Must-try: Experience a husky sledding adventure or take a wilderness tour to glimpse the northern wilderness in its raw, majestic splendor.

6. The Canadian Arctic & Nunavut

Frozen Wilderness & Aurora Glows
Venture into Arctic Canada's untouched realm. Cruise past icy fjords, see polar bears stalking the sea ice, and witness the ethereal Northern Lights dance across the polar sky—a celestial ballet that ignites the soul.

Must-try: Kayak amidst floating icebergs, or spend a night in an ice hotel under a sky ablaze with auroras—pure magic in its most primal form.

7. Icefields Parkway & Columbia Icefield, Canada

The Road of Glaciers & Waterfalls
Drive along one of the world's most scenic routes, where glaciers descend from the **Columbia Icefield**—a colossal frozen river—carving a pathway through towering peaks and shimmering blue lakes.

Must-try: Take a glacier tour on a massive ice explorer coach and feel the ancient ice beneath your feet—frozen relics of earth's earliest days.

8. Big Sur & California Coastline

Cliffs, Reefs & Oceanic Whispers
Drive the rugged Pacific coastline, where seaside cliffs meet crashing waves and secret coves. Spot sea lions sunning themselves on rocky islands, and bask in the sunrise over the **Pfeiffer Beach**, with its purple sands.

Must-try: Hike the **Julia Pfeiffer Burns State Park** trail to view waterfalls plunging into the ocean—a wild masterpiece of erosion and resilience.

The Call to the Wild

This isn't just a list of places; it's an invitation—a summons to awaken your senses to Earth's primal heartbeat. Whether it's witnessing geysers erupt with ancient power, hiking through mountain kingdoms, or drifting in quiet kayak lakes, these wildernesses are sacred grounds—spaces where the Earth's original essence still whispers to those willing to listen.

Travel here isn't merely about ticking off destinations; it's an immersion into the raw, unspoken poetry of the Earth itself. It's about surrendering to the ancient rhythm that pulses beneath your feet, feeling the whisper of wind across mountain ridges, listening to the lullabies of rushing rivers, and witnessing the silent grandeur of glaciers and forests that have withstood the test of time.

In these sacred wildernesses, every moment is an awakening—a reminder that we are temporary visitors in a realm where nature's power is both gentle and relentless. It invites you to rediscover forgotten parts of yourself—courage in the face of towering cliffs, awe beneath star-studded skies, serenity during tranquil lake mornings.

The wilderness calls — not just to adventure, but to reverence. To listen, to learn, and to honor the venerable pulse of Mother Earth. Here, in these vast, unspoiled landscapes, lies the most profound journey—back to the roots of who we are in a universe crafted with infinite beauty and timeless wonder.

So, listen closely to the silent songs of the wild, and let the ancient heartbeat of the Earth guide your soul. In the vastness of these uncharted realms, find your true reflection—an echo of eternity in the dance of mountains, water, and wind. Embark with an open heart, for in the wilderness, we do not just see the world—we become part of its timeless symphony, woven into the very fabric of nature's grand, eternal story.

The Caribbean Breeze: Islands of Paradise

Imagine a place where the sun paints golden streaks across turquoise waters, where calypso rhythms resonate through the air, and where the spirit of warmth and welcoming hospitality infuses every moment. Welcome to the Caribbean—a luminous archipelago of islands that embody pure paradise and pulsating life, wrapped in a constant, gentle breeze.

Here, life is a dance between relaxation and celebration—a mosaic of friendly faces, vivid landscapes, and a culture that invites you to breathe easy, laugh often, and embrace every moment as a gift from the sea.

An Invitation to the Caribbean's Heartbeat

The Caribbean isn't just a destination; it's an experience—an intoxicating blend of sun, sand, sea, and soul. Its islands are home to some of the world's most pristine beaches—powder-soft sands that stretch into endless horizons, kissed daily by the whispering ocean waves. It's a place where the water's color shifts with the sunlight, shifting from shimmering aquamarine to deep cobalt, inviting travelers for a swim, snorkel, or simply to stand in awe of nature's watercolor masterpiece.

The **island culture** is an exuberant celebration of life itself. The air hums with the sound of **calypso, reggae, and soca beats**, echoing from sun-drenched shores and vibrant villages. Every street, every beach, and every sunset is a festival—a testament to the resilience, joy, and unbreakable spirit of the Caribbean people.

A Culture as Warm as the Sun

The Caribbean's soul lies in its people—friendly, open, and radiating genuine warmth. No matter where you go—from the bustling markets of Kingston to the colorful streets of San Juan—hospitality flows effortlessly, wrapped in the aroma of jerk spices, fresh seafood, and island spirits.

Experience the **immersive culture** that defines the islands: learn to dance to reggae beats, participate in a **Junkanoo parade**, or share a drink in a seaside tavern, where stories are swapped and friendships are born in seconds. Taste **native dishes**—succulent seafood, spicy stews, and sweet tropical fruits that embody the very essence of island life.

The Caribbean is a melting pot of histories—African, European, Indigenous, and Asian—and its festivals reflect this cultural richness, full of dance, music, and colorful costumes. It's a place where every moment celebrates life, love, and legacy.

Nightlife & Adventure: Experience the Energy

While the sun's warm embrace invites countless travelers to relaxation, the Caribbean's nightlife erupts with vibrant energy, especially in destinations like Barbados, Puerto Rico, and the Dominican Republic. Beach clubs pulse with lively music, fire dancers light up the night sky, and dance floors overflow with young spirits eager to party beneath the stars.

For the adventurous at heart, key attractions include diving into coral reefs teeming with marine life, windsurfing across breezy bays, or exploring lush rainforests and waterfalls. Islands like Jamaica and Aruba boast exhilarating nightlife combined with cultural shows, street parties, and night markets—perfect for those seeking adventure after sundown.

The Allure of the Easy-Going Spirit

What makes the Caribbean truly special is its effortless **laid-back vibe**—a slow, carefree rhythm that soothes your soul. Here, time seems to move to the gentle sway of palm trees, and stress melts away amidst the panoramic beauty and friendly smiles.

Whether lounging in a hammock with a chilled drink, exploring hidden coves, or engaging with local artisans, every experience is imbued with a sense of joy and ease. The islands remind us that life is best enjoyed in small doses—of sunshine, laughter, and good company.

The Heartbeat of Humanity: The Caribbean's Historic Tapestry

The Caribbean is more than a collection of radiant islands; it is a crucible where history, culture, resilience, and artistry converge. For centuries, this region has been a crossroads of civilizations—where Indigenous peoples thrived long before explorers arrived, and where waves of conquest, revolution, and renewal have left indelible marks on the collective human story.

A Historic Crossroads of Human Ingenuity and Spirit

Long before Christopher Columbus set sail across the Atlantic, the Caribbean was home to vibrant indigenous civilizations—Taino, Carib, Arawak—whose rich cultural tapestries and philosophical understandings of nature shaped the land's soul. Their stories, art, and spiritual practices echo through remains, cave paintings, and folk traditions that still pulse in local rituals.

The age of exploration brought a tumultuous dance—European colonizers, traders, and explorers arriving with ambitions of wealth, conquest, and faith—reshaping landscapes and lives in equal measure. As sugar plantations thrived and the slave trade expanded, the region became a global hub of economic and cultural exchange, forging new identities born from resilience and adaptation.

The Legacies of icons and icons of influence

The Caribbean's influence on human civilization is profound:

- **Marcus Garvey:** The visionary Jamaican orator and political leader inspired movements for Black pride and independence worldwide. His teachings on self-empowerment and unity continue to resonate today.

- **Bob Marley:** The legendary Jamaican singer and activist's reggae rhythms became the soundtrack of peace, love, and resistance—guiding countless souls to hope amidst struggle.
- **Michelle Obama and Barack Obama:** Their roots in the Caribbean—Barack hailing from Hawaii and Chicago's heritage, Michelle with family in Jamaica and Kenya—embody the diasporic journey of identity, resilience, and global influence.

The Caribbean's diverse peoples—African, European, Indigenous, Asian—have woven a rich cultural fabric that continues to influence music, dance, cuisine, and social movements worldwide.

The Islands' Irresistible Allure

Yet, as enduring as its history is, the true essence of the Caribbean lies in its unparalleled beauty. The islands are sanctuaries of serenity and celebration—ephemeral paradises where turquoise waters caress soft sands, and lush green hills explode with life. They beckon travelers to find solace in the gentle sway of palm trees, to dance to reggae and calypso, and to surrender to the simple joy of island time.

The Caribbean is a canvas of endless colors—coral reefs, sunset skies, vibrant markets, and living folklore. Every island offers its own unique melody; every wave carries a story of resilience, revival, and hope.

A Final Note: An Experience Beyond Words

The Caribbean is not just a destination; it is a divine invitation to reconnect with the essence of humanity—joy, resilience, love, and mystery. It's a place where history is alive in every smile, every dance step, and every sun-drenched sunset. The islands' natural beauty, cultural riches, and soulful rhythms demand at least once in a lifetime to be truly experienced—and felt.

As you breathe in the salt air and feel the ocean breeze, remember: these islands are more than beautiful landscapes—they are the very heartbeat of human spirit and natural wonder. They remind us all that life, in its purest form, is a celebration—flawless, fleeting, and endlessly stunning.

An Invitation to Explore

The Caribbean breeze isn't just a literal wind; it's a metaphor for freedom, joy, and renewal. It invites you to forget your worries and immerse yourself in an endless paradise where every day is a celebration of life's simple pleasures.

So, whether you seek serenity on pristine beaches, vibrant cultural festivals, or energetic nights filled with dance and laughter, the Caribbean is calling. It's a place where the heart is light, the spirit is free, and every moment is as warm as the sunshine—an eternal embrace of paradise and pulse.

Let the Caribbean breeze take you away—on an unforgettable journey into the soulful, vibrant heart of islands that truly feel like home

Caribbean Island-Hopping Adventure: 7 Days of Paradise

Day 1: Arrival in Jamaica — The Heartbeat of Reggae & Roots

- **Morning:** Arrive in Montego Bay or Kingston.
- **Afternoon:** Settle into a beachfront resort, relax and soak in the warm Caribbean sun.
- **Evening:** Experience live reggae at a local beach bar, ignite your soul with the infectious rhythms, and enjoy jerk chicken and tropical drinks.
- **Must-do:** Take a sunset cruise along the coast, listening to Bob Marley melodies that define the island's spirit.

Day 2: Blue Hole & Waterfalls in Ocho Rios

- **Morning:** Explore the **Dunn's River Falls**, where cascading waterfalls invite you to climb and splash in crystal-clear waters—an invigorating refresh.
- **Afternoon:** Visit the **Blue Hole**—a hidden gem—offering cliff jumping, snorkeling, and deep swimming pools surrounded by lush jungle.

- **Evening:** Unwind on the beach or indulge in local seafood ceviche as the reggae beats carry you into the night.

Tip: Engage with local artisans and try a traditional **lime and ginger cocktail**.

Day 3: Saint Lucia — The Island of Pitons & Romance

- **Morning:** Fly to Saint Lucia, renowned for its majestic Pitons mountains and lush rainforests.
- **Afternoon:** Take a scenic drive through the **Sulphur Springs** volcano—sulfur baths that refresh your spirit.
- **Evening:** Dine in a cliffside restaurant overlooking the coastline, tasting Creole seafood and Caribbean spices.
- **Must-do:** Evening walk along the beach, drinking fresh coconut water, and reflecting on the island's enchanting allure.

Day 4: Snorkelling & Beach Relaxation in Saint Lucia

- **Morning:** Snorkel over coral reefs teeming with tropical fish, sea turtles, and vibrant marine life.
- **Afternoon:** Relax on the iconic **Anse Chastanet** or **Sugar Beach**, sinking into soft sands with a cocktail in hand.
- **Evening:** Experience a lively fire dance show—a hypnotic blend of music, movement, and celebration.

Day 5: Barbados — The Vibrant Vibrations & Nightlife

- **Morning:** Fly to Barbados, the island of unforgettable beaches and lively festivals.
- **Afternoon:** Explore **Bridgetown**, a UNESCO World Heritage Site, with colonial architecture and colorful markets.
- **Evening:** Dive into the island's thriving nightlife—reggae bars, beach clubs, and dance halls pulsate with energy.
- **Must-do:** Sip a rum punch on the beach at dusk and dance the night away under a canopy of stars.

Tip: Try local delicacies like flying fish and Cou-Cou—a traditional Bajan dish.

Day 6: Water Sports & Island Exploration

- Morning: Windsurf, kiteboard, or try paddle boarding in Folkestone Marine Park.
- Afternoon: Take a boat trip to Hitman's Cave or Animal Flower Cave, exploring hidden grottos and swimming in natural sea pools.
- Evening: Relax in a seaside restaurant with fresh seafood and steel drum music setting the mood for your final night.

Day 7: Return & Reflection in Antigua or The Bahamas

- **Morning:** Fly to Antigua or Nassau for your final day in paradise.
- **Relax:** Lounge on **Dickenson Bay** or **Cable Beach**, soaking in the Caribbean rays.
- **Experience:** Take a final snorkel along coral reefs, sip on tropical cocktails, and listen to the soothing sound of waves.
- **Departure:** Reflect on the week of adventures, the warm welcoming people, and the endless blue horizons.

Your Caribbean Escape Awaits

This adventurous escape is crafted to give you a taste of everything—the soulful rhythms of Jamaica, the romantic peaks of Saint Lucia, the lively beaches of Barbados, and the ultimate island bliss of Antigua or The Bahamas. It's a journey of sun-drenched mornings, dance-filled nights, and unforgettable natural wonders—highlighting the vibrant, spirited, and endlessly welcoming essence of the Caribbean.

Let the breezes, beats, and beauty of these islands transport you to a paradise where every moment is an eternal celebration of life's simple joys.

Mexico's Mysteries and Markets

Mexico's Mysteries and Markets: A Tapestry of Color, Culture, and Secrets

Imagine a land where ancient ruins whisper lost stories, where every alleyway and marketplace teems with life, color, and mystery. Welcome to Mexico—a country of enchanting contradictions and sublime treasures, where vibrant markets hide age-old secrets, and the spirit of the people echoes in every dance, song, and delicious bite.

Mexico is an intoxicating blend of history and folklore, of ancient civilizations and modern celebrations. It's a place that beckons explorers to peel back layers of time, to embrace the vivid chaos of its markets, and to uncover the mysteries written in its ancient stones and lively streets.

Markets of Magic: The Heartbeat of Mexican Life

Step into a bustling market—*mercado*—and you enter a sensory wonderland. Here, the air is thick with the aroma of freshly roasted coffee, spicy chilies, sweet tropical fruits, and smoky spices. Each stall is a story, each vendor a storyteller—selling handcrafted textiles, ornate jewelry, and delicately painted pottery.

Iconic Markets & Hidden Treasures:

- **La Mercado de Coyoacán** in Mexico City: A labyrinth of colors, with vibrant textiles, artisanal sweets, and street performers.
- **Oaxaca's Textile Market:** Woven blankets, intricate embroidery, and stories threaded into every piece.

- **Chichen Itza Market:** A place to discover local crafts, souvenirs, and the mysteries surrounding the ancient Mayan ruins.

Must-do: Bargain politely, taste freshly made tamales, and listen to heartfelt stories behind each handmade artifact—the market isn't just a place to buy; it's a gateway into Mexican life.

The Mysteries of Mexico: Ruins, Legends & Hidden Keys

Beneath the sunlit splendor of colonial cities and lush jungles lie mysteries that continue to fascinate:

- **The Pyramids of Chichen Itza:** Once a Mayan astronomical observatory and ceremonial center, these ruins are echoing witnesses to secrets of ancient astronomy, mathematics, and ritual.
- **Teotihuacán:** The "City of the Gods," whose colossal pyramids and mysterious glyphs still puzzle archaeologists, leaving us to wonder about the lost civilizations that built these marvels.
- **The Legend of the Aztec Calendar Stone:** Carved from a single massive basalt slab, its intricate patterns and symbols hint at cosmic knowledge and religious secrets lost in time.
- **Hidden Caves of Naica:** Deep beneath the Mexican desert, caves glow with immense sapphires and crystalline formations—nature's secret lab of creation.

Curiosity tip: Dive into local legends—stories of voodoo, ancient shamans, and spiritual gateways that still stir the imagination of those seeking to understand Mexico's mystical depths.

The Culture & People: Warmth, Faith, & Fiesta

Mexican culture is a vivid tapestry woven from indigenous roots and Spanish influence—a lively mosaic of traditions, art, dance, and faith.

- **People:** Warm, expressive, and spirited—Mexicans greet you with heartfelt smiles and open arms. The community-centered way of life is evident in colorful festivals, lively towns, and shared meals.

- **Family & Faith:** From the elaborate **Day of the Dead** celebrations to grand cathedrals like **Catedral Metropolitana**, faith and family are core to life's rhythm.
- **Music & Dance:** Mariachi bands, folk dances, and the legendary ** Ballet Folklórico** pulse with energy, inviting you to join the celebration.

Must-do: Participate in local festivals, learn a few dance steps, or simply share a *tlayuda* (toasted corn tortilla with toppings)—authentic moments that reveal the heart of Mexico.

The Flavors of Mexico: A Culinary Kaleidoscope

Mexican cuisine is as vibrant as its culture—rich, spicy, and soul-nourishing:

- **Tacos al pastor**, **enchiladas**, and **mole** sauces are gateways into centuries-old culinary traditions.
- Street food stalls serve **elotes** (grilled corn), **churros**, and **tamarind candies**, each bite an explosion of flavor.
- Drink **mescal** and **tequila**—the spirits of ancient agave traditions—and toast to new adventures.

Food tip: Engage in a cooking class—learn to craft authentic salsas or make fresh corn tortillas. Food isn't just nourishment here; it's a language of love.

Mexico's Hidden Treasures & Future Mysteries

Beyond the famous sights and vibrant markets lie countless hidden gems—secrets whispered by the wind through ancient caves, lost in the shadows of mountain temples, and preserved in the enduring traditions of indigenous communities. Every road unfurls a new story; every smile opens a window into centuries of resilience; and every sunset paints a promise of mysteries yet to be uncovered.

Forgotten Caves & Sacred Sites

Deep within Mexico's rugged terrains hide caves adorned with ancient glyphs and shimmering crystals—testaments to civilizations long vanished yet still whispering their knowledge in silent echoes. These sacred sites, often only accessible through guided journeys, are portals to the spiritual depths of cultures that revered nature as divine. Walk through labyrinthine passages, and feel the presence of shamans and prophets who sought to unlock cosmic secrets beneath the Earth's surface.

Mountain Temples & Remote Villages

High in the Sierra Madre or nestled in lush jungles are mountain temples and sacred sites where traditions have remained untouched for generations. These tranquil communities cling to their ancestral roots, practicing rituals, crafts, and beliefs that connect them to the land and cosmos. Visiting such places is like slipping into a living tapestry of faith, tradition, and harmony—an immersion in the soul of Mexico's spiritual legacy.

Coastal Villages & Marine Mysteries

Along the coastlines lie fishing villages where ancient stories are told at sunset—of spirits rising from the ocean, of lost treasures buried beneath the waves, and of dolphins and turtles that grace the seas, guarding secrets of the deep. Snorkeling or diving in these waters reveals vibrant coral reefs and marine life that have thrived for millennia, hinting at ecological mysteries still unfolding beneath the surface.

Indigenous Heritage & Future Frontiers

Mexico's indigenous communities—Zapotec, Mixtec, Maya, and others—carry the torch of ancient wisdom, weaving their stories into contemporary life. As they preserve rituals, language, and crafts, they become guardians of the past and bridges to the future. Engaging with these communities offers hopes, traditions, and wisdom that can illuminate new paths—reminding us that the future is rooted in respecting the deep, ancestral wellspring.

The Eternal Allure of Mexico: A Land of Enduring Mysteries

Mexico isn't just a country of sun-drenched beaches and lively fiestas; it is a land of profound secrets and everlasting marvels. Its mountains, jungles, and coastlines hold the keys to understanding human resilience, spirituality, and the endless capacity for discovery.

Every journey here is an invitation—a call to look beyond the surface, listen to the whispers of the past, and embrace the mysteries still unfolding. For in Mexico, every sunset paints the promise that future adventures and hidden truths are waiting patiently just beyond the horizon.

Come, wanderer of wonder, and let Mexico's secrets awaken the explorer within. The true treasures are not only in its sights, but in the heart's deep yearning to seek, to understand, and to belong—to the land, the stories, and the endless adventure of the soul.

Hidden Spots & Indigenous Stories: Mexico's Secret Treasures

Hidden Spots

1. Cueva de las Manos (Cave of Hands)

Deep within the Patagonian cliffs of Argentina's southern border lies a remarkable site — but similar stories echo in Mexico's remote caves. The **Cueva de las Manos** (Cave of Hands) in Patagonia is famous for its stenciled handprints from ancient hunters. In Mexico, lesser-known caves like **Sistema de las Cuevas de Cacahuamilpa** offer labyrinthine tunnels filled with stalactites, stalagmites, and mysterious petroglyphs—the silent language of ancient artisans, whispering secrets of their spiritual lives.

2. Sierra Gorda's Hidden Waterfalls

Nestled in the rugged Sierra Gorda of Querétaro, secret waterfalls like **Escalara de los Enamorados** beckon adventurers willing to seek the unseen. These lush, untouched spots are stories in themselves—where indigenous rituals once blessed the waters for healing and renewal—fading echoes from a long-lost world.

3. La Cañada de la Virgen (the Hidden Valley)

This secluded valley in the Yucatán Peninsula hosts ancient cenotes and subterranean rivers, guarded by legends of Mayan priests and spirits that still haunt its depths. Ancient stelae and carvings suggest sacred rituals performed in secrecy, connecting today's travelers to the mystic rites of the Maya.

4. The Río Usumacinta & Uncharted Jungle Temples

Flowing through Guatemala and Mexico's Chiapas region, the **Usumacinta River** winds past lost temples cloaked in moss and mystery. These ruins, still largely unexplored, are repositories of indigenous stories—centuries-old tales of gods and kings fighting, forgiving, and transforming the jungle.

Indigenous Stories & Mystical Legends

1. The Legend of the Popol Vuh

The sacred Mayan manuscript **Popol Vuh** is a poetic tapestry of creation stories, hero legends, and cosmic wisdom. It recounts how gods fashioned humans from maize—the sacred crop—and how the hero **Kukulcán** (Feathered Serpent) shaped the universe. These stories teach about balance, respect for nature, and the divine within every living being—a mindset still alive in indigenous practices.

2. The Spirit of the Jaguar in Totonac & Maya Cultures

In many indigenous beliefs, the jaguar is a spirit of power, rebirth, and mystery. Legends tell of shamans transforming into jaguars through sacred rituals, guiding souls through the spiritual realm. Temples and caves dedicated to jaguar deities reveal a mythic world where humans and animals are intertwined in a dance of life and death.

3. The Legend of Xtabay

In Yucatán folklore, the **Xtabay** is a mythical female spirit—an enchanting figure who lures travelers into the jungle, leading them to secret sites of ancient temples. Legend warns of her beauty and wickedness, symbolizing the thin line between the spiritual and the mysterious—a reminder to respect the unseen realms.

4. The Aztec & Zapotec "Tree of Life" Legends

Stories speak of sacred trees—like the **Yaxche** in Zapotec tradition—that hold the universe together. These spiritual symbols are believed to be gateways between worlds, places where stories of creation, transformation, and eternity are still whispered in the rustling leaves.

The Call of the Ancients

In every corner of Mexico—hidden caves, remote jungles, sacred ruins—there are stories waiting to be discovered. The land's mysteries are whispers of a deep, sacred past—a testament that beneath its vibrant celebrations and lush landscapes, lie legends that continue to dream, struggle, and inspire.

To seek these hidden spots and listen to these indigenous stories is to take part in an ongoing journey—an awakening that the oldest truths whisper softly: We are all part of an unbroken lineage of wonder, resilience, and sacred mystery.

Discover Mexico: A 14-Day Journey through Culture, Colors, and Timeless Treasures

Mexico is a living mosaic of ancient civilizations, colonial splendor, and modern vibrancy—a land where history breathes in every stone, and every turn offers a new story. Embark on this ultimate adventure to uncover the soul of Mexico—a country that ignites the senses, warms the heart, and invites endless discovery.

Day 1-3: Mexico City — The Heartbeat of Heritage

Explore & Immerse

- **Zócalo & Historic Center:** Start at the sprawling Main Square, home to **Palacio Nacional** and the grand **Metropolitan Cathedral**—testaments to Spanish conquest and indigenous resilience.
- **Templo Mayor & Anthropology Museum:** Dive into the Aztec empire's secrets and marvel at the Aztec calendar stone.
- **Frida Kahlo Museum & Coyoacán:** Walk through the artist's vibrant home, a burst of color and creativity.
- **Xochimilco:** Float through canals on colorful trajineras—dancing, singing, and celebrating life on old aztec waterways.

Travel Tip:
Rent a car for flexibility but also explore via metro—an affordable, immersive way to experience local life.

Day 4-5: Teotihuacán & Puebla — Mysteries & Colonial Charm

- **Teotihuacán Pyramids:** Climb the **Sun & Moon Pyramids**, walking through ancient avenues that whisper secrets of a lost civilization.

- **Puebla:** Wander colorful streets, explore Santa María Tonantzintla & San Francisco Acatepec churches, and enjoy traditional **mole poblano**.

Your Journey Style:
Use a self-drive to feel the pulse of small towns and scenic routes—maps and local tips will guide a memorable road trip.

Day 6-8: Oaxaca — Indigenous Heritage & Colonial Splendor

Discover & Taste

- **Historic Centro & Santo Domingo:** Admire baroque architecture, lively markets, and craft workshops.
- **Monte Albán & Hierve el Agua:** Explore ancient Zapotec ruins and surreal mineral springs with mineral-laden 'waterfalls.'
- **Food & Culture:** Join a traditional cooking class—Learn to craft tamales, tlayudas, and mole.

Travel Tip:
Self-driving or hire local guides for a deeper connection—this region is about slow, authentic exploration.

Day 9-10: Campeche & Yucatán Peninsula — Coastal Beauty & Maya Mysteries

- **Campeche's Colonial Walls:** Walk your way through UNESCO-listed streets, with colorful facades and fortress walls.
- **Mayan Temples:** Explore **Uxmal** and **Chichen Itza**—the legendary pyramids and ball courts that echo ancient earth-shaking rituals.
- **Hidden Cenotes:** Swim in natural freshwater caves, ancient portals to other worlds.

Travel Tip:
Rent a car for flexibility to explore remote cenotes and coastal villages—roads are well-marked, scenic, and safe.

Day 11-12: Mérida & Riviera Maya — Colonial Elegance & Caribbean Bliss

- **Mérida:** The cultural capital of Yucatán—visit churches, markets, and local artisans.
- **Riviera Maya & Tulum:** Relax on powdery beaches, snorkel in coral reefs, and visit the **Tulum Ruins** perched above the Caribbean.
- **Cenotes & Eco-Parks:** Dive into cenotes or explore eco-parks like Xcaret and Xel-Há.

Day 13-14: Mexico's Pacific Coast & Riviera

- **Acapulco & Puerto Vallarta:** Soak in vibrant nightlife, beaches, and water sports.
- **Mazatlán:** Discover lively markets, historic architecture, and fresh seafood.
- **Nightlife & Culture:** Experience authentic mariachi, lively festivals, and seaside charm.

Travel Tips & How to Get Around

- **Self-Drive:** Mexico's scenic byways are a joy for explorers; rent a comfortable, reliable car, and enjoy the freedom to customize your journey.
- **Public Transport:** For urban exploration, buses and metro systems are efficient and affordable.
- **Domestic Flights:** Use to save time when hopping between distant regions—Mexico's air network is extensive and economical.
- **Local Guides & Tours:** Deepen your understanding with curated tours, private guides, and community-led experiences—these add depth and authenticity.

The Essence of Your Mexico Adventure

This journey is your personal story—an unfolding tapestry woven with colorful landscapes, ancient whispers, vibrant traditions, and unforgettable encounters. It's a voyage that awakens your senses, ignites your curiosity, and deepens your understanding of a land where every corner holds a secret, every street a song, and every moment a sacred memory in the making.

Mexico isn't just a destination; it's an invitation to rediscover wonder in the everyday, to embrace the mysterious beauty of ancient ruins and lively markets, and to connect with its warm, resilient people. It's a place where history and heart beat as one, inviting you to write your own chapter in its grand story.

So go forth with open eyes and a bold heart. Embrace every adventure—big or small—and let Mexico's magic ignite the explorer within you. Because the most extraordinary journeys are not just about the places you see, but the soul's awakening that they inspire.

Your story is waiting—unfold it in the land of endless color, timeless mystery, and infinite charm. Mexico — a paradise that lives in your dreams, now ready to become yours.

South America

A Symphony of Passion, Rhythm, & Unforgettable Souls

Imagine a continent where the air is thick with excitement, where every heartbeat echoes with the rhythms of salsa, tango, and carnival beats—where the people live with an infectious zest for life. Welcome to South America—a land of vibrant colors, fiery landscapes, and joyful souls that dare to embrace every moment with zest and passion.

This is not merely a land of stunning mountains, lush rainforests, and endless coastlines—it's a living celebration of life itself, woven from the threads of diverse cultures, ancient traditions, and unbreakable spirits. It's a continent where storytelling is a dance, where football is a religion, and where every face tells a story of resilience, pride, and joy.

A Symphony of Cultures & Celebrations

South America's cultural landscape is a kaleidoscope—an ever-shifting mosaic of indigenous legacies and colonial influences. From the mesmerizing rhythms of samba in Brazil, the passionate tango of Argentina, the colorful festivals of Bolivia, to the rich Andean music of Peru, each region offers a unique melody that pulses with life.

The continent's carnivals, like Rio's famed **Carnaval**, are bursting festivals of color, costumes, and joy—an explosion of dance, music, and community spirit. In every city, in every village, the cultural heartbeat is alive in the streets, echoing the primal happiness of a people who cherish life deeply.

The Passion for Football & Sports

In South America, football is more than a sport—it's part of the continent's DNA. Football heroes like **Pelé**, **Maradona**, **Messi**, **Santos**, and **Riquelme** are not just legends—they are living embodiments of hope, skill, and pride. The joy of scoring a goal, the thrill of a last-minute victory, or simply the sound of a football bouncing in dusty streets encapsulates the continent's love for this beautiful game.

Argentina's **Maradona** and **Messi** have inspired generations, their names synonymous with hope and resilience. Brazil's **Samba nation** lives and breathes football, with legendary stadiums that echo stories of brilliance and heartbreak, uniting millions in shared passion.

The Dance & the Spirit of Joy

Dance in South America is more than movement—it's a language of the heart. Whether it's the sultry **Tango** in Argentina's Buenos Aires, the lively **Samba** in Brazil, or the energetic **Cumbia** and **Salsa** in Colombia and the Caribbean coast—you feel the pulse of life in every step, every move celebrating rhythm, love, and freedom.

It's a continent that teaches us that living is an art, and every day is a chance to dance, sing, and embrace the bliss of simply being alive.

South America: Where Passion Meets the Heartbeat of the Earth

Here, nature itself seems to breathe with the same exuberance as its people—the towering Andes, the lush Amazon Rainforest, the fiery deserts, and endless coastlines. It's a symphony of earth, water, and wind that invites you to lose yourself in its beauty, its rhythm, and its stories.

South America isn't just seen; it's felt. It's not only explored; it's embraced. It's a continent where the soul is set ablaze by its sights, sounds, and the unyielding spirit of those who call it home.

Come, let your heart beat to its rhythm. Enter its stories. Dance with its colors. Discover the magic of a continent where life is lived with passion, joy, and an unbreakable zest that stays with you forever.

Andean Adventures: Peru and Machu Picchu

High up in the breathtaking heights of the Andes, nestled within an emerald embrace of mountains and clouds, lies a mystery wrapped in stone—Machu Picchu, the forgotten city of the Incas. Yet the story of Peru extends far beyond this legendary site, into valleys carved by ancient civilizations, jungles teeming with life, and towns alive with heritage.

Peru is a land where history's echoes resonate through every step, where adventure beckons amidst towering peaks and sacred ruins, and where cultures—ancient and new—dance together in harmonious celebration of life.

The Marvel of Machu Picchu & the Inca Legacy

Imagine standing amidst the ruins of **Machu Picchu**, a marvel of engineering and spirituality shrouded in mist—a city lost to the ages yet alive with mystery. Built in the 15th century by the Incas, this citadel at the crown of the Andes embodies human ingenuity and sacred harmony with nature.

Climb the stone terraces, where sophisticated aqueducts and canals purr like ancient rivers of wisdom. Visit the **Intihuatana** stone, believed to be an astronomical device, and breathe in the aura of a civilization that thrived in perfect harmony with the mountain gods.

Must-do: Trek the legendary **Inca Trail**, a journey through lush cloud forests, ancient ruins, and breathtaking vistas—each step a pilgrimage through time and spirit. For the less adventurous, take a scenic train ride—a luxurious voyage through valleys and mountains, revealing Peru's natural splendor.

The Sacred Valleys & Beyond

Venture into the **Sacred Valley of the Incas**, where terraced vineyards, colorful markets, and Inca ruins tell stories of a divine civilization that revered mountain spirits and celestial cycles. Here, farmers still harvest quinoa, and artisans craft textiles woven with ancestral patterns.

The Enchanting Amazon & Rainforests

Deep in Peru's jungles, wildlife thrives amid the lush canopy—jaguars, macaws, and poison dart frogs remind us that life persists in the most primal corners of the Earth. Join guided excursions, visit indigenous villages, and learn ancient medicinal practices—immersing yourself in a living tapestry of tradition and nature.

Inca & Colonial Heritage

Explore **Cusco**, the historic capital of the Incas, where narrow cobblestone streets wind through colonial plazas. Visit San Blas artisans, and feel the pulse of a city where history's layers are woven into every adobe wall.

Adventure & Discovery: Activities for the Brave & the Curious

- **Hiking & Trekking:** From the snow-capped **Ausangate** peaks to the mysterious **Choquequirao**, the landscapes beckon explorers to walk paths steeped in legend.
- **River Rafting & Kayaking:** Feel the rush of white-water rapids on the Urubamba River or paddle the tranquil lakes reflecting the snow-tipped Andes.
- **Horseback Riding & Mountain Biking:** Traverse remote trails, feeling the earth beneath you, and witness an unspoiled world that seems untouched by time.
- **Wildlife Encounters:** Search for the elusive Andean condor, visit wildlife preserves, and witness llamas and alpacas grazing in open pastures.

Sacred Rituals & Cultural Celebrations

Partake in authentic ceremonies—offerings to Pachamama (Mother Earth), partake in traditional dances, or attend festivals celebrating local legends. Relish the vibrant music, color-drenched costumes, and the collective heartbeat of a culture that venerates nature, ancestors, and the cosmos.

The Spirit of Peru & the Andes
Peru isn't just a destination; it's an invitation to ascend into a higher consciousness, to step into a landscape that awakens your senses and stirs your soul. From the mysterious heights of Machu Picchu to the tranquil lakes and lively towns below, this is a land that inspires wonder, ignites adventure, and connects you to the very pulse of life itself.

Come, journey beyond the known, and discover the heart of an ancient world still beating strongly in the modern dawn. The Andes await—vast, awe-inspiring, and timeless. Your adventure into Peru's soul begins now.

7-Day Peru Adventure: From Machu Picchu to Hidden Valleys

Day 1: Arrival in Lima — The Gateway to Peru

- **Morning:** Arrive in Lima, the vibrant capital. Check into a boutique hotel in the historic district.
- **Afternoon:** Explore Plaza Mayor, the cathedral, and the colonial architecture that narrates the city's rich history.
- **Evening:** Dinner at a renowned ceviche spot and a stroll along Miraflores' seaside promenade, watching the sunset over the Pacific.

Tip: Spend the night in Lima to acclimate to the altitude and enjoy its bustling culinary scene.

Day 2: Cusco — The Heart of the Inca Empire

- **Morning:** Fly to Cusco, the ancient capital of the Incas (30-minute flight). Rest and acclimate to the altitude.
- **Afternoon:** Walk around the Plaza de Armas, visit the **Coricancha** (Temple of the Sun), and wander through the cobbled streets of San Blas.

- **Evening:** Sample Cusqueña craft beers or join a local dance and music show.

Tip: Take it slow—altitude sickness can strike; stay hydrated and avoid strenuous activity until acclimatized.

Day 3: Sacred Valley & Pisac

- **Morning:** Drive through the Sacred Valley, a lush corridor of terraced fields and ancient sites.
- **Visit:** The Pisac Market—an explosion of textiles, jewelry, and local crafts.
- **Afternoon:** Explore the **Inca fortress of Ollantaytambo**, with terraces cascading down mountain slopes, whispering secrets of their builders.
- **Evening:** Relax in a charming inn in Urubamba or Ollantaytambo village.

Tip: Engage with local weavers and artisans—immerse yourself in living Inca traditions.

Day 4: Machu Picchu — The Lost City of the Incas

- **Early Morning:** Take the scenic train ride from Ollantaytambo or transfer via Inca Trail (if booked in advance)—the journey itself is breathtaking.
- **Tour:** Guided walk through Machu Picchu, exploring terraces, temples, and mysteries of this ancient citadel hidden high in the mountains.
- **Afternoon:** Optional hikes to **Huayna Picchu** or **Sun Gate** for panoramic views.
- **Evening:** Return to Cusco by train or stay overnight near Machu Picchu for a quieter experience.

Tip: Wear comfortable shoes, bring water, and engage your senses—this is a place to feel stories centuries old come alive.

Day 5: Cusco to Sacsayhuamán & Rainbow Mountain

- **Morning:** Visit the impressive **Sacsayhuamán** fortress—massive stone walls that defy explanation.

- **Afternoon:** Embark on a full-day excursion to **Rainbow Mountain** ("Vinicunca"), a surreal landscape of multi-colored stripes—an awe-inspiring natural spectacle.
- **Evening:** Return to Cusco and relax in a cozy local café.

Tip: Book a guided tour, stay hydrated, and prepare for a high-altitude trek. The view is worth every breath.

Day 6: Lake Titicaca & Uros Floating Islands

- **Morning:** Travel to Puno, on the shores of Lake Titicaca—the world's highest navigable lake.
- **Visit:** The floating Uros islands—clusters of reed mats where indigenous communities maintain ancient traditions.
- **Afternoon:** Experience local music and crafts, or explore Taquile Island's terraced hills and textile artistry.
- **Evening:** Return to Puno or stay overnight by the lake for a mystical sunset.

Tip: Engage respectfully with local communities—these living cultures are the soul of Andes' traditions.

Day 7: Return to Lima & Departure

- **Morning:** Fly back to Lima for your international connection.
- **Optional:** If time permits, visit the **Museo Larco** for its world-class pre-Columbian art collection.
- **Transfer:** To the airport, carrying memories of high peaks, ancient mysteries, and vibrant cultures.

Final Inspiration

Your week in Peru will take you through a land where every step uncovers a new story—of ancient civilizations, sacred mountains, and resilient peoples. It's an adventure that awakens your spirit, a journey that leaves you profoundly humbled and endlessly inspired.

Are you ready to step into the lost worlds of the Incas, the mysterious valleys, and breathtaking peaks? Peru's magic beckons—your extraordinary chapter starts now.

Amazonian Mysteries

The Amazonian Mysteries: Nature's Living Legend

In the heart of our planet lies a sprawling, enthralling wilderness—an emerald labyrinth that whispers secrets of time, life, and transformation. Welcome to the Amazon—the lungs of Earth, a living cathedral of biodiversity, mystery, and timeless wonder.

Stretching over nine countries, this colossal rainforest is more than a jungle; it is an intricate symphony of life—a vibrant tapestry woven from countless species, ancient spirits, and natural marvels. Here, nature awakens in a riot of colors and sounds, a dance of survival, evolution, and renewal, echoing the primal song of our very origins.

The Enchanting Essence of the Amazon

What Is the Amazon?

At its core, the Amazon is a vast hydrological and ecological network—an intricate system of rivers, lakes, floodplains, and dense rainforests that span approximately 5.5 million square kilometers. The **Amazon River**, over 4,000 miles long—second only to the Nile—is its mighty artery, nourishing a thriving maze of ecosystems that support the richest diversity of life on Earth.

The Soul of the Jungle

In this lush, humid cradle of life, every leaf, wing, and stream has a story—a symphony of symbiosis that sustains the planet's balance. It is a sanctuary for endangered species, a birthplace for evolution, and a prophetic window into Earth's primordial past.

And what incredible creatures call this realm home? Brace yourself:

- **Giant River Otters:** Playful, social, and curious, these majestic mammals paddle through the waterways.
- **Pink River Dolphins:** Mystical and rare, their elusive forms glide beneath the surface, woven into local myths.
- **Harpy Eagles:** The undisputed queens of the sky, with expansive wingspans and piercing gaze, guardians of the canopy.
- **Poison Dart Frogs:** Brightly colored little warriors, wielding potent toxins and iridescent beauty.
- **Anacondas & Pythons:** The giants of the rivers, silently lurking, embodying Mother Nature'sRaw power.
- **Harpy & Macaw Parrots:** Vibrant, intelligent, and noisy—colorful symphonies of wings and song.

The Diversity

The Amazon is a realm of extremes:

- Over **390 billion trees**, representing **16,000 species**, cast an incessant canopy of green—each a tiny universe.
- The rivers teem with **more than 2,200 fish species**—from tiny tetra to monstrous piraruccu.
- The forest shelters countless mammals, birds, insects, amphibians, and reptiles, many yet to be discovered—it's an ongoing mystery of life in motion.

Unveiling the Mysteries: Adventures in the Amazon

The Amazon is a world of adventure, awe, and discovery—an explorer's paradise tailor-made for those eager to embrace the unknown.

Itinerary of Wonders & Realms

Day 1-2: Arrival & River Safari

Begin your journey in Manaus, Brazil's gateway to the Amazon. Take a boat cruise along the mighty river, watching the sunrise ignite the forest canopy, and listen to the calls of cacophonous wildlife awakening to a new day.

Day 3-4: Rainforest Lodge & Canopy Walks
Stay immersed in the jungle at an eco-lodge nestled within the rainforest. Walk among ancient trees on swinging bridges, spotting sloths hanging lazily, or toucans flashing their colors overhead. Dive into night walks—silent excursions where every rustle could reveal a mysterious creature.

Day 5-6: Indigenous Village & Cultural Connection
Meet indigenous communities—learn their traditions, crafts, and secrets of survival. Share stories around fires, taste wild fruits, and gain insight into the spiritual layers of the forest—where every leaf whispers ancient knowledge.

Day 7: Wildlife & Birdwatching Expedition
Enhance your senses in a birding boat tour, spotting elusive species—kingfishers, harpy eagles, herons—and marvel at the symphony of calls echoing through the canopy.

Day 8: Kayaking & Floating Forests
Paddle silent canoes through flooded forest areas, discovering hidden wildlife and exploring the mysterious "floating" trees—tales of the flood cycle that sustains this lush world.

The Living Secrets of the Rainforest
Beyond its captivating scenery lie mysteries—hidden species, ancient medicinal plants, and ecological secrets. The Amazon is nature's living legend—continually evolving, endlessly inspiring.

Why the Amazon?
Because this is where Earth's primal heart still beats fiercely—where every breath connects you to life's

Secrets of the Green Abyss

Deep within the dense emerald heart of the Earth lies a realm shrouded in whispered legends and shimmering shadows—a vast, living enigma that refuses to reveal all its secrets. The Amazon rainforest is more than a forest; it is a mystery—an ongoing story

written in the language of shadows and light, where time itself seems to pause, holding its breath in reverence.

The Veiled Legends

For centuries, explorers, shamans, and jungle dwellers have spoken of unseen realms—hidden temples swallowed by vines, caves echoing with lost voices, and spirits said to guard the balance of life. Ancient petroglyphs etched into rocks, cryptic symbols hidden in the foliage, and mysterious patterns on butterfly wings whisper tales older than history itself—secrets waiting patiently beneath layers of moss and myth.

The Forest's Silent Guardians

The richness of the Amazon isn't just in its creatures; it's in its silent sentinels—trees that harbor long-forgotten tales, rivers that carve passages into eternity, and soil that cradles mysteries of Earth's earliest days. Many species, unclassified and unknown, pulse beneath the surface, guardians of ecological secrets that can redefine our understanding of life itself.

Missing Pages of Nature's Manuscript

What does the Amazon hold? Perhaps a species of plant so rare it's only a legend, a medicinal flower with powers no modern science fully understands, or a hidden chapter of Earth's evolutionary story that remains cloaked in fog. Some believe it is a place where souls come to transform—an earthly gateway between worlds, where the line blurs between myth and reality.

The Thrill of Untouched Discovery

Venturing into the Amazon is an invitation into a realm of endless wonder—a quest to find what has yet to be seen or named:

- **Unearthing the secrets of ancient medicinal plants** used by indigenous shamans—each leaf and root a whisper from the past.
- **Treading the unmarked trails** where rare orchids bloom in silent ecstasy, and elusive predators stalk in muted shadows—artists painting their stories in natural ink.

- **Listening for whispers of the forest**—the subtle symphony of life, where every chirp, hum, and croak may hide a story of adaptation, resilience, and ancient wisdom.

The Enchanted Unknown

Every discovery, every new species, every unexplored cavern—or even a quiet, unseen corner of the jungle—serves as a reminder that this world is still a vast, unfolding mystery. It whispers that the Amazon is more than a limitless green maze; it is the storyteller of Earth's secret history, waiting to reveal its next chapter to the patient, the curious, the brave.

The Living Enigma

The Amazon isn't just a place to explore; it's an invitation to listen—listening carefully to the echoes of bygone ages, the silent whispers of nature's ancient wisdom, and the mysteries that only unveil themselves to those willing to embrace the unknown.

Dare to step into the green abyss, and you may find yourself not only discovering hidden secrets but unlocking parts of your own soul—because in this mysterious wilderness, the greatest secrets are always waiting for those brave enough to seek them.

In the heart of the green abyss, where shadows dance and whispers linger, lies a realm of eternal secrets—an untamed universe waiting patiently for those brave enough to listen.

Here, time slows, and the ancient soul of Earth breathes softly, inviting us to uncover its hidden stories, to walk the silent corridors of forgotten worlds, and to awaken the explorer within.

Dare to step into this lush, mysterious sanctuary, and you may find that the greatest discoveries are not only in the treasures you unearth but within the depths of your own spirit—calling you to remember that the universe's most sacred secrets are written in the language of wonder and wonderment.

And in that sacred dance with the unknown, you will realize—you are part of this vast, unfolding mystery—a vital voice in the eternal song of life.

The Amazon awaits—not just as a place of discovery but as a mirror of your own endless possibilities, a journey into the soul's most profound mysteries.

South American Spirit: Argentina & Brazil

Imagine a continent pulsing with unrestrained passion—a place where every heartbeat resonates in the tango and samba, where the air hums with the rhythm of life itself. Welcome to Argentina and Brazil—two nations that embody the raw, fiery soul of South America, each a storyteller of resilience, love, and ceaseless energy.

In these lands, history dances with modernity, and tradition is painted in sweeping strokes of dance, music, and vibrant festivals. From the windswept pampas to the famed beaches of Copacabana, this is where the true spirit of South America lives—bold, beautiful, and alive.

Argentina: The Land of Passion & Panoramas

In Argentina, the pulse is in its deeply rooted love for dance, food, and soccer—the lifeblood that courses through its cities and countryside alike. The passionate tango—born in the smoky dance halls of Buenos Aires—captures the longing and zest that define Argentine soul. The city's streets breathe not only history but an undeniable vibrancy—elegant, yet wild.

Venture into the pampas, Argentina's sprawling plains, and witness the rhythm of life among cattle ranches and gauchos. Feel the pride in a traditional asado, the fiery Argentine barbecue that's as much a social ritual as a meal.

And in the Andes, explore the mystical landscapes of Patagonia—where glaciers carve the southern skies, and the wind whispers stories of explorers and ancient spirits. Argentina invites you to embrace its boldness—its beauty in chaos, passion, and poetic longing.

Brazil: The Heartbeat of Joy & Diversity

Brazil erupts with life in every corner—a carnival of colors, sounds, and spirits. The rhythmic pulse of samba, the vibrant extravagance of carnival, and the lively streets ofRio de Janeiro embody Brazil's unbreakable zest for life. Here, the joy of dance is contagious, and the freedom of expression is celebrated in every song, every move, and every smile.

Venture into the Amazon rainforest, the ecological gem of the world—an immense, living cathedral teeming with creatures both magnificent and mysterious. Experience the energy of the Pantanal, one of the world's largest wetlands, where jaguars prowl and exotic birds fill the sky in a riot of colors.

Brazil's spirit is written in its diversity—indigenous traditions, African rhythms, European influences—all woven into a vibrant tapestry of life, festa, and hope.

A Symphony of Passion, Rhythm, and Love

These twin giants of South America are not merely places to see—they are experiences that ignite your senses and touch your soul. They challenge perceptions, inspire dreams, and remind us that life's greatest joys come from embracing the wild, beautiful chaos of living.

Argentina and Brazil are the beating hearts of South America—where the dance of life is eternal, and every moment is an invitation to love, celebrate, and live wildly.

The Colors of Life — An Invitation

South America is a living masterpiece painted with the brightest hues of passion, resilience, and celebration. Its cities sing with rhythmic beats, its landscapes sparkle with natural wonders, and its people embody the fierce joy of life—a continent where every heartbeat is a drum, and every breath is a song.

It beckons explorers with open arms and invites them to see with eyes unclouded by routine. To listen with hearts unburdened by doubt. To immerse in a land where the traditional and the modern dance together in vibrant harmony, creating a kaleidoscope of endless stories waiting to be told.

A Tapestry Woven in Heartbeats

Imagine waking up in Rio, the city alive with samba, its streets a mosaic of color and life. See the smiling faces of children playing football on the beaches, their laughter mingling with the roar of waves. Walk through vibrant markets where artisans craft their dreams in textiles, jewelry, and murals—each piece bursting with history and hope.

Travel to the ancient ruins of Machu Picchu, shrouded in mist, where the stones whisper secrets of a civilization that reached for the heavens. Feel the magic of the Amazon's lush canopy, where every leaf whispers stories of survival, and every creature embodies nature's endless capacity for renewal.

And then, venture further—into the highlands of Colombia, the vineyards of Argentina, and the colorful streets of La Boca—where life bursts forth in a carnival of culture, music, and dance. These are the living colors of a continent that refuses to be muted, a palette ever-changing—outrageous, luminous, divine.

The Heartbeat Beneath the Surface

Beyond the external vibrancy lies the deep pulse of resilience—an unbreakable spirit born from centuries of ancestral stories, revolutionary struggles, and unyielding hope. The indigenous traditions, African roots, and colonial echoes have twisted, twined, and blossomed into a unique cultural renaissance—setting the stage for a people who live life with unrelenting passion, fierce pride, and joy.

Every festival, every dance, every song is a testament—a living affirmation that the true essence of life is found in celebrating the now, in embracing every moment as precious, and in dancing to the rhythm of our shared human story.

An Invitation to Embark on Your Own Colorful Journey

This continent isn't merely a destination; it's an awakening—a divine call to embrace the vibrancy within and without. To surrender to the music that never stops, to taste the fiery spices of life, and to feel the beat of the world echoing in your own heart.

So, dear traveler, let go of hesitation. Dust off the doubts and step boldly into the chromatic whirlwind that is South America. Its stories are waiting—exampled in the shimmering waters of the Galápagos, the spirited dances of Argentina, the ancient stones of Peru, and the unbreakable resilience of its people.

This is your moment. The colors of life are a permanent invitation—dancing in the wind, shining in the sun, living in the soul. Join the celebration. Your adventure of a lifetime is calling—ready to paint your story in hues of joy, discovery, and endless wonder.

Open your heart, ignite your spirit, and let South America remind you that life, in its purest form, is a celebration—a voyage of color, rhythm, and love that never truly ends.

Beaches & Beyond: Nature's Most Colorful Creations

The continent's pristine beaches are a paradise of turquoise waters and golden sands. From the seductive coast of Costa Rica and Panama to the wild shores of the Galápagos, nature has painted a picture so magnificent that it seems almost unreal.

- **Bocas del Toro, Panama:** Tropical islands where the water is so clear you can see the reef below and the sunsets burn with fiery intensity.
- **Galápagos Islands, Ecuador:** Living proof of evolution's artistry—unique creatures like giant tortoises, marine iguanas, and blue-footed boobies in their natural wonderland.
- **Machu Picchu & Sacred Valleys:** Beyond the ruins, discover lush cloud forests and ancient terraces humming with the energy of centuries ago.

Football: The Soul of South America

No exploration of South America would be complete without paying homage to its soul—**football (soccer)**. Passion pulses through the veins of every city from the streets of Buenos Aires to the stadiums of Rio, and the games aren't just sport—they're visceral experiences shared by millions.

- **Boca Juniors vs. River Plate:** The legendary rivalry that ignites the heart of Argentina—an electrifying spectacle of skill, passion, and history.
- **Maracanã Stadium:** A cathedral of football where heroes are born, legends are made, and every cheer echoes with dreams of glory and heartbreak.

Football isn't just a game—it's a living, breathing cultural phenomenon that unites nations, fuels dreams, and embodies the unyielding spirit of South America.

Oceania

A Personal Ode to Paradise

Imagine a vast, shimmering ocean cradling a continent of wonder—where every island is a jewel, every wave whispers a legend, and every sunset paints a masterpiece of hue and harmony. Welcome to Oceania—a land of endless azure, lush green, and untouched paradise that is truly a world apart.

For centuries, Oceania has beckoned explorers, dreamers, and lovers of the sublime. Its islands are the living embodiment of nature's artistry—volcanoes rising dramatically from the sea, beaches so pristine they seem unreal, and rainforests echoing with the songs of native birds and ancient spirits.

This is our personal favorite—a place where the soul finds peace in the gentle embrace of the ocean, and the heart awakens to the profound beauty of living in harmony with nature.

An Archipelago of Endless Wonder

Oceania isn't a single place; it's a constellation of islands, each with its own story, song, and soul:

- **Australia:** A continent and island of paradoxes—desert landscapes, vibrant cities, and an extraordinary array of wildlife. Uluru's majestic presence awakens ancient dreaming stories, while Sydney's Opera House sings with modern elegance.
- **New Zealand:** A land of storytellers, with rugged mountains, fjords, and Maori heritage. Lord of the Rings landscapes come alive here, inviting adventurers to step into scenes of mythic grandeur.

- **Fiji & the South Pacific Islands:** Tropical havens with crystal-clear waters, coral reefs, and a welcoming spirit that makes every visitor feel like family.
- **Papua New Guinea:** A treasure of tribes, rainforests, and untouched traditions—an immersion into one of the world's last true frontiers of cultural diversity.

But Oceania's magic isn't just in its landscapes; it's in its soul—its profound rhythm of life, its embrace of the Wild, and its invitation to reconnect with the essence of being human.

Why Oceania Is Unmissable

- **Unique Wildlife & Marine Life:** From kangaroos and koalas to humpback whales and manta rays, the biodiversity here is unparalleled.
- **Indigenous Cultures & Traditions:** Maori haka, Aboriginal Dreamtime stories, and Pacific islander rituals weave deep cultural tapestries that connect the past with the present.
- **Unspoiled Beaches & Coral Reefs:** Surf, snorkel, or simply lounge on beaches where time slows and worries melt away.
- **Adventure & Serenity:** Dive into world-class surfing, hike ancient volcanoes, or meditate in tranquil rainforests—each experience offers a rebirth of the spirit.

A Heartfelt Invitation

Oceania isn't just a part of the world; it's an experience that touches the core of the human heart. It's a symphony of beauty, resilience, and harmony—a place where everything feels alive, boundless, and sacred.

It is our personal favorite—an endless journey into wonder, crafted by the ocean's lullabies and the land's ancient stories. So, whether you seek adventure, serenity, or a profound reconnection with nature and yourself, Oceania awaits with open arms, ready to transform your soul and inspire your dreams.

Island Paradises: Australia & New Zealand

Imagine a stretch of earth and sea where the sky kisses wild, rugged landscapes—an unspoiled dreamscape of vibrant reefs, ancient forests, and rugged mountains. Welcome to Australia and New Zealand—two extraordinary island nations that redefine what it means to be a paradise.

These lands are nature's masterpieces—painted with the brushstrokes of time and resilience, where every island whispers a story of survival, innovation, and unyielding beauty. From the coral kingdoms beneath the waves to the soaring peaks that pierce the clouds, this is a world where adventure and serenity dance together in a harmonious embrace.

For travelers seeking the extraordinary, Australia and New Zealand are not just destinations—they are a call to awaken the explorer within, to dive into adventures, to breathe in pure, untainted air, and to connect with the primal magic of Earth's most magnificent islands.

The Land of Wide Horizons & Deep Mysteries

Australia, a continent wrapped in endless deserts, lush rainforests, and iconic wildlife—kangaroos, koalas, and the mysterious voices of the Dreamtime. The **Great Barrier Reef**, the world's largest coral system, invites snorkelers and divers into an enchanted world of color and life. Uluru's silent grandeur is a spiritual monument, whispering stories of the Aboriginal Dreaming.

New Zealand—a land of mythic landscapes, where towering mountains, fjords, and forests mirror the fantasy worlds of legend. The lush Fiordland and Milford Sound are nature's cathedral, inviting explorers to take a cruise into the depths of untouched beauty. It's also the birthplace of **adventure sports**—bungee jumping, skydiving, and jet boating—all in a landscape that seems crafted for daring dreams.

An Unforgettable Canvas of Life

Together, Australia and New Zealand are a symphony of life in all its forms:

- **Biodiversity:** From the uniquely bizarre **platypus** and **kiwi** to ancient kauri trees and vibrant coral gardens—this is a realm where nature's diversity defies imagination.
- **Indigenous & Maori Heritage:** Aboriginal Dreamtime stories and Maori legends weave a rich cultural fabric—spirits, myths, and rituals that live on in song, dance, and art.
- **Adventure & Soulful Serenity:** Surfer's paradise on Bondi Beach; hiking in glowworm caves; discovering glow-in-the-dark beaches; or simply gazing into star-studded skies—each experience awakens your senses and reconnects you with nature's primal pulse.

An Invitation to Explore Your Inner Wilderness

Australia and New Zealand are more than destinations—they are landscapes that stir something primal, something wild, and something profoundly alive within us. They teach us that adventure and peace, discovery and reflection, are all part of one eternal dance.

Come. Dive into their turquoise waters, scale their rugged peaks, wander through their ancient forests, and open your heart to the boundless beauty that these island paradises hold.

Because in these lands of myth and marvel, every moment is a voyage into the extraordinary—crafted by nature's finest brushstrokes and waiting for you to step into the masterpiece.

Come, awaken your spirit where the ocean meets endless sky, and the mountains whisper ancient secrets. Step into a realm where every wave, every breeze, and every star invites you to explore the depths of wonder—and to discover the boundless universe that lives within your soul.

In Australia and New Zealand, the earth's most majestic masterpieces await your touch—terra firma and coral kingdoms, lush rainforests and fjords of fire and ice—all calling you to dive into adventure, embrace serenity, and dance beneath the stars.

This is your moment—your invitation to journey beyond the familiar, to breathe in the pure magic of island life, and to piece together the incredible story of your own wild, beautiful adventure.

So, open your heart, trust your dreams, and let these magnificent lands awaken the explorer within you—because the voyage of a lifetime begins where your spirit is set free.

The islands are waiting—are you ready to answer the call?

Australia: The Land of Vast Horizons and Infinite Wonders

Australia is a continent of contrasts—a sprawling canvas of rugged Outback, lush rainforests, pristine beaches, and vibrant cities. It's a land where nature's raw power is captured in towering cliffs and great deserts, and life pulses with an unbreakable spirit of innovation and resilience.

Imagine standing beneath the mighty Uluru, feeling the heartbeat of the Dreamtime stories etched into ancient stone. Picture yourself snorkeling among coral gardens teeming with color, or hiking through rainforests whispering secrets of time's earliest days. From cosmopolitan Sydney to the wilds of the Kimberley, Australia welcomes the curious with open arms and endless possibilities.

But here's a truth—covering the vast expanse of Australia in one trip is an impossible feat. Its beauty is too immense, its landscapes too diverse, and its wonders too numerous for a single journey to capture. To truly experience Australia's magic, one must savor it in

deliberate, soulful exploration—each region a chapter of discovery, waiting to be read slowly and savored.

New Zealand: The Land of Legend and Lush Landscapes

New Zealand is a spellbinding island kingdom of mythic mountains, emerald fjords, and forests alive with the songs of native birds. It's a realm where every landscape feels like a scene from a fantasy—raw, majestic, and endlessly inspiring.

Picture yourself navigating the rugged alpine passes of the Southern Alps, marveling at mirror-like lakes beneath towering peaks, or exploring lush rainforests bursting with life. Known as the adventure capital of the world, New Zealand is where heart-stopping hikes, bungee jumps, and jet-boating adventures awaken your wild side.

And just as with Australia, attempting to see the entirety of New Zealand in one trip would be like trying to contain a universe in your hands. Its beauty demands patience, deep exploration, and appreciation of every unique corner. To truly embrace its essence, you need to experience each island—each set of landscapes and stories—on its own terms.

A Deliberate Choice: Experience Each in Its Full Glory

Australia and New Zealand are sister lands—each a masterpiece crafted by nature and time. But the truth remains: these are two worlds, each deserving a dedicated voyage. Attempting to run through both in one journey is an exercise in haste—an injustice to their beauty, their stories, and their soul.

Choosing one allows you to immerse deeply, to truly taste the heartbeat of each land, and to unlock the secrets they hold.

Sample Itineraries

Australian Odyssey: 12 Days of Wonder

- **Day 1-3:** Sydney—Climb the Harbour Bridge, explore the Opera House, and relax on Bondi Beach.

- **Day 4-5:** Blue Mountains—Hiking through mist-shrouded valleys and waterfalls.
- **Day 6-7:** Great Barrier Reef—Snorkel among vibrant coral or take a liveaboard cruise.
- **Day 8-9:** Uluru & Ayers Rock—Experience sacred sunrise and sunset, and learn about Dreamtime stories.
- **Day 10-12:** Melbourne or Brisbane—Vibrant arts scenes, coastal drives, and wildlife encounters.

New Zealand Adventure: 12 Days of Magic

- **Day 1-3:** Queenstown—Bungee jumping, jet-boating, and exploring Fjordland's stunning scenery.
- **Day 4-5:** Milford Sound—Cruise through shimmering fjords surrounded by soaring peaks.
- **Day 6-7:** Rotorua—Soak in geothermal springs, visit Maori villages, and enjoy traditional performances.
- **Day 8-10:** Wellington & Tongariro National Park—Hiking volcanic landscapes, exploring film locations from The Lord of the Rings.
- **Day 11-12:** Auckland—Harbor cruises, city markets, and Waitakere Ranges waterfalls.

Final Thought

Australia and New Zealand are jewels glittering in the same celestial crown—each offering a universe of wonder. But in their splendor and depth, they command dedicated journeys, savoring every breathtaking vista and soulful encounter.

Choose your path wisely, and let each land reveal its true magic—layer by layer, moment by moment—in a voyage that transforms, humbles, and inspires in ways words can only hint at.

Pacific Dreamscapes

Pacific Dreamscapes: Nature's Whispers in the Endless Blue

Close your eyes and imagine an ocean without end—a shimmering, iridescent realm where every wave caresses a secret, every island whispers ancient stories, and the horizon stretches beyond the bounds of imagination. Welcome to the Pacific Dreamscapes, a mystical sanctuary where water and wonder fuse into a symphony of serenity and adventure—an eternal dream woven into the very fabric of Earth.

In this celestial expanse, time takes on a gentle, languid rhythm. The waters ripple with life—vibrant coral gardens like kaleidoscopic tapestries beneath the surface, schools of luminous fish darting like fleeting dreams, and majestic whales breaching in a ballet of grace. Here, the land and sea dance in a harmony so pure, it awakens a primal longing—an invitation to lose oneself in the poetry of the infinite blue.

Imagine drifting in the tranquil lagoons of Bora Bora—those mystical, lagoon-ringed islands, where overwater bungalows seem to float like dreams on crystal waters.

Walk along the pristine beaches of Fiji, where palms sway in choreographed elegance, and the sands invitingly shimmer, whispering promises of relaxation and renewal.

Or venture into the lush rainforests of Papua New Guinea, where towering waterfalls cascade into emerald pools—refreshing the spirit with whispers of the jungle's ancient secrets.

In Hawaii, the volcanic islands—big, bold, and alive—tell stories of fire and ice, where molten lava once shaped the landscape, creating a paradise of stark beauty and vibrant life.

And in the Marquesas, Tahiti, and the Cook Islands? Every atoll, every reef, every secluded cove is a sacred fragment of Earth's enduring dream—the ultimate reflection of life's purest poetry.

The Pacific Dreamscapes are not merely a place to visit—they are a state of being. They whisper to the heart: "Dream bigger. Explore deeper. Find the magic that awakens when you surrender to the endless dance of water and sky."

This realm urges you to dive into aquamarine mysteries, paddle along silent coral walls, and watch dawn's first light ignite the sea in hues of pink and gold. It's a symphony of peace and thrill—a place where worries drift away with each gentle wave and the soul awakens to the eternal song of the ocean.

The Pacific Dreamscapes call to those who seek to dream with open eyes, to explore with open hearts, and to immerse themselves in the endless poetry of water, wind, and wonder—an unending celebration of life's most beautiful mystery: the universe's deep, silent song.

Nature's Whispers in the Endless Blue

Close your eyes and imagine an ocean without end—a shimmering, iridescent realm where every wave caresses a secret, every island whispers ancient stories, and the horizon stretches beyond the bounds of imagination. Welcome to the Pacific Dreamscapes, a mystical sanctuary where water and wonder fuse into a symphony of serenity and adventure—an eternal dream woven into the very fabric of Earth.

In this celestial expanse, time takes on a gentle, languid rhythm. The waters ripple with life—vibrant coral gardens like kaleidoscopic tapestries beneath the surface, schools of luminous fish darting like fleeting dreams, and majestic whales breaching in a ballet of grace. Here, the land and sea dance in a harmony so pure, it awakens a primal longing—an invitation to lose oneself in the poetry of the infinite blue.

Imagine drifting in the tranquil lagoons of Bora Bora—those mystical, lagoon-ringed islands, where overwater bungalows seem to float like dreams on crystal waters.

Experience: Snorkel through vibrant coral reefs bursting with color, swimming alongside gentle manta rays and curious parrotfish. Glide on a glass-bottom kayak over a teeming reef, feeling the ocean's heartbeat beneath you.

Walk along the pristine beaches of Fiji, where palms sway in choreographed elegance, and the sands invitingly shimmer, whispering promises of relaxation and renewal.

Experience: Dive into the world's softest sands, then embark on a jungle trek to see waterfalls cascading into clear pools, perfect for a refreshing swim amid untouched greenery.

Venture into the lush rainforests of Papua New Guinea, where towering waterfalls cascade into emerald pools—refreshing the spirit with whispers of the jungle's ancient secrets.

Experience: Join a guided river rafting adventure, navigating wild rapids beneath emerald canopies, or trek through dense jungles searching for exotic bird species like the King-of-Saxony bird of paradise.

In Hawaii, the volcanic islands—big, bold, and alive—tell stories of fire and ice, where molten lava once shaped the landscape.

Experience: Hike across volcanic trails in Volcanoes National Park, watch the lava glow at night, or surf the legendary waves of Maliko Gulch, feeling the primal power of the Pacific.

And in the Marquesas, Tahiti, and the Cook Islands? Every atoll, every reef, and every secluded cove is a sacred fragment of Earth's enduring dream.

Experience: Paddle in peaceful lagoons, snorkel through underwater caves, or catch a sunset cruise along jagged coastlines to witness nature's fireworks in pinks and purples.

The Call to Adventure

The Pacific Dreamscapes are not merely a place to visit—they are a state of being. They whisper to the heart: "Dream bigger. Explore deeper. Find the magic that awakens when you surrender to the endless dance of water and sky."

Dare to dive into aquamarine mysteries, paddle along silent coral walls, and watch dawn's first light ignite the sea in hues of pink and gold. Feel the thrill of zip-lining over waterfalls, surf the legendary breaks, or trek to mountain summits that offer vistas of eternity.

These waters are alive with adventure, serenity, and endless possibility. The Pacific Dreamscapes beckon the brave, the dreamers, and those who yearn to rediscover the soul of Earth's most magnificent oceanic realm.

And as the waves whisper their ancient lullaby, and the skies ignite with dawn's first light, remember—you are part of this boundless, shimmering universe.

The Pacific's endless horizons beckon not just with their breath-taking beauty but with a call to your innermost explorer—the part of you eager to sink into the wild poetry of water, wind, and wonder.

Here, in these shimmering waters and lush islands, life's greatest secrets are written in the language of waves and sunsets. The ocean invites you to dive deeper—the voyage of discovery, renewal, and joy begins when you surrender to its eternal song.

Embrace the Dreamscapes, breathe the magic, and allow your spirit to wander beyond borders—into the infinite embrace of the ocean's heart, where every dawn promises a new beginning, and every sunset sings the lullaby of eternity.

The Pacific awaits—you only need to listen to its song and step into its endless, luminous dance.

Part - III
Personal Stories & Lessons Learned

Top 10 Unforgettable Encounters from Our Travel Experiences

1. Australia: Hand-feeding Kangaroos & Wombats in Kangaroo Island

In Australia's rugged heart, we found ourselves among the gentle giants of the outback—the kangaroos and wombats. The surreal experience of hand-feeding these curious creatures in their natural habitat, watching their eyes light up with trust and wonder, is etched into our memories forever. It's an intimate moment where nature's innocence and beauty become a part of your soul.

2. Romania: Meeting the Protectors of the Transylvania Forest

Deep within the mystical Carpathian mountains, we had a chance to sit alongside a local forestry team dedicated to preserving Romania's ancient woods. Listening to tales of reforestation, wildlife conservation, and the age-old legends of the forest guardians, we realized that real heroism lies in protecting life's most fragile wonders.

3. New Zealand: Sharing a Maori Welcome Ceremony

In New Zealand's lush valleys, we participated in a traditional **Powhiri**—a Maori welcoming ceremony that connected us to the land's ancient roots. The powerful chants, carved wooden Atua figures, and heartfelt hospitality created a moment of profound cultural communion, reminding us how human stories are woven into the fabric of the natural world.

4. Morocco: Dancing with Berber Nomads Under a Sahara Sunset

In the endless sands of the Sahara, a group of Berber nomads shared their stories, songs, and dances around a flickering campfire. As the golden sun dipped below the horizon, we danced with these resilient souls—

living legends of the desert—feeling the pulse of life, love, and resilience in every beat.

5. **Norway: Witnessing the Aurora Borealis with Locals**

High in the Arctic circle, we joined Sami herders beneath the shimmering curtains of the Aurora Borealis. The silent, swirling lights seemed to breathe magic into the night—an awe-inspiring spectacle that stirred the ancient spirits of Earth and sky. It was a moment of silent reverence and cosmic connection.

6. **Sweden: Ice Hotel & Candlelit Aurora Experience**

In the icy embrace of the Swedish Lapland, we slept in an ice hotel, marveling at intricate sculptures illuminated by flickering candles. Later, we stood entranced under the dancing auroras, feeling as if we'd stepped into an ephemeral dream—an encounter with nature's most fleeting masterpiece.

7. **India: Sharing a Spiritual Morning in Varanasi's Ghats**

On the sacred ghats of the Ganges, we witnessed a dawn ceremony of pilgrims bathing and offering prayers. Amidst the sacred melody of conch shells and chants, we felt the river's eternal energy—an encounter that reconnected us to spirituality, life, and the mysteries of existence.

8. **Tanzania: Watching the Great Migration under a Serengeti Sunrise**

As the endless plains awoke, we watched a staggering herd of wildebeest and zebras migrate in a sea of dust and life, crossing roaring rivers beneath a fiery sunrise. The raw power of nature's eternal cycle—so fierce, so fragile—etched itself into our hearts forever.

9. **South Africa: Coming Face-to-Face with the Big Five**

While on safari in Kruger National Park, we had a close encounter with a lion's majestic gaze, a moment of primal connection that reminded us of the fragile balance of life. It's a meeting with the wilderness that awakens respect, awe, and humility.

10. Brazil & Argentina: Celebrating Life at Local Festivals & Football Matches

In Brazil, we joined a riotous **Carnaval** parade, dancing among thousands of samba dancers, feeling the pure euphoria of collective joy. Meanwhile, in Argentina, we watched passionate fans cheer wildly at a Boca Juniors match—a raw, emotional experience of community, pride, and unbreakable spirit.

Challenges on the Road

Embracing the Wild, Imperfect Beauty of Travel

Traveling is often portrayed as a montage of picturesque sunsets, perfect landscapes, and seamless adventures. But the truth, as every seasoned explorer will tell you, is that the journey is as much about overcoming challenges as it is about celebrating triumphs.

Each trip is a tapestry of emotional highs and lows—moments of awe, joy, and discovery, intertwined with hurdles that test patience, resilience, and humility. These challenges are not obstacles to be feared, but the silent teachers guiding us toward deeper understanding—of ourselves, others, and the world.

The Unexpected Storms: When Nature Tests Your Spirit

I remember wandering into a vibrant market in a remote village, immersed in the colors and sounds, when suddenly, a torrential downpour transformed the narrow alley into a rushing river. The wind howled fiercely—an uninvited reminder that nature's temperament is wild and unpredictable.

In that storm, I learned patience—in waiting, in seeking shelter, and in understanding that sometimes, the universe humbles us with its mighty power, asking us to surrender control and trust in the moment.

Lesson: Respect the rhythms of nature. Pack for the unexpected, and embrace every shower as a reminder that life, like weather, changes swiftly—and often beautifully.

The Language Barrier: Silent Conversations of the Heart

One evening, I found myself in a tiny café in a distant city, trying to order food with gestures and a few broken words. The staff smiled kindly, but communication was a puzzle—an incomplete dance of expressions and patience.

In those moments, I realized that language is more than words—it's a bridge of empathy. When words falter, kindness bridges the gap. When gestures fail, a genuine smile speaks volumes.

Lesson: Cultivate humility and openness. Let your actions and heartfelt intent be your language, for kindness has no barriers.

The Lost Moments: When Maps and Plans Fall Apart

There was a time I missed an entire day because I took a wrong turn and ended miles away from my itinerary. The initial frustration melted into wonder—I found a quiet village, a forgotten alley, and a story I would never have encountered otherwise.

Travel isn't about ticking boxes; it's about embracing the detours as opportunities for magic. The unplanned moments, the missteps—they are often the richest chapters.

Lesson: Release the need for perfection. Trust your intuition, stay flexible, and discover that sometimes, the best stories happen in the uncharted.

The Cultural Clashes: When Worlds Collide

One morning, I unintentionally disrespected local customs in a sacred site, and the silent disappointment was a lesson in humility. It was an uncomfortable reminder that respecting traditions enriches your understanding and forms genuine bonds.

Every encounter with a different culture is a mirror reflecting our own assumptions. Embrace the unfamiliar with reverence.

Lesson: Approach differences with curiosity and respect. Every tradition holds a story—listen, learn, and honor it.

The Emotional Challenges: Facing Your Own Shadows

Travel often brings feelings of loneliness, vulnerability, or homesickness. Sitting alone in a foreign landscape, I realized that these emotions are part of the voyage—the inner journey of growth.

Travel confronts us with our own shadows, pushing us to heal, forgive, and become stronger.

Lesson: Be gentle with yourself. Allow your feelings to flow, trusting that every challenge is shaping a more resilient, compassionate you.

The Final Reflection

Yes, travel can be challenging—sometimes chaos, sometimes discomfort. But through these moments, we learn what it truly means to live fully: to face uncertainty with courage, to embrace imperfections with grace, and to discover that even in difficulty, beauty blooms.

The road isn't always smooth, but every bump, every storm, and every unexpected turn is a sacred part of your story—a chapter of transformation that turns travellers into warriors of the soul.

So, step forward with an open heart, knowing that every challenge you face is a gift—an invitation to grow, to deepen your connection to life, and to find the courage that turns the ordinary into the extraordinary.

In the whisper of the wind and the roar of the storm, truths are revealed—hidden treasures within the chaos, the silent songs of the soul.

Every challenge faced along the road is a sacred verse—a gentle reminder that the greatest journeys are within, where resilience blooms in the face of adversity and wisdom grows in the soil of humility.

Embrace the storms that come your way, for they are the storms of rebirth—transforming fears into strength, doubts into dreams, and wounds into the shining armor of your spirit.

Trust that every detour, every stumble, every silent tear is a step closer to the truth—an awakening to the divine masterpiece that resides within each of us.

Walk boldly into the unknown, for the road of life is not merely a path of destination, but an endless dance of discovery—where every challenge is merely a verse in your song of becoming.

And in that luminous dance, you will find—
the greatest adventure of all—the journey back home, to the infinite sanctuary of your own heart.

The Unexpected Joys of Travel: The Hidden Fire of Life's Greatest Gift

Travel is often painted as a chase for the famous sights—the grand monuments, the iconic landscapes, the must-see waterfalls. But beneath the surface, far beyond the guidebooks and well-trodden paths, there lies a hidden universe of surprises. These are the moments that crack open your soul, set your heart ablaze, and remind you that the greatest joys are often the unplanned, the unexpected, and the rawly authentic.

This is a celebration of those uninvited gifts—the spontaneous encounters, the quiet epiphanies, and the luminous surprises that turn ordinary journeys into extraordinary revolutions within.

The Fire of Spontaneity: When the Unexpected Sparks Joy

Imagine wandering through a village market, when suddenly, a local musician invites you to dance. Or stumbling into a tiny tea shop, where strangers become friends through shared stories and heartfelt laughter. These un scripted moments—raw, unfiltered, and unpretentious—are the true flames of adventure.

In their unpredictability, they ignite sparks of joy that music cannot reproduce nor plans can contain. They remind us that life's biggest treasures often arrive unannounced—wrapped in a smile, a shared meal, a fleeting glance.

The secret? Let go of rigid plans. Embrace every twist, turn, and detour. The universe has a habit of surprising us when we least expect it—and those surprises are the fire that fuels true joy.

The Beauty of Vulnerability: When Fears Turn Into Triumphs

Travel demands vulnerability—stepping into the unknown, speaking a new language, navigating unfamiliar streets. Sometimes, miscommunications lead to awkward laughter; other times, they forge bonds stronger than words.

Losing your way in a labyrinth of narrow alleys or a tangled jungle path can feel daunting—until you realize that these "failures" are the fertile ground for authentic connection, personal growth, and profound joy. Every mistake becomes a story, every setback a triumph—proof that the true victory lies in resilience, in daring to be vulnerable.

The fiery truth? The greatest joy comes from shining despite fears—turning uncertainty into an unbreakable spirit of adventure.

The Joy of Connection: When Strangers Become Family

On the road, you discover that the world is filled with kindred souls—strangers who, in a moment, become friends, teachers, or unexpected family. Whether it's sharing a meal with a local family, dancing in a festival, or exchanging stories in a hut on a mountain slope, these human connections are the glowing embers that remind us: we are all part of one luminous universe.

The most fiery of all? The realization that, amidst differences, kindness and love are universal languages—gifts more precious than any monument.

The Thrill of Discovery: When Nature and Culture Reveal Their Secrets

Hiking into a hidden valley, swimming beneath a rainforest waterfall, or stepping into an ancient temple—these are the moments where the world reveals its secret fires. Unexpected discoveries—an elusive animal, a breathtaking view, or an ancient carving—set your heart racing and leave indelible marks on your soul.

The true joy? That the world is an endless source of marvels—waiting patiently, almost daring you to uncover its secrets.

The Fire Within: How Travel Reignites Our Inner Passion

Most powerful of all, the unexpected joys of travel light the fire within ourselves—the passion, curiosity, and spirit we sometimes forget amid daily routines. Every unanticipated moment reminds us: life is meant to be lived fiercely and authentically.

Faith, love, adventure—these aren't just moments to chase; they are the flames that burn within us, ignited anew by every journey, in every unexpected joy.

FINAL FLAME: Your Journey of Unpredictable Wonder Awaits

Don't merely seek the grand landmarks; chase the sparks of surprise. Seek the moments that make your heart race, your soul sing, and your spirit roar—because in the unpredictable, in the unplanned, lies life's most exhilarating, fiery gifts.

Go forth boldly. Embrace the unknown. And let every unexpected joy fall like fiery sparks—lighting up the grand adventure of your life. Because the most beautiful moments aren't scheduled; they're born from the fearless pursuit of wonder.

Reflections: How Travel Transforms Us

The Heart of the Journey: An Ode to the Spirit of Travel

As we come to the end of this voyage—yet, in truth, the journey never truly ends—we stand at the heart of what travel has always been: a sacred dance between the outward and the inward, an eternal quest to discover, to understand, and to transform.

Travel is more than the mere act of moving through space; it is a timeless voyage that awakens parts of us we never knew existed. It's a mirror reflecting our deepest truths—our fears, hopes, resilience, and awakening. It's the sacred key that unlocks the door within, revealing a universe of boundless potential and infinite stories.

The Transformative Power of Travel

Every step along the road—whether admiring ancient ruins, wandering through lively markets, or gazing at star-filled skies—becomes a mirror to our own inner landscapes. It's in the clash of unfamiliar sounds, the taste of new foods, the colors of foreign lands—that we discover the vibrant, resilient core of who we are.

Travel doesn't change us; it reminds us. It reminds us that life's true magic lies in curiosity, in openness, and in the willingness to be humbled by the vastness of the world—and, ultimately, of ourselves.

The Journey Beyond Borders

Borders are just lines on a map, echoes of old divisions echoing in the corridors of fear and separation. But the real journey—*the one that ignites the soul*—transcends borders. It unites hearts, dissolves prejudices, and reveals the interconnectedness of all beings.

This voyage leads us to see ourselves not as isolated individuals but as explorers of the infinite, forever seeking new horizons—both outside and within. It teaches us that the greatest discoveries aren't in the places we visit, but in the depths we reach within ourselves—our courage to face the unknown and our capacity to love unconditionally.

The Calling to Embrace the Unknown

Every adventure whispers a sacred truth: that life's richest blessings come from stepping into the unknown—into new cultures, unfamiliar landscapes, and uncharted territories of our own hearts. It is in daring to venture beyond comfort, to embrace the unpredictable that we find our fullest selves.

And so, the most profound journey is not just through distant lands but through the uncharted terrains of our spirits. It's a voyage that encourages us to listen more deeply—to the silent stories of the universe, to the subtle whispers within, and to the infinite dance of life itself.

A Reflection on the Soul's Wanderlust

In the end, travel is a sacred pilgrimage—a continual awakening of wonder, compassion, and purpose. It is a calling that echoes in our deepest core: to seek truth, to cherish beauty, and to recognize that every moment, every encounter, every challenge is a sacred thread woven into the tapestry of our existence.

The world outside is a mirror reflecting the vast universe within. And every time we step into the unknown—whether on distant shores or within the silent chambers of our mind—we are heralds of awakening—a testament that the journey is eternal, and the possibilities are boundless.

The Final Embrace

So, carry this truth close to your heart:
Your journey of discovery is a divine dance—a sacred unfolding of life's eternal story. Every adventure, every challenge, every moment of awe is a gift—a reminder that the true magic of travel lies in the transformation it ignites within you.

Embrace the wanderer within. Celebrate the eternal odyssey. And remember—wherever you go, the most important journey is the one inward, where the universe's deepest mysteries await your discovery.

Because in the end, the world is not just what you see. It's who you become—an infinite explorer, forever traveling, forever growing, forever alive in the endless dance of wonder and love

"Beyond every shoreline, within every breath, lies a universe waiting—silent yet shouting, vast yet intimate. The greatest voyage is not across distant skies, but inward into the infinite depths of your soul.

For in every step you take into the unknown, you ignite the eternal flame—a light that guides you through the shadows, awakens your spirit, and whispers the sacred truth:
we are travelers not just of places, but of endless wonder—the infinite dance of discovery within and beyond."

Part - IV
Inspiring the Traveler in You

Inspiring the Travel within You

Travel isn't just about crossing borders or ticking off destinations; it is an ongoing voyage of the soul—an awakening that stirs your deepest passions, broadens your perspective, and reminds you of the infinite wonder woven into the fabric of life.

It's a gentle whisper in the quiet mornings when you gaze at a distant mountain, a roaring call in the bustling markets of foreign lands, and a sacred reminder in moments of solitude beneath a star-studded sky. Travel, in essence, is a mirror reflecting the boundless universe within—a journey into the uncharted territory of your own spirit.

The Inner Journey: Discovering the World's Reflection

Every place you visit is an extension of your own story—every sunset, whisper, and encounter becomes an invitation to look inward. The mysterious forests, sprawling deserts, and vibrant cities are not just landscapes; they are chapters in your ongoing saga of creation, curiosity, and growth.

Travel teaches you to listen better—to the stories of strangers, the silent language of nature, and the quiet voice of your own heart. It's about breaking free from routines, shedding fears, and awakening a sense of wonder long buried beneath the layers of everyday life.

The Power of Presence and Mindfulness

In the fast-paced world of modern living, the true art of travel is immersing yourself fully into each moment—feeling the texture of soil beneath your feet, inhaling the aroma of unfamiliar spices, or watching a sunset dissolve into a canvas of colors. These moments aren't just souvenirs; they are sparks igniting awareness and gratitude.

The grandest voyage begins within, where your mind and spirit embrace the unknown with open arms. When you travel with intention—curiosity, patience, and humility—you transform every experience into a sacred lesson, every obstacle into an opportunity for growth.

Cultivating a Travel Mindset in Daily Life

The essence of travel isn't confined to distant lands; it's a way of living. Practice seeing beauty in the ordinary—notice the way sunlight filters onto your window, or how an old street might whisper stories if you listen closely. Be curious about people's lives and cultures—treat every encounter as a chance to learn, to expand your horizon, and to cultivate kindness.

Bring the spirit of discovery into your everyday routines—try a new cuisine, explore a different neighborhood, or simply pause to breathe and appreciate the present moment. These small acts are, in fact, the seeds of a lifelong adventure.

Your Inner Explorer Awaits

Look beyond the maps and itineraries—your greatest journey is the one that unfolds within. Wander into the terrains of your imagination, your dreams, and your aspirations. Embrace the unknown within yourself—your fears, hopes, and endless potential. Trust that the world outside and the universe within are mirrors, each reflecting new chapters waiting to be written.

A Call to Your Inner Traveler

Remember: The greatest discoveries are often the ones we make inside—moments of clarity, peak experiences of connection, and sparks of creativity ignited by unfamiliar sights and sounds. Each step you take on the outside is a step closer to understanding your true self—your passions, your purpose, your unique contribution to this wondrous tapestry called life.

So, ignite your curiosity. Be brave. Embrace every unfolding chapter—inside and out. For the world is a mirror, and your journey begins with the first step … inward.

The Inner Voyage: Embracing Your Innate Desire to Travel

Every heart beats with a silent echo—a whisper of longing, a flicker of curiosity. Deep within, there exists an unwavering, universal desire to explore—the innate dream to wander through exotic lands, to immerse oneself in unseen worlds, to touch the divine in every corner of the Earth.

This isn't merely a fantasy—it's the very essence of what it means to be human. From every mountain peak to every coral reef, from ancient cities to remote islands, the longing to discover is etched into our nature, whispering that somewhere beyond the horizon lies a part of ourselves waiting to be awakened.

The Dream of Exotic Destinations

Perhaps it's the allure of the Caribbean's turquoise waters, the mystique of the Middle Eastern bazaars, or the majesty of the Nordic fjords—each destination calls us with a siren's song, promising moments of awe, wonder, and transformation. It's an age-old story—the explorer's instinct—that beckons from within, urging us to break free from routine and step into the adventure of a lifetime.

And yet, this longing isn't just about ticking off places on a map. It's an internal journey—a quest for meaning, joy, and connection. It's about shedding the layers of everyday life and rediscovering the parts of ourselves that are wild, poetic, and free.

The Great Inside-Outside Bridge

The truth is, every trip we take out into the world is a mirror of our inner landscape. The mountains we climb, the rivers we cross, and the cultures we embrace present us with opportunities to shed fears, ignite passions, and awaken the deepest parts of our spirit.

When we are lost in a jungle, marveling at its lush chaos; when we sit silently in a monastery amid ancient chants; or when we dance under the stars at a Caribbean festival—this is the universe's way of reminding us that life is a grand adventure, both outward and inward.

Connecting the Dots: Travel as Transformation

Whether it's the icy silence of Arctic fjords, the vibrant chaos of a Moroccan souk, or the serenity of a Santorini sunset, each journey ignites a spark—an awakening to new possibilities, perspectives, and dreams. It is within this sacred dance of exploration that we find ourselves: curious, humbled, inspired.

In the depths of exploring distant lands, we discover the Earth's most profound gift: a reflection of the limitless universe within our own soul. The mountains whisper wisdom; the oceans teach patience; the cities inspire innovation. And in every encounter, we realize that the world is an endless mirror of the uncharted territories within ourselves.

The Inner Explorer's Invitation

So, dear traveler, imagine the adventures your soul yearns for—exotic beaches, bustling markets, ancient temples, majestic forests, and starry skies. Picture yourself stepping into new worlds with wonder and reverence, knowing that each step, each glance, each moment of awe is a journey into the divine within you.

The world is a vast, open book waiting to be read, and your story—a unique tapestry—begins the moment you decide to turn the page. Unlock your inner explorer, trust your dreams, and remember: every destination you seek is a reflection of your own boundless spirit—your courage, curiosity, and yearning for the extraordinary.

Final Reflection

The great secret of travel isn't only in discovering distant lands but in uncovering the vast, limitless universe that resides within. It is a sacred dance—connecting the outer world with the inner realm—inspiring us to believe that life itself is a journey without end, a masterpiece crafted by our dreams, daring us to explore both the world "out there" and the universe "inside."

So, embrace your innermost longing to wander. Let the road beckon you beyond the familiar, and step boldly into the adventure that is both the world and your soul—one awe-inspiring voyage of eternal discovery.

Travel Tips & Cultural Etiquette: Navigating the World with Respect & Grace

Embarking on a journey into new lands is an exciting adventure—an opportunity to expand your horizons, embrace different ways of life, and connect deeply with diverse cultures. Yet, to truly immerse yourself and leave a positive impression, it's essential to approach each destination with awareness, respect, and thoughtful sensitivity.

Here are carefully curated **travel tips and cultural etiquette** to help you traverse new terrains gracefully, making your experiences not only richer but also more meaningful.

1. Respect Local Customs and Traditions

Every region has its own sacred sites, rituals, and social norms—an unwritten code of respect that honours the community's identity. Before visiting temples, mosques, or sacred sites, **learn the appropriate attire**—covering shoulders and knees when required—and **observe silence or reverence** during rituals.

Tip: When in doubt, follow the local crowd's lead. If they're removing their shoes before entering a home or shrine, do the same. Small acts of respect create lasting bonds.

2. Mind Your Body Language

Gestures can carry very different meanings across cultures:

- In some countries, **a nod means yes**, but in others, it can mean no or simply acknowledgment.
- **Pointing** with your finger might be considered rude; use your whole hand or nod politely instead.

- **Public displays of affection** may be frowned upon in conservative regions—lean into local modesty norms.

Tip: Observe how locals interact—what's natural to them will often be respectful and appropriate.

3. Use Polite Language and Greetings

A warm smile, a friendly "hello," or a customary greeting—like **"Namaste," "Bonjour,"** or **"Salam"**—can open doors to authentic connection. Use basic polite phrases; showing effort to speak a few words in the local language demonstrates respect and willingness to engage.

Tip: Always say **"please"** and **"thank you"**—kindness is a universal language.

4. Be Mindful of Photography

Taking photos of people or religious sites can be sensitive. Always ask permission before photographing locals, especially in rural areas or markets. Respect signs indicating **"No Photography,"** and avoid capturing vulnerable or private moments.

Tip: When photographing cultural performances or rituals, ask politely; sometimes, a small gift or smile can express your gratitude.

5. Handle Money and Bargaining Respectfully

In markets and shops, bargaining can be part of the cultural experience, especially in regions like Asia or Africa. Approach with a smile, polite tone, and a friendly attitude. When paying, use the **correct currency and avoid showing disrespect** toward vendors—remember, behind every transaction is someone's livelihood.

Tip: If offered tea or a snack during negotiations, graciously accept—this is part of a warm hospitality tradition.

6. Be environmentally conscious and leave no trace

Every traveller has a responsibility to protect the breathtaking landscapes they visit. Dispose of waste properly, avoid disturbing wildlife, and opt for eco-friendly options whenever possible. Support local eco-tourism initiatives.

Tip: Carry reusable water bottles, use biodegradable toiletries, and respect conservation rules.

7. Adapt to Local Dietary Norms

In some places, eating with your hands is customary, or certain foods are eaten at specific times. Observe and adapt—this shows respect for the local way of life.

Tip: Carry small snacks or tissues, and dress modestly if dining at local eateries or religious sites.

8. Be Patient and Open-Minded

Travel often involves unexpected delays, language barriers, or cultural differences. Approaching these moments with patience and humor transforms potential frustrations into opportunities for understanding and growth.

Tip: Embrace every experience as a lesson—sometimes, the most memorable moments come from the simplest acts of kindness or curiosity.

Final Word: Your Journey of Respect and Connection

Travel is about more than seeing new sights; it's about feeling the heartbeat of each place, honoring its stories, and weaving your own into the fabric of generations past and traditions alive. Respectful curiosity and genuine kindness turn fleeting encounters into lasting friendships and meaningful understandings.

So, travel with an open heart, a respectful mind, and a spirit eager to learn. In doing so, you don't just visit the world—you become a part of it.

Creating Your Own Path: Planning Your Adventures

Every traveller dreams of a journey that reflects their unique spirit—the places that call to their soul, the moments that ignite their passion, and the stories that become etched in their hearts. The magic of travel isn't only in discovering new horizons; it's in daring to craft a path that is truly your own.

Whether you're exploring the distant corners of a continent or retracing footsteps of ancient civilizations, your journey begins with intention, curiosity, and imagination. Here's how to transform dreams into reality and craft an adventure as distinctive as you are.

1. Define Your Inspiration

Start by asking yourself:

- What draws me most? Is it history, nature, culture, adventure, or relaxation?
- Do I seek solitude among ancient ruins, adrenaline-charged hikes, or vibrant festival celebrations?

Allow your passions to guide your choices—your adventure is a reflection of your inner voice.

2. Research & Dream Big

Dive into stories, documentaries, blogs, and maps—immerse yourself in possibilities. List the destinations, activities, and experiences that resonate most deeply. Don't limit yourself to popular hotspots; often, the most unforgettable moments happen off the beaten track.

Tip: Keep a journal or digital folder of inspiring sights, local traditions, and personal goals to help refine your vision.

3. Curate Experiences, Not Just Destinations

Design your journey around meaningful activities:

- Attend local festivals or ceremonies
- Join workshops—cooking, crafts, dance, or storytelling
- Hike remote trails or explore sacred sites
- Engage in community-based tourism—supporting local artisans and initiatives

This focus transforms travel from sightseeing into deep cultural immersion.

4. Choose Your Pace & Balance

Everyone's ideal journey looks different.

- Do you prefer slow travel, savoring each moment?
- Or a fast-paced voyage packed with adventures?

Balance moments of exploration with rest. Your path should nourish your body, mind, and spirit.

5. Plan Flexibly & Embrace Spontaneity

Be prepared but leave room for serendipitous discoveries. Sometimes, the best experiences are unplanned—an unexpected festival, a local's recommendation, or a sunset that steals your breath away. Cultivate an open attitude and trust your instincts.

6. Connect with Locals & Fellow Travelers

The essence of memorable journeys lies in authentic connections. Engage with local communities, try a traditional meal, learn a few words of the language, or share stories around a fire. Fellow travelers can also become lifelong friends and companions on your path.

7. Respect & Give Back

As you craft your personal adventure, remember: traveling is also a responsibility. Support local businesses, respect indigenous cultures, and leave a positive impact. Choose eco-friendly options and be a mindful guest.

8. Capture & Reflect

Create a journal, photo album, or blog of your journey. Reflecting on your experiences deepens your connection and helps you learn from each step. More importantly, cherish those moments—they become the stories that inspire others and your own future adventures.

Your Unique Journey Awaits

Every path you forge is a story waiting to be written—an expression of your curiosity, courage, and heart. Your adventure is yours alone, illuminated by your passions and shaped by your dreams.

So, dare to create your own path. Step into the unknown with excitement and respect. Trust your intuition, follow your dreams, and let each experience be a brushstroke on the canvas of your extraordinary life.

Because at the end of the day, the most beautiful journey is the one that is uniquely yours

The Power of the Journey: Love, Discovery, and Growth

Travel isn't merely a path from one place to another; it is a profound voyage into the depths of our souls—a journey that awakens the heart, expands the mind, and nurtures the spirit. It's a dance of love, discovery, and growth, woven into every step, every encounter, and every new horizon.

Love: The Heartbeat of Every Journey

Love is the silent currency that fuels every voyage. It begins with an open heart, eager to embrace the unfamiliar and to see the world through another's eyes. Whether it's the warm smile of a local artisan, the gentle undulation of waves on a distant shore, or the shared laughter over a simple meal, travel teaches us that love transcends borders—connecting us in our shared humanity.

In distant lands, love manifests in moments of genuine connection. It is in the act of listening, understanding, and respecting. The more we open ourselves to love—be it for new cultures, new landscapes, or new friends—the more our world expands, enriching our lives with compassion, empathy, and wonder.

Discovery: The Gift of Seeing with New Eyes

Every journey presents a chance to see the world anew—to shift perspectives, challenge assumptions, and uncover hidden truths. Discovering new cuisines, traditions, and histories awakens the curiosity dormant within—reminding us that the universe is vast, beautiful, and endlessly surprising.

Travel invites us to venture beyond comfort zones, into places where perceptions are challenged and the mind is stretched. It's a lesson in humility—a humbling realization that we are but a tiny part of an infinite cosmos of stories and spirits. As we discover landscapes and cultures different from our own, we not only learn about the world but also about ourselves—our fears, our passions, our limitless potential.

Growth: The Transformation of the Soul

The most profound magic of travel lies in its power to transform. Each journey—whether a day trip or a once-in-a-lifetime expedition—imprints upon us. We return changed—more compassionate, resilient, inspired, and wise.

Growth manifests in quiet moments of reflection, in overcoming challenges, and in embracing vulnerability. It's in the realization that beauty exists both in the grandeur of mountains and in the little acts of kindness shared along the way.

In traveling outward, we inevitably travel inward. We discover strength in our fragility; courage in our fears; hope in places of despair; and joy in the simplest of pleasures. The journey teaches us that life's true richness lies in continual unfolding—like the petals of a blooming flower, stretching towards the sun.

Embrace Your Infinite Adventure

Your journey is a sacred dance—a lifelong symphony of love, discovery, and growth. Every step taken outside the familiar is a step inward, a chance to meet your true self amid the vast, beautiful universe.

So, embrace the adventures that call your name. Dare to wander beyond the known, open your heart to the unfamiliar, and listen to the whispers of the world around you. Each moment, each encounter, is an offering—a gift of love and transformation.

Because the greatest journey isn't measured by miles or destinations; it's measured by the love you give, the truths you uncover, and the person you become along the way.

Let every journey be a testament—an expression of your courage to love, your curiosity to discover, and your strength to grow. And in doing so, you'll find that the most extraordinary adventure is the one within—the endless story of a soul forever yearning to evolve.

Epilogue

The Endless Passage: Future Adventures & Dreams

As you close these pages, a gentle whisper lingers—a call from the horizon, urging you onward. The journey does not end here. It is an endless passage—an eternal dance between where you've been and where your spirit dares to go.

Every story shared, every destination explored, is but a stepping stone in the infinite voyage of your soul. The world is a vast, luminous canvas awaiting your touch, your curiosity, and your dreams.

The Horizon of Unwritten Adventures

Close your eyes and imagine the tapestry of futures woven with threads of possibility. Perhaps it's the call of distant mountains waiting to be conquered, or the silent allure of forgotten temples seeking your discovery. Maybe it's the quiet desire to reconnect with nature in unspoiled wilds, or to immerse yourself in cultures that continue to dance and sing through generations.

The horizon is not a boundary; it's an invitation—an open door to new stories, new friendships, and new depths within yourself. Your next adventure might begin in your own backyard, in a new chapter of life, or somewhere whispered about in your dreams.

Dreams as the Compass of Tomorrow

Let your dreams be your compass—bright, bold, and boundless. Hold onto that unspoken desire to learn, to feel, and to grow. The universe cooperates with those who dare to dream awake—turning visions into realities, fears into courage, hypothesis into experience.

Every day is an opportunity for a new beginning—an uncharted voyage waiting to unfold. Trust in your inner explorer, for the greatest discoveries are those waiting patiently inside your heart.

The Spirit of Everlasting Curiosity

Remember, the true traveler is never finished—each step, each breath, each moment is part of an ongoing story of wonder. The world is a mirror reflecting your endless curiosity and creative spirit.

Whether you seek the quiet serenity of a mountain trail or the vibrant rhythm of a distant city, each adventure shapes your narrative—an opus of love, discovery, and transformation.

To the Dreamer & the Explorer

To all who carry within the spark of wanderlust—this is your call: keep seeking, keep exploring, keep dreaming. The roads and skies are wide open, waiting for your footprints and your visions. Your journey is eternal; your story, unfinished.

Step forward with courage, gratitude, and an open heart. The universe itself is an endless passage—an infinite dance of boundless adventures, forever inviting your soul to soar.

Because life's greatest treasures are not only found in distant lands but are discovered anew with every heartbeat, every dream, and every step you take beyond the known.

The adventure continues…

Go forth, dream bigger, and remember: the horizon is only the beginning. Your passage is endless, and the universe's wonders await your discovery. The voyage is yours—crafted by your passions, fuelled by your curiosity, and guided by your dreams.

HOUSEHOLDERS' DISCIPLINE IN JAINISM

(A Study of Amṛtacandra's Puruṣārthasiddhyupāyaḥ with the edited text in Sanskrit in Devanāgarī script)

Dr. Madhusudan Mishra

M.A. (Utkal). M.Phil., Ph.D. (Poona),

Lecturer, Post-graduate Department of Sanskrit,

G.M. College (Autonomous), Sambalpur.

BOOK EASTERN EBL LINKERS

EASTERN BOOK LINKERS

DELHI : : INDIA

Publishers :
EASTERN BOOK LINKERS
5825, New Chandrawal, Jawahar Nagar,
Delhi-110007 Ph.: 2520287

First Edition : 1996

ISBN : 81-86339-23-X

Laser typesetting & Printing at :
Unique Print Media
Phone : 7252362

IN MEMORIUM
MY LATE LAMENTED FATHER
DAITYARI MISHRA
WHO TAUGHT ME THE FIRST ALPHABET.

PREFACE

The present work is the outcome of the research I did in the University of Poona during 1986-87. Initially it was published under the title : A Critical Study of Amṛtacandra's Puruṣārthasiddhyupāyaḥ (Punthi Pustak, Calcutta, 1992). In that edition the text of the Puruṣārthasiddhyupāyaḥ was transliterated into Roman script with a view to help foreign scholars study the text. In the mean time I received a number of requests from Indian scholars to go for another edition of the work with the text in devanāgarī script. Moreover, a number of printing errors noticed in the first edition were to be corrected. The study-portion of the text also needed certain changes. This second edition takes care of all this. While presenting it to the world of scholars, I deem it a duty to speak a few words as a prologue to the study proper, as it involves a highly important aspect of Indian culture i.e. the *puruṣārtha*-s.

Traditionally, *puruṣārtha*-s are categorised as *dharma, artha, kāma and mokṣa.* It is the argument of scholars that it was initially the *trivarga* theory which constituted the essential feature of Hindu system of thought, *mokṣa* having been added to later on. Since no detailed and coherent account of this four-fold goals of human life is found in any religio-philosophical literature, it is indeed extremcly difficult to ascertain their exact nature. However, this much is clear that while the first three objectives i.e. *artha, kānıa* and *dharma* are essentially related to the empirical world, the fourth one, *mokṣa,* is related to the transcendental one.

The concept of *puruṣārtha* has been traditionally explained as : "*yasmin kṛte puruṣasya prītir bhavati saḥ puruṣārthaḥ padārthaḥ* (*Śārīrabhāṣya* on *Manusmṛti* 4.1.2) R.N. Dandekar ("The theory of Puruṣārtha-s: A Rethinking," Annals of the Bhandarkar Oriental Research Institute, Vol. LXVIII, Poona, 1987, p.663) defines the *puruṣārtha*-s as "motivations of human needs or desires to be satisfied", or "the ingredients of experience conducive to human fulfilment", or "human values consciously pursued by man". Literally, the word denotes the sense "objects of human life". Recapitulaling the general view on these ends Dandekar (ibid, p. 664) writes that through the proper coordination of these four, "one is expected to build up a truly integrated personality, and to realize a truly full life—a life which is materially rich (*artha*), aesthetically beautiful (*kāma*), ethically sound (*dharma*) and spiritually emancipated (*mokṣa*)." However, *mokṣa* always falls out of the orbit due to its intimate relation with the transcendental world, quite opposite to the first three's with the empirical one. While the first three are intensely engrossed in this world of action, *mokṣa* implies the transcendig of the phenomenal world.

Just like the concept of four-fold human ends, the idea of four-fold *āśrama* is also unique to Indian tradition. If the whole human life is taken as a pilgrimage, the four *āśrama*-s may well be conceived as four resting places. The four *āśrama*-s are *brahmacarya, gārhasthya, vānaprastha* and *yativrata*. Even though each one of them has its own significance, still the second one i.e. *gārhasthya* is first among all its equals. It is the pivot around which the whole social order revolves. The prestige is commands for its unique role in imparting training to the novices (to enter into householder's life), fulfilling the disires of the child and old alike, and preparing for the journey to be undertaken by itself in future (i.e. preparation for *vānaprastha* and *yativrata* days) is to be noted down. Thus it occupies a central position in our social fabric. Probably for this unique position it holds, Hinduism-nay, Brahmaṇic Culture, lays emphasis on it.

Jaina tradition also shares the concept of four-fold *puruṣārtha*-s, but divides human life into two major disciplines, namely, monk's discipline and householder's discipline. Since Jainism constitutes a part and parcel of the ancient Śramaṇic culture, it lays more emphasis on ascetic life. The reason is that since a householder's life is bound by so many limitations, it is not so easy to practise the religion in its true spirit in comparison to that of an ascetic. Thus, the status of being the most ideal discipline has always been given to monkhood. However, householder's discipline also runs parallel, only next to it. Even though both the ways are equally competent to achieve the ultimate goal, in monk's discipline one gets a speedy progress and in househonder's it is slow and gradual.

Attainment of *mokṣa* consititutes the essentical goal of both Hinduism and Jainism. But while Hinduism lays more emphasis on householder's discipline as a means to attain *mokṣa,* Jainism lays more emphasis on monk's discipline. The attainment of *mokṣa* is possible through a proper coordination of *samyag-darśana, jñāna* and *cāritra* (cf. *samyagdarśana-jñāna-cāritrāṇi mokṣamārgaḥ* : Tattvārthasūtra of Umāsvāti), claims Jainism. For that attainment, Jainism expects its adherents to follow a definite code of conduct. Even though Jainism lays more emphasis on monk's disipline, still Mahāvīra has also built an order where there is a scope for householders also. Thus we have two sets of code of conduct : one for the monks and the other for the householders called *Śrāvaka*-s. In the ancient canonical literature of Jaina Śvetāmbara texts, we have got independent works dealing with both the disciplines separately, e.g. the Uvāsakadasāo deals with householder's discipline and works like Ācārāṅga and Uttarādhyayana-sūtra deal with monk's discipline. On the other side, we have, in the Digambara tradition, Vaṭṭakera's Bhagavatī-Ārādhanā, which is the oldest work related to the same topic. Samantabhadra's Ratnakaraṇḍa-Śrāvakācāra contitutes the oldest treatise dealing with householder's discipline in Digambara Jaina tradition. Actually, the reality is : by both the ways one can attain the highest end. But depending on one's own capacity he will have to choose the order. However, mank's discipline has always been given the highest status in Jainișm and the one of the householder's occupies a lower status. The last stage of householder's discipline is the initial stage of monks' disipline. The aim behind advocating a subordinate discipline like the one of the householders is to introduce the laymen to monkhood, but by a slow and gradual manner. Then only the obtainment of the highest human end becomes more feasible and possible.

Amṛtacandrasuri, belonging to the 10th Century A.D., has presented a work entitled Puruṣārthasiddyupāyaḥ which deals with householder's discipline i.e. *Śrāvakācāra*. In this work he lays more emphasis on the fourth ultimate goal i.e. *mokṣa* or emancipation. A definite and well organised code of conduct has been ordained by him which will ensure a gradual development of householders towards the status of the monks. An absolute success in adopting and following the twelve *vrata*-s (vows), namely, the five *aṇuvrata*-s three *guṇavrata*-s and four *Śikṣāvrata*-s constitutes the focus of this text. The uniqueness of this work lies in its attempt to initiate the householders to monk's discipline with a view to making them familiar with the principal order of Jaina tradition. The code of concuct is just like the various means in the way of progress of human life towards the ultimate goal. The code of conduct prescribed and described in the *Śrāvakācāra*-s is just like a schooling or training for the adoption of monkhood at the final stage.

The Puruṣārthasiddhyupāyaḥ of Amṛtacandra is one of the many *Śrāvakācāra*-s which highlights householder's discipline in a unique way. Its systematic way of presentation, lucid language, rudimentary thinking and high pholosophical tone have made it occupy a distinct position in the rich firmament of Jaina *Śrāvakācāra* literature. Unlike other writers, Amṛtacandra adopts Kundakunda's dialectic of *vyavahāranaya* and *niścayanaya* (practical and real standpoints) while elucidating the main principles of householder's discipline, which makes the treatise a unique one by combining jaina mysticism in householder's order. This prompted me to critically study the treatise afresh which is being introduced to the scholarly world. I shall feel my labour rewarded it constructive suggestions come from discerning readers so that I whould be in a position to take note of them in future editions.

ACKNOWLEDGEMENT

It is indeed a matter of great pleasure and privilege for me to record my deep sense of gratitude and indebtednes to a number of people who have rendered their invaluable help to me in bringing out this volume.

First and formemost, my profound sense of gratitude is due to Prof. S.M. Shaha, University of Poona, but for whose apt guidance and fatherly affection, this work would not have seen the rays of the day.

Prof. A.C. Swain and Dr. U.N. Dhal the leading Indologist-duo from Orissa, have constantly inspired me by their candid assessment and constructive comments. I offer my sonly obeissance to both of them.

I gratefully acknowledge the assistance of my family members, especially of my elder brothers-Mr. Srikanta Mishra and Mr. Tarakanta Mishra, who sacrificed all their comforts for the sake of my higher studies.

My wife, Naliniprabha, deserves my words of apreciation for sharing the domestic responsibilities and thereby relieving me from those burdens to concentrate on academic activities.

I have no words to thank Messrs Eastern Book Linkers, Delhi for their remarkable zeal in bringing out this volume within such a small compass of time.

ā no bhadrāḥ kratavo'yantu viśvataḥ

G.M. College, Madhusudan Mishra
Sambalpur,
Rajasaṁkrānti
15.6.1995

ABBREVIATIONS

PṢ. .. *Puruṣārthasiddyupāyaḥ*
Rb. .. Right belief
Rc. .. Right conduct
Rk .. Right knowledge
Sc. .. *Saṃyak-cāritra*
Sd. .. *Samyagdarśana*
Sj .. *Samyagjñāna*

CONTENTS

INTRODUCTION

The present work aims at critically studying Amṛtacandra's *PS,* a treatise on the rules of conduct for Jaina laymen. The work belongs to the *Caraṇānuyoga* section of Jaina literature which deals with householders' and monks' discipline. The Jaina *Śrāvakācāra*-s are one of the important sources of information regarding Jaina lay community. They have been composed not only in Sanskrit and Prakrit but also in Modern Indo-Aryan languages like Hindi, Gujarati, Marathi, etc. There are some *Śrāvakācāra*-s which are composed in Dravidian languages such as, Tamil, Kanarese also. The study of Jaina *Śrāvakacāra* literature is very valuable for understanding Jaina community with its socio-religious aspects. Scholars like Mrs. Stevenson, R. Williams, Dr. Vilas Sangave etc. have attempted to present such survey of Jaina householders' life with a historical and sociological perspective. There are works studying individual *Śrāvakācāra*-s independently also. For example, in India a group of Digambara scholars like J.L. Jaini, Champatray Jain, Nathuram Premi, Hiralal Jain, A.N. Upadhye have produced editions of works such as *Ratnakaraṇḍaśrāvakācāra, PS, Dvādaśānuprekṣā,* Vasunandi's *Śrāvakācāra* etc. However, the critical study of the contents of some of the *Śrāvakācāra*-s is still a desideratum. Amṛtacandra's *PS* is one of such works which await a critical analysis of their contents. Hence an attempt has been made here for the first time to present a critical and comparative study of householders' discipline as reflected in the *PS*.

Though the text of the *PS* has been edited and translated by Ajit Prasad in English, by Nathuram Premi and Saranaram Jain in Hindi, none of them has tried to evaluate the contents of this work with a comparative and critical approach, which constitute the main thrust of the present study.

Amṛtacandra's Life—

As we have already mentioned Amṛtacandra is the author of this work. We know nothing about his personal life. He gives no information about himself in his works. Āśādhara while quoting a verse from *PS* addresses him as *Ṭhakkura* which might be either Amṛtacandra's surname or another name. Except that nothing at all is known of the life of this *Ācārya*.

Amṛtacandra's Date—

Without any direct historical evidence it will be very difficult to settle his date too. Scholars like Dr. A.N. Upadhye,[1] Nathuram Premi[2] place him somewhere between 10th century A.D.

Amṛtacandra's Works

Apart from the *PS* which is also know as *Jīnapravacanarahasyakośa*, Amṛtacandra has composed

1. *Pravacanasāra*, Introduction (ed.) *Upadhye*, A.N. p.96.
2. *Premi*, Nathuram, *Jaina Sāhitya aur Itihās*,. pp. 309-310.

Tattvārthasāra (a metrical exposition of the *Tattvārthasutra* of Umāsvāti), commentaries on Kundakundācārya's *Pravacanasāra, Pañcāstikāya* and *Samayasāra* and *Samayasārakalasa,* which is often treated as an independent work.

Amṛtacandra's Position

As a commentator, Amṛtacandra's position is really unique because, so far as we know, he is the first commentator on the authoritative works of Kundakunda. He does not aim at verbal explanation, but to simply propound the philosophical contents of the original texts. His zeal for *anekānta* logic is remarkable. That is quite clear from his commentaries and other works. He shows close acquaintance with *Digambara* as well as *Śvetāmbara* works. His mastery over Sanskrit idioms is remarkable. According to Dr. A.N. Upadhye Amṛtacandra is more a poet than a prose writer.[3] As a spiritual poet his position is simply unique and unequalled by any Jaina author before or after him.

Puruṣārthasiddhyupāya—

As we have already said, the *Ps* deals with the duties of the Jaina householders. It is in a highly philosopholical tone. After short introduction giving certain basic principles of Jainism, it discusses the *ratnatraya,* the twelve *vrata*-s and *Sallekhanā* with their *aticāra*-s, the *tapa*-s and the *pariṣaha*-s. It is in the spirit that animates it, that work differs from all others of its kind. In rather harsh verse,

3. *Pravacanasāra,* Introduction, (ed.) A.N. *Upadhye,* p.94.

Amṛtacandra sings the praise of *Ahiṁsā* with the fervour of a mystic, always stressing his theme that all the evil man can do in some sense is an expression of *Hiṁsā*.[4] Thus we see that in the *Ps*, Amṛtacandra's explanation of *Ahiṁsā* and the relation between the *Vyavahāranaya* and *Niścayanaya* are important contributions to the understanding of the subject. There is a feshness about his treatment and some of his illustrations are original and striking.[5] Thus it is clear that Amṛtacandra's *PS* occupies an important place in Jaina *Śrāvakācāra* literature. In the present work we have compared Amṛtacandra's treatment of householders' discipline with that of his predecessors like Kundakunda, Umāsvāti and Samantabhadra. The outcome of our research is that Amṛtacandra, unlike his predecessors and followers, attaches unique importance to *Ahiṁsā* as the core of Jaina householders' discipline and tries to interprete all others vows in the same light.

Outline

The outline of the present work is as follows:

Chapter One - Right belief

Chapter two - Right knowledge

Chapter three - Right conduct

Chapter four - Conclusion.

At the end, a critically edited text of the PS in Sanskrit is given.

---

4. *Williams*, R. *Jaina yoga*, p. 25.
5. *Upadhye*, A.N. *Op.Cit.* p.93

CHAPTER I

SAMYAGDARŚANA OR RIGHT BELIEF

0.1. INTRODUCTION

The edifice of Jainism is erected on the three basic tenets namely, Right belief (Rb), Right knowledge (Rk) and Right conduct (Rc). They are called as *Samyagdarśana* (*Sd*), *Samyagjñāna* (*Sj*) and *Samyakcāritra* (*Sc*) respectively. These are the three gems or *'ratnatraya'* in Jainism. Since Rk andRc presuppose Rb, we shall here first deal with the latter.

The term *'Samyagdarśana'* is a compound and it has two components namely, *'samyak'* and *'darśana'*. Etymologically *'samyak'* means 'going alongwith' and *'darśana'* means 'insight' or 'perfect realization'. Thus etymologically *sd* renders the meaning as 'going alongwith the perfect realization'. However, the secondary meaning of the term *Sd* is 'right belief'. It generally means firm and unshakeable faith in the seven fundamentals of Jainism namely, *Jīva, Ajīva, Āśrava, Bandha, Saṁvara, Nirajarā* and *Mokṣa*. It also means the unswevering faith in the Holy Trinities : *Āpta, Guru* and *Śāstra*.

0.2. VARIOUS VIEWS ON SD.

A good number of definitions of *Sd* are found in various Jaina scriptures. The idea remains the same while the way of presentation only differs. Kundakunda (1st century A.D.), the great ethico-religious Jaina philosopher, in his *Darśana Pāhuḍa* characterises the nature of *Sd* as the posession of firm belief in the six kinds of *Dravya*-s, the nine *Padārtha*-s, the five *Astikāya*-s and the seven *Tattva*-s.[1] Nemicandrācārya represents the belief in the six *Dravya*-s, the five *Astikāya*-s and the nine *Padārtha*-s as indicative of *Sd*.[2] The *Mokṣa Pāhuḍa* recognises the belief in the non-violent *Dharma*, in the *Deva* bereft of the eighteen kinds of faults and in the sermons of the Omniscient as constitutive of Rb.[3] Again the *Niyamasāra* regards the belief in the perfect Souls, the scriptures and the six *Dravya*-s determining the nature of Rb.[4] Besides, according to the *Mūlācāra* and *Uttarādhyayana*, the belief in the nine *Padārtha*-s expresses the nature of *Sd*.[5] Vasunandi in his *Śrāvakācāra* describes the nature of Rb as the true and unshakeable conviction in the perfect souls, the scriptures and the seven *Tattva*-s.[6] Some great *Ācārya*-s like Umāsvāti,[7] Amṛtacandra[8] and the author of *Dravyasaṁgraha*[9]

1. *Darśana-Pāuḍa*, 19
2. *Gommaṭasāra Jīvakāṇḍa*, 560.
3. *Mokṣa-Pāhuḍa*, 19
4. *Niyamasāra*, 5
5. *Mūlācāra*, 203; *Uttarādhyayana*, 28. 14-15.
6. Vasunandi's *Srāvakācāra*, 6.
7. *Tattvārthasūtra*, 1.2.
8. *Ps*. 22
9. *Dravyasaṁgraha*, 41

unanimously depict *Sd* as the belief in the seven *Tattva*-s. Samantabhadra defines it as a belief in true deities, true scriptures and true teachers as against the follies of belief in psuedo-*deva*, psuedo-*guru* and psuedo-scripture.[1]

0.3. AMṚTACANDRA ON SD

In the *Puruṣārthasiddhyuapāyaḥ* (*PS*) at the outset Amṛtacandra justifies the need of *Sd* as one of the three constituents of the pathway leading to liberation. According to him, unless and until *Sd* is obtained no attainment of the other two *i.e.*, *Sj* and *Sc* is possible, as it prepares a way for them. Thus Rb is the threshold to Rk and Rc.

Amṛtacandra prescribes certain procedures for a successful attainment of Rb. Traditionally emphasis has been laid on their static aspects; but in our opinion since they have much more practicality in them, their dynamic aspects cannot be underminded.

First of all, like his predecessors, he advises to keep unflinching faith in the seven predicaments *viz.*, *jīva*, *Ajīva* etc. as they are free from perverse notions. It is the nature of the soul. No doubt should be entertanied regarding the matter whether all these multisided views of things proceeding from the Omniscient, are true or false. A true believer should not desire worldly material prosperity in this life, or an elevated position of sovereign or deityhood in the next life. It also prohibits any sort of inclination or adherence to any other religion contaminated by the adoption

1. *Ratnakaraṇḍaśrāvakācāra*, 4

of one-sided theories. A believer should not also exhibit a feeling of disgust at the various conditions of life caused by hunger, thirst, cold, heat etc., or at the sight of filthy things such as, excrement etc. In this world, he who keeps his faith in the *Tattva*-s should never have a superstitious belief in a fallacious scripture, an unreal doctrine, or a spurious deity. To evolve the virtue of *Upavṛṁhaṇa* or an enlargement of the adhered faith, one should ever cultivate the true nature of *Jīva* by meditating upon tenderness and the like attitudes. One should take measures to conceal others' vices. In case of deviation from the religious path, under the influence of anger, pride, bodily passion etc., he should strengthen his knowledge of the Self and that of others by logical scriptural argument and should stick to the righteous path. One should ever cherish feelings of deep affection for the adhered religion, which in turn brings about the treasure of spiritual happiness, and for the principle of non-injury and also for all co-religionists. One should ever make his self radiant by the light of the three jewels, and should add to the glory of Jainism by exceptional charity, austerity, worship of *Jīna,* the conqueror, and by profound learning.[1]

0.4. THE NATURE OF MOKṢAMĀRGA.

A philosophical doctrine in India is called *Mokṣaśāstra,* the science of liberation. The aim of all the systems of Indian philosphy (except that of Cārvāka) is to show us the means for the attainment of liberation. Jaina philosophy is not an

1. *Ps.* 21-30.

exception to this phenomenon. It aims at the liberation of the soul from the Kārmic matter and the realisation of the true nature of self. Now we shall undertake a discussion regarding the nature of *Mokṣa-mārga* as has been treated by some jaina pioneers in the field of philosophy. We shall restrict our discussion to Amṛtacandra who happens to be our main concern, and to other three authors namely, Kundakunda, Umāsvāti and Sāmantabhadra who seem to have influenced his thought mainly.

Jaina philosophy views everything from the two stand-points, *Vyavahāra* (empirical) and *Niścaya* (transcendental). Since *Mokṣa-mārga* is constituted of the '*ratnatraya*-s'[1], it can also be viewed from the above two standpoints and here, we have '*Vyavahāra ratnatraya*' and '*Niścaya ratnatraya*' accordingly. The following discussion aims at analysing the nature of the two and therefore we intend to pick- up the idea of the noted philosophers in that regard.

Kundakundācārya never contradicts the traditional doctrine that Rb, Rk and Rc together constitute the path or means of liberation. On the contrary, he holds it to be the universal and eternal law for the purification of soul and calls it a '*Niyama*'. One of his works '*Niyamasāra*' primarily discusses what is a '*Niyama*'. He says: '*niyamo mokṣopāyaḥ*' or '*Niyama*' (is) the way to liberation. Moreover, the remaining works like *Pravacanasāra, Pañcāstikāya, Samayasāra* etc. also elaborately expound the concept of Rb, Rk and Rc as constituting

1. *Tattvārthasūtra,* 1.1

the path of liberation. But by employing the terminology of his conceptual viewpoints of *Vyavahāra* and *Niścaya* in this respect, he marvellously gives a somewhat new dimension to the traditional meaning of *Mokṣa-mārga*. He observes: "Belief in soul etc. (the nine categories) (is) Rb; the knowledge of them is Rk and the giving up attachment etc. is Rc. This certainly is the way of liberation. The learned doesn't indulge in the practical (path), giving up the real substance (*i.e.* the pure soul), because only in the saints who depend upon the highest substance, the destruction of *Karma*-s takes place."[1] According to Kundakunda, it is only from the practical point of view that Rb, Rk and Rc can be predicted of soul. But from real, non-differential standpoint, there is neither knowledge, nor conduct, nor belief. The knower is the pure knower itself. Thus he says:

"vavahāreṇuvassadi ṇāṇissā catittadaṁsanam ṇāṇam

ṇa vi ṇāṇaṁ ṇa carittam ṇa daṁsaṇam jāṇago suddho[2]

Umāsvāti, in his *Tattvārthasūtra* sticks to the *Vyavahāra* aspect of *Mokṣa-mārga*. He says: "*Sd*, SJ and *Sc* together constitute the way of liberation.[3] He is of the opinion that after annihilating the bondage and its causes, the absolute spiritual development is *Mokṣa-mārga*. In the last chapter of *Tattvārthasūtra* he speaks that an absolute decay of *karma*-s (*i.e. nirjarā)* and an absence of the causes of bondage *(i.e. saṁvara*) lead to the destruction of

1. *Samayasāra*, 162-163
2. *ibid*. 7.
3. *Tattvārthasūtra*, 1.1

all *karma*-s and it is *Mokṣa* or Salvation.[1] From such a type of treatment we can say that while describing *Mokṣa* etc. he generally lays more emphasis on the practical standpoint.

The standpoint of Samantabhadra in his *Ratnakaraṇḍaśrāvakācāra* is the same as that of Umāsvāti. He also refers to the three tenets *i.e.* *Sd, Sj.* and *Sc* to be constituting the path to liberation. He designates *Mokṣa-mārga* as *'Dharma'*. The opposite of all these three are the causes of wordly sorrow etc.[2]

Amṛtacandra ditto follows Kundakunda in his treatment of *Vyavahāranaya* and *Niścayanaya,* and *Vyavahāra-ratnatraya* and *Niścaya-ratnatraya* *i.e.,* *Vyavahāra-Mokṣa-mārga* and *Niścaya-Mokṣamārga* respectively. Both of them accept the utility of *Vyavahāranaya* as the means of explaining *Niścayanaya* to an ignorant person who is in the lower stage of spiritual evolution. Again, once a person is capable of comprehending Truth asserted by *Niścayanaya, Vyavahāranaya* is to be discarded, while in direct self-realization there is no scope for both *Vyavahāranaya* and *Niścayanaya* which are the means of indirect knowledge *i.e.* scriptural knowledge. Thus *Samayasāra,* the pure self, transcends both *Vyavahāranaya* and *Niścayanaya.* This state is described by Amṛtacandra as a condition of becoming *Mādhyastha* or equanimous. In this state an aspirant is neither inclined towards *Vyavahāra* nor to *Niścaya,* since their purpose being served they are of no use to him.

---

1. *ibid.* 10. 2-3.
2. *Ratnakaraṇḍaśrāvakācāra,* 3.

Mokṣa-mārga is described by Amṛtacandra from real standpoint. He says: "This is the means of realising human goal (*i.e.* liberation) that constitutes the renunciation of wrong belief, Rk of one's real nature and non-deviation from it (*i.e.* self)." Amṛtacandra contends that *Mokṣa-mārga* characterised by Rb, Rk and Rc is propounded by the knowers of *Vyavahāra* and *Niścaya* from both *Vyavahāra* and *Niścaya* standpoints. Like *Kundakunda* he lays more emphasis on *Niścaya-ratnatraya*. This is also obvious from the fact that according to him *'vatnatraya'* in itself is not the cause of bondage, but the element of *rāga* or attachment is its cause. Similarly, when he says that even householders' partial observance of the *'ranatraya'*, devoid of *rāga*, leads to liberation, he is emphasizing real standpoint only. In short, we may conclude that though Amṛtacandra discusses both *Vyavahāra* and *Niścaya ratnatraya*, he certainly shows his inclination to *Niścayaratnatraya*.

Though the pathway to liberation may be described from practical and real standpoints, it is not two in number. The two-fold description of *Mokṣa-mārga* does not require to presuppose two independent paths or two means of liberation. That's to say the disticntion between *Vyavahāra ratnatraya* and *Niścaya ratnatraya* may elucidate *Mokṣa-mārga* from two standpoints. However, the *Mokṣa-mārga* is the one and the same.

Though the real standpoint is preferable to practical standpoint, it is not an end in itself. These are the two means of knowing *Mokṣa* and *Mokṣa-mārga* indirectly on the basis of scriptural knolwedge. Once the purpose is served one has to be impartial, indifferent and equanimous towards them. Because in direct realization of self there is not scope for indirect means of knowledge viz., the practical and real standpoints.

0.5. AMṚTACANDRA'S TREATMENT OF SD FROM TWO STANDPOINTS:A RETROSPECTIVE ANALYSIS.

Amṛtacandra devotes ten verses in his *PS* for the discussion of *Sd*. He defines it from both *Vyavahāra* and *Niścaya* standpoints as follows: *Sd* from the practical standpoint, according to him, means right faith in seven categories or *Tattva*-s such as, *Jīva, Ajīva* etc. while this, from the real standpoint means faith in the nature of *Ātman* itself which is devoid of wrong belief.

If we analyse the *aṅga*-s of Rb laid by him, we see that they have two aspects: negative and positive. In total, he deals with eight factors or *aṅgas* of Rb viz. *Śaṅkā, Ākāṁkṣā, Vicikitsā, Mūḍhadṛṣṭitva, Upavṛmhaṇa, Sthitikaraṇa, Vātsalya,* and *Prabhāvanā*. The first four are negative whereas the last four are positive in nature. The first four are also seen to be included in the list of five blemishes. In the first phase he advises to give up the first four vices, and in the second phase he advises to stick to the last four virtues or essentials. These eight limbs or pillars are prescribed by him for supporting Rb. While the renunciation of the first four deals with the spiritual progress of individual's life, the practice of the last four is concerned with one's social life. As we have already seen, he prefers to impart a full- fledged knowledge of *Mokṣa-mārga* from both *Vyavahāra* and *Niścaya* standpoints, laying more emphasis particularly on the latter; he does not want to adhere exclusively or one-sidedly to either of the two because, like Kundakunda and other Jain authors, he is also on *Anekāntin*. Now we shall undertake a detailed discussion of these eight pillars of Rb.

Amṛtacandra starts with *Niḥśaṅkita-Aṅga*. In this connection, he advises a right believer to have an absolutely doubtless conviction regarding the validity of the Jain doctrines. The relevancy of this limb is as follows: individual intellect is so limited that it is impossible to possess a complete knowledge through it. So one should have strong faith in the Omniscient's words yielding the indirect knowledge of *Tattva*-s of Jainism. This is the *Niḥśaṅkita-Aṅga* from practical standpoint, while from the real standpoint faith in the soul itself is the *Niḥśaṅkita-Aṅga*.

Secondly, he advises to give up every sort of desire. A true believer does not hanker after worldly pleasure and positions. One should not also aspire for the doctrines of the heretics contaminated by onesidedness. From the *Niścaya* standpoint one should aspire for one's pure self only. This is *Niḥkāṁkṣita-Aṅga* from *Vyavahāra* and *Niścaya* standpoints respectively.

The third pillar, *Vicikitsā,* from the practical standpoint means not to entertain the feeling of disgust or apathy or dislike towards different physical and mental conditions caused by hunger, thirst, cold or heat etc. It also means not to experience the sense of disgust towards dirty things viz. excrement etc. While from the real standpoint the absence of disgust towards unpleasant things is caused by the real knowledge of the *Ātman*. Since the *Ātman* is entirely different from physical conditions viz. hunger etc., it is not affected by them. It is the only knower of such non-self things.[1]

In the *Amūḍhadṛṣṭi - aṅga* he warns a disciple not to deviate from the righteous path. One who has understood *Tattvas* should never have a belief in a fallacious scripture, a plausible doctrine or a spurious deity. This is the *Amūḍhadṛṣṭi-aṅga* from *Vyavahāra* standpoint; while from; *Niścaya* standpoint, taking interest in one's own pure self is *Amūḍhadṛṣṭitva*.

These four limbs are negative in nature aiming at abstinence from doubt, desire, disgust and folly. After the annihilation of all these four one becomes unpurturbed and starts his real journey for the attainment of Rb. Justifying the need of these four we can say that one who makes himself victim of his own ill-considered actions cannot concentrate his mind. Detachment in its true nature is the result of one's making out the real nature of an object. Permanent and undecaying bliss comes from inside and not from sensual enjoyments. Thus we see that faith in seven categories viz. *Jīva* etc. is the means of strengthening faith in *Ātman* itself, which is the most important thing for an aspirant.

In the second phrase of his discussion on *Sd* Amṛtacandra takes into consideration some of the social aspects. First of all, he advises to enhance the spiritual quality of one's self by means of contemplation and practising the ten rules of piety namely, highest forgiveness, tenderness,

1. See commentary of *PS. ed.* S.Jain, Saharanpur, 1959.

straightforwardness, purity, truth, self-restraint, austerities, charity, detachment and chastity. This is the real aspect of *upavṛmhaṇa,* whereas its practical aspect is called *upagūhana* which means concealing faults, weaknesses or discripancies of others.

Sthitikaraṇa or steadiness is the sixth pillar of Rb. By constant reasoning and logical argumentation one should avoid scepticism. It is its practical aspect while from the real standpoint, it means remaining oneself firm in the pure state of *Ātman* by avoiding passions like anger, pride etc., whereas to help others to do so is *sthitikaraṇa* from the practical standpoint.

In the *Vātsalya-Aṅga* he includes fraternity for both *Dharma* and *Dharmātmā.* A religion of love is the sole cause of blissful spiritual state. It is nothing but an actual practice of the uncorrupt '*ratnatraya*-s'. Thus from the pratical point of view possessing love for all co-religionists is *Vātsalya-Aṅga,* while the same for pure *Ātman* is *Vātsalya-Aṅga* from the real standpoint.

In the last limb *Prabhāvanā* he advises to cultivate and cherish soul through the lustre of the three jewels. It is the inward procedure of elevating the self. This is *Prabhāvanā* from the real standpoint. But from the practical standpoint one should propagate Jainism by forming religious organisations, building temples, practising physical penance, giving donations and by learning the Jaina scriptures.

These eight pillars are prescribed for both laymen and monks. The monks lay more emphasis on *Niścaya* aspect whereas the householders on *Vyavahāra* due to their limited capacity. Thus we see that Amṛtacandra deals with both real and practical aspect of these eight limbs of *Samyaktva*, either explicitly or implicitly in these verses (*i.e.* 23-30) of the *PS*.

0.6. PLACE OF SD IN MOKṢA-MĀRGA.

Sd plays a very significant role in the pathway to liberation. Many a Jain treatise have given it a foremost place among all the requirements to march towards the ultimate human goal, *i.e.* liberation. As we have already stated that jainism treats everything from two standpoints, *Vyavahāra* and *Niścaya;* so let us consider the role of *Sd* as *Vyavahāra Sd* and *Niścaya Sd* in *Mokṣa-mārga.*

In all Jaina scriptures related to *Mokṣa-mārga,* we observe that the beginning is made with *Vyavahāra Sd* which forms a stepping-stone towards the realization of the self. Moreover, it is an indirect means of liberation.

Regarding *Niścaya samyaktva* it can be said that it is nothing but an obsorption in the self itself. It begins from the fourth stage of the fourteen *guṇasthānas i.e., samyaktva guṇasthāna* or the stage of *Rb* which is devoid of wrong faith and *anantānubandhi-krodha-māna-māyā-lobha.*

Amṛtacandra defines *samyaktva* as faith in one's self or discernment of one's self. Rest of the *Tattva*-s become secondary in *Niścaya samyaktva*. Thus *Niścaya samyaktva* is the direct cause of liberation. According to *Darśana Pāhuḍa* of Kundakunda, without *Sd* austere penance and profound learning even of thousand years become unyielding and futile.[1] Again in the same text he states that a person who deviates from the right conduct is not the real deviator; but he who deviates from right faith is the real deviator. Samantabhadra in his *Ratnakaraṇḍaśrāvakācāra* places *Sd* on the lofty peak of spirituality. He says: *Sd* is nobler than *Sj* and *Sc*. It is the helm-man or pilot of the ship of the '*ratnatraya*-s', which comes to the rescue of people drowning in the worldly ocean of misery etc.

Amṛtacandra uses the term '*ādau*,'[2] meaning, first and foremost, for *Sd* which is to be practised with all sorts of care and propriety; because only on the acquisition thereof knowledge and conduct become right. Faith indicates the first spark of both empirical and transcendental Truth. In the Ṛg *veda*[3] faith has been highly praised. *Śrīmadbhagavadgītā*[4] also urges a devotee to possess right faith. *Chāndogyopaniṣad*[5] strikes the same point. In short, everywhere ethics begins with Rb. Kundakunda in his *Niyamasāra* also treats *Sd* at the outset. Samayasāra of the sanee author gives prime importance to SD as it prepares a pathway to liberation. *Sd* dispells all types of bondage. Thus it paves the way for Rk and Rc without which no spiritual progress is possible.

---

1. *Darśana Pāhuḍa*. 4-5
2. *PS*. 21
3. Ṛgveda,.. 10. 151.1-5
   "Śraddhayāgniḥ samidhyate śraddhayā hūyate haviḥ..."
4. *Gītā*. 4.39
5. *Chāndogyopaniṣad*, 6. 12.3.

0.7. RELATION OF SD WITH SJ AND SC.

According to the *PS, Sd* is the edifice on which *Sj* stands. One who has attained *Sd* can enable himself for an acquisition of *Sj*. These two are contemporaneous to each other. Eventhough they evolve at one and the sametime still there is a distinction between them, as they do have different characteristics. Amṛtacandra declares Rk to be the effect and Rb, the cause. A causal relation exists between them which is similar to a lamp and its light. Regarding its relation with *Sc* we may contend that eventhough *Sd* does not have a direct relation with *Sc*, through *Sj* it is linked with *Sc*.

CHAPTER II

SAMYAGJÑĀNA OR RIGHT KNOWLEDGE.

INTRODUCTION.

Like *Sd, 'Samyagjñāna'* is also a compound. It has two components, namely, *'Samyak'* and *'Jñāna'*. The term *'Samyak'* is an adjective of *'Jñāna'* which means 'going alongwith' or 'going together' or 'right'. Knowledge being the essential characteristics of Soul or Self, that knowledge would be called right which goes alongwith or goes together with the Self or Soul. From the real point of view, it refers to the real knowledge of the Self or a knowledge in which a clear-cut distinction is made between the Self and the non-Self.[1]

0.1. VARIOUS VIEWS ON SJ

Samantabhadra in his *Ratnakaraṇḍaśrāvakācāra* defines *Sj* as follows: the knowers of the scriptures call it (right) knowledge that knows a (thing) as actually exists, neither less nor more, and is devoid of perversity as well as doubt.[2] Kundakunda in his *Niyamasāra* treats *Sj* in the following way:

1. *...Yaḥ sva-parāntaraṁ jānāti sa jānāti, Iṣṭtopadesa.*
2. *Ratna. Śrāvakācāra*, 42.

(knowledge) free from doubt (*saṁśaya*), perversity (*vimoha*) and vaccilation (*vibhrama*) is Rk. Moreover, correct understanding (*adhigama*) of the fact that which priciples are worth renouncing and whihc are worth realising, (is) Rk.[1] He declares Soul to be characterised by *upayoga* which is constituted of both *Jñāna*[2] and *darśana*. Thus Rk has been one of the important characteristics of Soul. Kundakunda further divides Rk into natural (perfect) and un-natural. Un-natural is four-fold, viz., *mati, śruta, avadhi* and *manaḥ-paryaya-jñāna*.[3] The first three may be both right or wrong whereas the last one, *manaḥ-paryaya* is always right in nature.

Tattvārthasūtra of Umāsvāti does not give any categorical definition of *Sj*. However, it first gives a five-fold division of it and further suggests *Sj* to be the real knowledge of the seven *Tattva*-s attained by means of both *naya* and *pramāṇa*. *Naya* is a standpoint which gives us a partial knowledge of an object or the characteristic of a given object, while *pramāṇa* presents a comprehensive knowledge of the totality of all aspects. As we have already stated, his five-fold division [4] of knowledge is as follows: *mati, śruta, avadhi, manaḥ-paryaya* and *kevali* out of which the first three can be both right and wrong, and the last two are necessarily right. By *Sj* he means the knowledge that is associated with Rb.

---

1. *Niyamasāra*, 51-52.
2. *ibid*, 10.
3. *ibid*, 11-12.
4. *Tattvārthasūtra*, 1.6,9.

0.2. AMṚTACANDRA ON SJ

PS devotes six verses to the discussion of *Sj*. At the outset emphasis has been laid on the point that one who has attained Rb can only be able for the acquisition of Rk. Such type of eligibility comes through following the tradition as well as applying one's reasoning. Knowledge devoid of Rb cannot be called right. Though Rb and Rk exist simultaneously in Soul, they are different due to their difference in characteristics. We have already seen that there exists a causal relation between the two. Amṛtacandra explains this causal relation through the illustration of a lamp and its light. Thus Rb is just like a lamp whereas Rk is like its light. In the penultimate verse he advises to comprehend Truth or Reality which is of indeterminate nature. This knowledge should be free from doubt, perversity and ignorance. Rk is verily the nature of the Soul only. In the concluding verse he proposes eight components of Rk viz., correct knowledge of the words of Jaina scriptures, their meanings, proper time for reading them, modesty, etc. These eight components deal with the manner of acquiring knowledge. We shall deal with them later on.

0.3 SJ FROM REAL AND PRACTICAL STANDPOINTS : A RETROSPECT

Barring the *Cārvaka* school, generally in each and every school of Indian philosophy *e.g. Vedānta*, Buddhism etc., knowledge has been treated from two standpoints, namely, *vyāvahārika* and *pāramārthika*. Jaina philosophers also divide it into *Niścaya* (*i.e. pāramārthika*) and *Vyavahāra* (*i.e.* empirical) standpoints.

Kundakunda in his *Samayasāra* observes that although from the empirical point of view (*i.e. Vyavahāra*) there is a difference between Soul and knowledge, yet from the transcendental point of view (i.e. *pāramārthika*) it suffices to state that Soul is the knower and nothing else. Thus knowledge occupies a unique position in Jains system. Again it is one of the signal features of jains philosophy that it divides *upayoga* or consciousness into two types: *Darśana* (perception) and *Jñāna* (cognition). *Darśana* is that undifferentiated, detailless, indefinite, hazy, first stage of knowledge which always precedes *Jñāna* which is detailed, definite, certain knowledge of an object. Kundakunda further divides *Jñānopayoga* into two kinds: *svabhāva Jñāna* (natural knowledge) and *vibhāva Jñāna* (non-natural knowledge). The first one, *i.e.* natural knowledge is perfect and independent. Unassisted by sense Non-natural knowledge is of two types: Right knowledge and wrong knowledge. He further divides Rk into four kinds:

Sensory knowledge (*Mati-jñāna*)

Scriptural knowledge (*Śruta-Jñāna*)

Visual knowledge (*Avadhi-Jñāna*)

Mental knowledge (*Manaḥ-Paryaya-Jñāna*)

Wrong knowledge is also of three kinds: *Kumati* (wrong sensory knowledge), *Ku-śruta* (wrong scriptual knowledge), and *Ku-avadhi* (wrong visual knowledge). When knowledge is combined with Rb, it is called Rk; when it is associated with wrong belief, it is called wrong knowledge. Kundakunda strongly establishes his view that it is from the practical standpoint only that one can differentiate between *Darśana* and *Jñāna*;[1] but from real standpoint they are inseparable. In *Samayasāra*[2] also he contends that it is from the practical standpoint only that we make distinction among the different attributes of Soul such as, perception, knowledge and conduct. But from real standpoint, there is no distinction as such in Soul. Kundakunda further asserts his view by saying that knowledge is nothing but Soul itself.

Samantabhadra's approach towards *Sj* is purely from the empirical standpoint. In his *Ratnakaraṇḍaśrāvakācāra*[3] he observes: The knowers of the scriptures call it (right) knowledge that knows a (thing) as it actually exists, neither less nor more, and is devoid of perversity as well as doubt. It is obvious that here by Rk Samantabhadra means scriptual knowledge only. The Jaina tradition divides scriptures subjectwise into four kinds: (1) *Prathamānuyoga* dealing with the biographies of illustrious Jaina heroes like the *Tīrthaṅkara*-s, *Cakravartin*-s etc. Which are called *Purāṇas* also; (2) *Karaṇānuyoga* literature deals with the Jaina concepts of Universe, time etc. cover their cosmological literature and mathematical calculations related to it; (3) *Caraṇānuyoga* is related to the discipline of householders and monks, while (4) *Dravyānuyoga* contains a metaphysical literature dealing with substances such as, *Jīva, Ajīva* etc. Samantabhadra, taking into consideration these four types of scriptures, divides Rk also into similar four types.

---

1. *Niyamasāra*. 158-171
2. *Samayasāra*. 7and 116.
3. *Ratna*. *Śrāvakācāra*. 42-46.

This substantiates our observation that he treats Rk from the practical standpoint.

Regarding the *Tattvārthasūtra* it can safely be said that Umāsvāti's definition of the five-fold knowledge is purely from the practical standpoint; because the very division of anything into different attributes or aspects is the function of practical standpoint. Again it makes a statement of onething in relation to other foreign things. The five types of knowledge such as, *mati, śruta, avadhi, manaḥ-paryaya* and *kevala* presented by Umāsvāti are in relation to the presence or absence of knowledge-obscuring *Karman* which is responsible for this distinction. Though Omniscience is a pure and perfect knowledge of the Self, it is in relation to the previous four types. Therefore, strictly speaking, the five-fold division of knowledge comes in the arena of practical standpoint.

Following Kundakunda's *Samayasāra* we may divide *Niścayanaya i.e.* the real standpoint into two types: *Aśuddha Niścayanaya* and *Śuddha- Niścayanaya*. We may say that *mati,* śruta, *avadhi* and *manaḥ-paryaya* can be asserted from the practical standpoint, whereas *kevala* from the impure real standpoint (*Aśuddha Niścayanaya*). while from the pure real point (*i.e. Śuddha Niścayanaya*) no distinction exists in Soul whatsoever.

Amṛtacandra paticularly sticks to the real aspect of *Sj* when he advises a true believer to make endeavour for knowledge and the realization of Reality which is *Sat* (existent) and *Anekāntātmaka* (indeterminate). That is, from the real standpoint *Sj* means knowledge of the nature of soul. This knowledge is devoid of doubt, perversity and uncertainty. However, from the practical standpoint, by *Sj* he means scriptural knowledge. He further gives eight limbs or pillars of acquiring scriptural knowledge such as, *grantha* (text or wording of scripture), *artha* (meaning of scripture), *ubhaya* (both wording and meaning), *Kāla* (proper time for reading scripture), *vinaya* (modesty), *Sopadhāna)* (retention or memorisation), *Bahumāna* (showing respect to the sources of knowledge) and *Anihnava* (not concealing the source of knowledge such as, scripture or preceptor). Now we shall discuss the nature of these eight pillars or limbs of acquiring scriptural knowledge in detail.

0.4. EIGHT LIMBS OR PILLARS OF SJ FROM VYAVAHĀRA STANDPOINT.

(i) *Grantha*: In scriptural study textual wording is the most important thing. In the olden days there was an oral tradition in India. The scriptural knowledge was handed down by a *Guru* to a disciple through oral transmission only. So it was expected that the pronunciation of words should be grammatically correct.

(ii) *Artha*: Mere proper recitation does not serve the purpose. One has to pay attention to the authentic meaning of the text. Thus the semantic aspect of scriptural study is as important as the grammatical aspect.

(iii) *Ubhaya*: This limb of scriptural study is nothing but the combination of both *grantha* and artha as given above.

(iv) *Kāla*: It is very interesting to know that the Jains have prescribed proper time for reading scriptures and have described the improper times in which scriptural study was utterly prohibited. For example, at the time of solar and lunar eclipses, earth-quake, storm, mid-night, evening, falling of meteor, appearance of rain-bow etc. scriptures are not to be studied.

(v) *Vinaya*: This refers to thee respect to be shown to the scriptures while studying them. This includes washing of hands and feet with clean water before handling the scriptures and assuming a particular posture prescribed for a reader. In short, a student is supposed to respect scriptures as the source the knowledge.

(vi) *Upadhāna*: In oral tradition, retention and memorisation occupy an important position, the deficiency regarding which may lead to inaccuracy of scripural knowledge.

(vii) *Bahumāna*: This comes close to *vinaya* with the only difference that *vinaya* is internal feeling of respect, while *bahumāna* is its external expression, such as, placing scripture on a raised platform etc.

(viii) *Anihnava*: From the standpoint of knowledge this 'limb' has modern relevance. Even today, in research, authenticity depends upon quoting and acknowledging the source of knowledge. In olden days also it was expected to acknowledge the debt of a preceptor or scholar or a particular work.

Thus we see that these eight 'limbs' or 'pillars' of scriptural knowledge deal with the manner of studying and acquiring scriptural knowledge.

CONCLUDING REMARKS

From the above discussion it may be concluded that

(1) Knowledge cannot be called right unless it is preceded by right faith.

(2) Though right faith and Rk exist simultaneously in Soul, there is a causal relation between them. Right faith is the cause and Rk is the effect. The former is just like a lamp while the latter is just like its light.

(3) Rk from the real standpoint means the knowledge of the Self, while from the practical standpoint it means scriptural knowledge (*śruta jñāna*) which indirectly gives information of entities, such as, Self, non-self, bondage, liberation etc.

(4) And lastly, Rk preceded by right faith transforms into Rc. This we shall undertake for our study in the succeeding chapter.

CHAPTER III

SAMYAK-CĀRITRA OR RIGHT CONDUCT

INTRODUCTION

like *Sd* and *Sj*, *'Samyakcāritra'* is also a compound having two components, such as, *'samyak'* and *'cāritra'*. *'Cāritra'* again is a *Taddhita* derivative or secondary derivative. While *'samyak'* means 'going alongwith' or 'going together with' or 'right', *'cāritra'* renders the meaning as 'the manner of acting' or 'conduct'. Thus *'samyakcāritra'* or *'samyakcāritrya'* means 'going alongwith or right manner of acting'. In Jainism it refers to the prescribed code of conduct for its adherents, both monks and laymen.

0.1. VARIOUS VIEWS ON SC OR RIGHT CONDUCT.

As Jainism views everything from the real and practical standpoints, so also it happens in case of *Sc*. Kundakunda has treated it from the above two standpoints. In his *Samayasāra* he observes. "It should be known that the knowledge of *ācārāṅga* etc., the belief in *Jīva* etc., and protection of six kinds of living beings is called (right) conduct from the pratical standpoint. From the real point of view the Soul is my knowledge, the Soul, my belief and conduct. The Soul is renunciation, the Soul (is) stoppage (of inflow of *Karmas*), and concentration."[1] While treating *Sc* in his *Niyamasāra* he clearly says: Rc, from the practical point of view, is to practise Ousterities while from the real standpoint it means observing austerities from the real point of view.[2] That is to say that when Ousterities are practised with the aim of attaining real Rc *i.e.*, self-obsorption, they are said to be practical Rc. To be absorbed in one's own true nature is the real austerity and the same is real Rc also.

The treatment of *Ratnakaraṇḍa-Śrāvakācāra* of Samantabhadra is as follows: Abstinence from the channels of sins, such as, injury, untruth, theft, copulation, possessiveness is Rc of a real knower.[3] This definition is obviously from the practical standpoint. While Amṛtacandra defines *Cāritra* from the real standpoint he says, "due to the renunciation of all censurable activities, *Cāritra*, free from all passions, (actually) becomes the pure and indifferent (*i.e.* equanimous) Soul (itself)[4] This code of conduct is called right only when it follows Rk; otherwise not.[5]

In short, according to Jaina authors, from the practical point of view, *Cāritra* means an ethical code of conduct prescribed for both householders and monks; while from real standpoint, it is same as self-absorption or self-realization or pure nature

---

1. *Samayasāra*, 294-295.
2. *Niyamasāra*, 55.
3. *Ratnakaraṇḍa-Śrāvakācāra*, 49.
4. *Ps*, 39.
5. *ibid*, 38.

of the Self. Again we have already seen that practical conduct or *vyavahāra cāritra* is of two types: *Śrāvakācāra* or householders' discipline and monks' discipline. Let us first discuss *Śrāvakācāra* as it institutes the main thrust of our study.

0.2. ŚRĀVAKĀCĀRA AND ITS BASIS.

The term '*Śrāvakācāra*' is also a compound which has two components, such as, '*śrāvaka*' and '*ācāra*'. Etymologically, '*śrāvaka*' means 'a hearer' or a 'disciple' or 'one who listens to the discourse of a preceptor' and *ācāra*' means 'conduct' or 'day-to-day behaviour.' But in later ages the term 'śrāvaka' has changed its principal meaning and it refers to householders in general. Thus '*Śrāvakācāra*' generally means 'the conduct of householders'. This code of conduct varies from religion to religion as it is seen that each and every religion prescribes its own independent code of conduct for its adherents. It is also true in case of Jainism. In Jainism he is a *Śrāvaka* who has already attained right faith. He either observes the vows partially (*aṇuvratas*) or does not observe them but sticks to the right faith (*avirata- samyagḍṛṣṭi*) only.

0.3. WHO IS A REAL SRĀVAKA?

According to Jainism, there are two obstacles in the pathway to liberation. They are the vision-deluding *karma*-s (*darśanamohanīya*), and the character-obstructing *karma*-s (*cāritramohanīya*). Having conquered the vision-deluding *karmas*, the *Śrāvaka* continues to struggle against the character-obstructing ones. He adopts the twelve vows prescribed for a layman and then proceeds to limit is desires till he is able to follow absolute vows (*mahāvratas*) by becoming a monk.

The twelve vows of householders' discipline are: (1) five partial vows (*aṇuvrata*-s), (2) three meritorious vows (*guṇavrata*-s), and (3) four disciplinary vows (*śikṣāvrata*-s). The five *aṇuvrata*-s are: *Ahiṁsā, Satya, Acaurya, Brahmacarya* and *Aparigraha*. The three meritorious vows include in them the *Digviratiśīla, Deśaparimāṇaśīla* and *Anarthadaṇḍaśīla*. The four *Śikṣāvrata*-s are constitutive of *Sāmāyika, Proṣadhopavāsa, Bhogopabhoga,* and *Atithisaṁvibhāga*. After a continous and gradual observance of these vows, a *Śrāvaka* reaches the highest peak of spiritual evolution. At the end of his life he undertakes the *Sallekhanāśīla*-s and becomes submerged in Soul itself. We will deal with these twelve vows in detail in succeeding order as prescribed by Amṛtacandra who happens to be our main concern. In the course of discussion, for a comparison, we shall refer to the *Tattvārthasūtra, Ratnakaraṇḍa-Śrāvakācāra* and a few other *Śrāvakācāra*-s whenever necessary.

AHIṀSĀṆUVRATA

(I) THE VOW OF NON-VIOLENCE : A BRIEF SURVEY.

As a basic tenet of all religions, the doctrine of *Ahiṁsā* has been universally accepted. Gautama Buddha has been called the compassion Incarnate. The Allah of Muslims is called Al-Rahman and Al-Raheem, the Beneficent and the Merciful. Hindu *Īśvara* is described as *dayālu* and *kṛpālu*. "Thou shall not kill" is one of the ten commandments in the

Holy Bible. The great sage Veda-Vyāsa exclaims in the *Mahābhārata*:

"aṣṭādaśapurāṇānāṁ vyāsasya vacanadvayaṁ

paropakāraṁ hi puṇyāya pāpāya parapīḍanam"

That means: "All the eighteen Purāṇas have been condensed by Vyāsa in two phrases : The good of others lead to religious merit, causing pain to others is sin."

(II) JAINISM AND OTHER RELIGIONS ON HIṀSĀ AND AHIṀSĀ

At the hour of contrasting the vow of non-violence we find that every religion, except Jainism, has permitted, approved of, encouraged or injuncted *Hiṁsā*, the anti-thesis of *Ahiṁsā*, in the guise of sacrifice, help, protection etc. The Vedic injuctions of *Aśvamedha, Gomedha* (horse and cow sacrifice) are worth mentioning. The reference to *Yūpa* (a tying post) to tie an animal before slaining it is certainly an instance of injucted *Hiṁsā*. The Muslim community celebrate the Id-Ud- Zuha to commemorate the sacrifice of his son by Abraham. the Christians call a religious performance as sacrifice which is derived from the Latin word 'Sacrificium' meaning to santify, where sacrifice of life of any living being always takes place. Even to-day, many Hindu festival are there *e.g. Dāsaharā* etc. where animal-slaughter is still in practice. Moreover, barring the *Hiṁsā* in thought, they also call an injurious act as *Hiṁsā*. Thus Jainism is the only religion which not only abstains itself from all these cruelities, but also preaches *Ahiṁsā* as its first and foremost tenet. It considers thought as the root of action. Thus we commit *Hiṁsā* in thought before we commit it in action. Therefore, it divides *Hiṁsā* into two types: *Bhāvahiṁsā* and *Dravyahiṁsā*. *Bhāvahiṁsā* refers to the injury aimed at any vitality in thought, whereas *Dravyahiṁsā* is the real portrayal of the former. Jainism calls the first one to be real, grave and ghastly. Therefore, mere taking away the life of any being does not constitute complete definition of *Hiṁsā*. Violence in general has been defined as injury to one's vitalities out of negligence (*pramāda*). Negligence means, in short, the passionate ideas of attachment and aversion. Entertaining such ideas is violence[1] Thus Jainism treats violence from two standpoints and it is, therefore, full- fledged in nature.

(III) BHĀVAHĪṀSĀ VERSUS DRAVYAHIṀSĀ.

Bhāvahiṁsā or violence in thought has predominated the discussion on *Ahiṁsā* by Jaina thinkers. Umāsvāti defines it as "kiling the life of a vitality out of negligence caused by passions is *Hiṁsā*."[2] Ācārya Kundakunda contends that nto withstanding the killing or non-killing of a being a negligent person assuredly commits Hiṁsā.[3] Amṛtacandra holds the view that in the mental condition of negligence, caused by passions, such as, attachment etc. certainly violence proceeds, whether a living being is killed or not. Moreover, any injury whatsoever to the material or conscious vitalities through passionate activity of mind, body or speech is assuredly violence. More or less, we

1. *Ps.* 44.
2. *Tattavārthasūtra*, 7-8.
3. *Pravacanasāra*. 3.17.

see, each and every jain philosopher gives the idea that any passionate activity of mind is the root-cause of all violent physical acts. Therefore, one should first give up violence in thought. Then only observance of obsolute non-violence is possible. This description of *Hiṁsā* is from the real standpoint.

From the practical point of view, any kind of injury to any of the ten vitalities of a living being is violence. These ten are five senses, three powers of mind, speech and body, age and respiration.[1] Violence thus includes not only killing or physical injury but also curtailing the freedom of thought and speech of others. While other Jain philosophers such as Samantabhadra etc. give importance to action, Amṛtacandra has explicitly shown the importance of the intention of the agent.[2]

(IV) AMṚTACANDRA'S TREATMENT OF HIṀSĀ AND AHIṀSĀ.

Amṛtacandra holds the view that conduct can be of two types.[3] It is distinguished by total and partial abstinence from five evils, such as, injury, falsehood, theft, unchastity, and wordly attachment. Since these five (sins) destroy the pure thought activity of Soul, they are same as violence. Just for explaining the nature of non-violence five-fold distinction, such as, falsehood etc. is made (by a teacher). He strengthens his views by saying that any injury whatsoever to the material or

1. Gaṇin, Siddhasena on *Tattvārthsūtra*, Surat, 1930, 7-8.
2. *Ps.* 42-43; also 52-53.
3. *ibid.* 40.

conscious vitalities caused through passionate activity of mind, body or speech is violence. To say his viewpoints in a nutshell : Non-appearance of attachment and other passions in soul is *Ahiṁsā,* and their appearance is *Hiṁsā.*

Amṛtacandra has done a thread-bare discussion on this aspect and after illustrating his views he concludes that if *Bhāva- Hiṁsā* is renounced, then only a *Śrāvaka* can be said to be following the *Ahiṁsāṇuvrata*. This is clear from his view that there doesn't occur *Hiṁsā* when mere vitalities are injured, but when a person is not moved by any sort of passion and is carefully following Rc. On the contrary, if one acts carelessly being moved by passions, there certainly advances *Hiṁsā,* whether a living being is killed or not. Thus he says that under the influence of passions, a person first injures the Self through the self, whether there is any injury caused to others or not. One who has not adopted the vow of non-violence, has certainly an inclination towards its opposite, i.e. *Hiṁsā,* whether he actually indulges in it or not.

Subsequently he discusses the various types of *Hiṁsā*. The whole discussion can be brought under three heads: *kṛta* (done by self), *kārita* (got done by agents) and *Anumata* (approved). Moreover, the degree of passion determines the frequency and intensity of its result. So he says : "To one, triffling *Hiṁsā* brings serious result at one time; to another severe violence at the hour of fruition causes small consequence. Again the same *Hiṁsā* committed by two persons at one time may yield different results due to the variations in the intensity of passion. One's violent activity may prove to be beneficial for another fellow and for the injurious act of one person many others may suffer."

After illustrating the various consequences, varieties and causes of *Hiṁsā* he suggests the ways and means to avoid violence, and narrates the evils done by the causes prompting for committing violence. We shall discuss them in the following section which particularly deals with *Ahiṁsāṇuvrata*, the first among the twelve vows as well as the first among the five *aṇuvrata*-s or partial vows.

(V) TREATMENT OF AHIṀSĀṆUVRATA BY AMṚTACANDRA AND OTHERS.

The style followed by Amṛtacandra is simple and systematic. Throughout his discussion he first mentions the causes of violence and their nature and then describes the consequences of being addicted to them. He always advises for a complete abstinence from all these evil things and lastly gives a little concession to the *Śrāvaka*-s who cannot follow absolute renunciation.

At the very outset he advises to renounce wine, flesh, honey and the five *Udumbara* fruits.[1] This renunciation is treated as the basic qualities or *mūlaguṇa*-s of a householder. The earlier writers like Samantabhadra also have enumerated five *aṇuvrata*-s *and* abstinence from wine, flesh and honey as the eight *mūlaguṇa*-s.[2] Kundakunda had nothing to say regarding them as he primarily deals with monks' discipline. But *Ācārya* Somadeva has introduced an altogether different tradition by

1. *Ps.* 61.
2. *Ratnakaraṇḍaśrāvakācāra*. 66.

replacing the five *aṇuv̌rata*-s by abstinence from the five *Udumbara.*[1] Amitagati only adds the avoidance of night-eating to the eight *mūlaguṇas* of Amṛtacandra. From the above observation we can say that a majority of Jaina ethico-philosophers include *mūlaguṇa*-s in the *Ahiṁsāṇuvrata*.

We have already noted that *Ahiṁsā* is the main concern for Amṛtacandra. Throughout his discussion on the eight evils, such as, wine, flesh etc. he tries to prove how *Hiṁsā* is involved in them, sometimes explicitly and sometimes implicitly.

In the biginning he says that wine stupifies mind which in turn forgets piety. Unpious persons commit *Hiṁs ā* unhesitatingly. Moreover, wine is the birth-place of many liquor-born creatures. That is why those who enjoy it commit *Hiṁsā*. Pride, fear, disgust, ridicule, unmindfulness, grief, sex-passion, anger etc. are nothing but concomitats of *Hiṁsā* and wine is their root-cause. Likewise, flesh cannot be procured without causing destruction to life. So using flesh undoubtedly causes *Hiṁsā*. Even the flesh of dead bodies is prohibited because of the spontaneous birth of many creatures in them. Thus neigher raw flesh, nor cooked flesh, nor even meat in the process of cooking is to be taken, as there is a continuous creation of creatrues of the same genus there. For the same reson, honey is to be given up. The five *Udumbara*-s (gular, fig, pippal, pakar and banyan) are the place of birth of numerous mobile beings for which they are forbidden. Even dry fruits are forbidden because

1. *Handiqui*, K.K., Yaśastilaka and Indian tradition, sholapur, 1968, p.262.

Hiṁsā will occur there. Lastly, he advises to give up these eitht, the abode of unwanted things, the producer of invincible consequences as well as grave and ghastly vices. Then only one becomes worthy being a Jaina householder.

As a little concession he ordains that householders should renounce *Hiṁsā* of mobile beings, if they are unable to give up violence of immobile beings. According to him, perfect renunciation means abstinence from the nine-fold commission. They are *kṛta, kārita, anumata* violence multiplied by *vāk* (speech), *kāya* (body), and *manaḥ* (mind). Kundakunda also propounds for three *guptis* or rtstriction of *vāk, kāya* and *manas*. At the end of his discussion of the first phase, he concludes that it would be proper for a householder to possess only necessary articles so as to avoid unnecessary destruction of immobile beings.[1]

In the second phase[2] he elaborately deals with the wrong ideas of people regarding *Ahiṁsā*, where actually *Hiṁsā* is committed. He cites various examples of committing *Hiṁsā* under the guise of *Ahiṁsā* from various practices in the society. In the initial four verses (*i.e.* from 79 to 82), the author deals with the various excuses advocated by flesh-eaters. Slaughter of animals for the sake of sacrifices or to entertain guests or persons of rank has been deprecated. He rejects the idea of slaining a big animal in stead of killing many small ones and thereby supposing that non-violence is practised. Even harmful creatures are not to be killed

1. *PS*, 61-77
2. *ibid*, 78-90

with the belief that their destruction leads to the protection of many others. Nor at the killing of animals that injure others, with the intention to relieve them from their propsed sinful acts, should happen. The idea of extincting the life of a suffering being to relieve him from agony is also prohibited. A person who is always happy, if killed, continues to be happy; keeping such idea in mind one should not kill him. Similarly, a fallacious idea of killing a preceptor to enable him to achieve a better condition in the next life is also to be discarded. He further advises to give up the doctrine of 'pot-breaking immediate salvation' of the *Khārapaṭika*-s, impelled by their thirst for small riches. Even killing of one's own self for the sake of a starving person is strictly denied. This is the gist of his duscussion on various types of *Hiṁsā* practised under the guise of *Ahiṁsā*. Thus he asks for an absolute abstinence from all these varieties of *violence*.

(VI) AMṚTACANDRA'S TREATMENT OF AHIṀSĀṆUVRATA : A CRITICAL ANALYSIS.

Amṛtacandra has devoted about fifty verses to the discussion of *Ahiṁsāṇuvrata*. The observance of the vow of non-violence may be *autsargikī* (complete) or *apavādikī* (partial). The former is nine-fold (vide. verse No. 76 of *Ps*) and the number of the latter is innumerable. Amṛtacandra asks for complete renunciation of violence by adopting monkhood as much as possible because householders' discipline gets its culmination .

The main aim of Amṛtacandra is to refute the fallacious doctrines of different religions. Many a time he has vehemently criticised them. Eventhough he does not categorically mention the name of any religion, it is obvious that he aims his refutation mainly against the ill practices prevailing in Hinduism and the contemporary society. His observation of different factors leading to violence is very minute. His main concern is to point out *Hiṁsā* as the cause of all evils. That is why he gives utmost importance to renounce it. We have devoted one section to this primary aspect for a critical assessment and analysis which is not followed in other sections, because, acccording to Amṛtacandra, the twelve vows are nothing but different illustrations of *Ahiṁsā* bearing different names only.

(VII) TRANSGRESSIONS OR THE ATICĀRAS OF AHIṀSĀṆUVRATA.

While adopting the vow of non-violence a householder ought to know those acts that may transgress his vow so as to avoid them. *Tattvārthasūtra*[1] gives five such transgression. They are: *bandha* (tying up of living beings tightly), *vadha* (killing them), *cchaviccheda* (mutilating them), *atibhāra* (overloading) and *annapānanirodha* (withholding their food and drink). *Ratnakaraṇḍa-Śrāvakācāra*[2] and *Upasakadaśāṅga* [3] also mention the same. Amṛtacandra too ditto follows them.[4] Out he adds that such acts would not be transgression if inflicted for correction or by the way of

1. *Tattvārthasūtra*, 7. 19-20.
2. *Ratna. Śrāvakācāra*, 54.
3. *Upasakadaśāṅga*, 1.45.
4. *Ps*. 183.

punishment by one having due authority, and without an ill-will.

2. SATYĀṆUVRATA OR THE VOW OF TRUTHFULNESS.

The vow of truthfulness is the second among the five partial vows. It refers to the total abstinence from untruth and adherence of truth at the same time. In Brāhmaṇism it also refers to the *Brahaman*.[1] But in jainism it is taken as an ethical principle rather than an abstract metaphysical entity.

Following his own style of presenting definition of the vow, Amṛtacandra defines its opposite and thereby explains what truth is. He contends: "wherever any wrong statement is made through *pramādayoga* (careless activity of body, mind and speech), it is certainly known as fasehood."[2] Thus any factual statement which is made without carelessness is Truth. He divides untruth into four types:[3]

(i) Denial of the existence of a thing with reference to its position, time and nature, *e.g.*" "Devadatta is not here", (when he is actually present).

(ii) Asserting the existence of a non-existent thing with reference to its position, time and nature, *e.g.*"pitcher is here", (when it is not really there).

(iii) Representing a thing as something else, *e.g.* a horse is said to be a cow.

1. *Taittirīyopaniṣad*. 2.1.1
2. *Ps.* 91.
3. *ibid*. 92-98.

(iv) The fourth type of falsehood includes:

(a) Condemnable speech (*garhita*)

(b) Sinful speech (*sāvadya*)

(c) disagreeable speech (*apriya*)

Garhita or reprehensible speech is said to be all that is harsh, unbecoming, non-canonical and of back-biting nature. All types speches which make another engage in piercing, cutting, beating, ploughing, trading, stealing etc., is *sāvadya* or sinful as it leads to destruction of life. The last one is *apriya* speech which causes uneasiness, fear, pain, hostility, grief, quarrel or anguish of mind to another person. In short, in all these speeches, carelessness, the whole and sole cause of *Himsā*, is inevitably present. Therefore, *Himsā* takes place certainly in falsehood. At last Amṛtacandra gives a little concession to the householders and says" those who are not able to shun such *sāvadya* untruth, as it is unavoidable in arranging the bare necessities, should renounce all other forms of untruth for ever. It is the real observance of *Satyāṇuvrata*."

Regarding the nature of untruth, *Tattvārthasūtra*[1] speaks," Any thing false is called untruth." Here *pramattayoga* is to be understood as negligence on the basis of the previous definition of *Ahimsāṇuvrata*. According to Samantabhadra, "One who does not speak gross lie, nor even prompts anybody to speak the same, nor even speak the truth if it leads to disaster, and renounces untruth, he actually follows the vow of truthfulness."[2] In conclusion , we can say that all types

1. *Tattvārtha*, 7.9.

untruth being caused by negligence necessarily involve violence; so it must be renounced with all care.

TRANSGRESSION OF SATYĀṆUVRATA.

The *Ps,*[1] *Tattvārthasūtra* [2] and *Sāgāradharmāmṛta*[3] mention the following five transgressions of *Satyāṇuvrata.*

(i) *Mithyopadeśadāna* (false preaching)

(ii) *Rahasobhyākhyāna* (divulging one's secret)

(iii) *Kūṭalekhakṛti* (forgery)

(iv) *Nyāsāpahāra* (breach of trust)

(v) *Sākāraka-mantrabheda* (disclosing inferences drawn from gesture).

Besides these, Samantabhadra[4] considers *paiśunya* (culumny) and *parivāda* (reproach) as the *aticāras* of *Satyāṇuvrata.*

TRUTH IN INDIAN RELIGIOUS TRADITION.

Truth occupies a prominent place in Indian Thought. In the *Ṛgveda, ṛta,* a synonym of truth, is considered to be the chief divine quality.[5] *Śatapatha Brāhmaṇa* identifies truthfulness with *Dharma.*[6] The great *Bhāgavata-purāṇa*[7] mediatates

---

6. *Ratna.Śrāvakācāra,* 55.
1. *Ps.* 184.
2. *Tattvārthasūtra,* 7.21.
3. *Sāgāra.* 4.45.
4. *Ratna. Śrāvakācāra,* 56.
5. *Ṛgveda,* 10. 190.1
6. *Yo vai sa dharmaḥ satyaṁ vai tat : Śatapatha Br.* 14.4.2.26.
7. *...satyaṁ paraṁ dhīmahi : Bhāgavata Purāṇa* : benedictory verse.

upon the highest Truth at the outset. The *Upaniṣads* search for the ultimate Truth. This is also the case with all religions. Thus *Satyāṇuvrata* has a universal significance and it cannot be set aside.

3. ACAURYĀṆUVRATA OR THE VOW OF NON STEALING.

The third among the five partial vows is *Acauryāṇuvrata*. Etymologically it means non- stealing. But in Jainism it has a much wider meaning. It refers to an abstention from taking a thing which is not given. Because *'adattādānagrahaṇa'* or acceptance of something not given to you incurs violence. Wealth is, as if it were, an external vital force of a man, and whosoever takes away commits violence. According to Amṛtacandra careless taking anything which is not given is deemed as theft, and that is *Hiṁsā*,[1] because it injures the purity of one's own inner nature. It is the first type of theft. The second one is seizing the property of a person. As property is as dear as life, any loss of it is acutely felt. He who deprives a person of his property causes him severe pain and thus injures him. Thus thee is no distinction between violence and theft. It is quite evident that one would not take the property belonging to others unless he is actuated by a desire to have it. The presence of desire, the injury to the Self in the form of a moral and spiritual fall and injung to the person deprived resulting therefrom, constitute *Hiṁsā*. Thus Amṛtacandra gives most importance to the presence

1. *Ps.* 102-106.

of *pramatta-yoga* or carelessness and urges us to renounce it. Stretching the point to the extremity he advises an adherent not to accept even water-well if not given to him. Lastly, as a little concession to the householders he advises them to abstain from accepting ungiven things only as they are unable to follow the rigorous discipline of monks.

The *Tattvārthasūtra* defines *asteya* negatively and says: "*adattādānaṁ steyam*" or "acceptance of anything not given is theft". According to Samantabhadra" "when one does not accept does not steal something kept to left somewhere or forgotten or not given by others, he observes the vow of gross non-stealing'.[1]

ATICĀRAS OF *ACAURYĀṆUVRATA*

The following five transgressions of the vow of non-stealing have been mentioned in the *Ps*,[2] *Ratnakaraṇḍaśrāvakācāra*,[3] *Tattvārthasūtra*[4] etc.

(i) *pratirūpavyavahāraḥ* (adulteration)

(ii) *stenaniyogaḥ* (instigating theft)

(iii) *tadhṛtādānam* (receiving stolen property)

(iv) *rājavirodhātikarama* (violating state rules)

(v) *hīnādhikamānakarana* (false weight and measure)

---

1. *Ratnakaranda. Śrāvakācāra*, 57.
2. *Ps*. 185.
3. *Ratna. Śravaka*, 58.
4. *Tattvārtha*. 7.22.

4. BRAHMACARYĀṆUVRATA OR THE VOW OF CELIBACY.

The vow of celibacy is the fourth one among the five partial vows. Literally, it means 'treading or stepping into the soul'. But, matter as a of fact, it refers to the abstinence from sexual intercourse

Since the Vedic[1] period the importance of this vow has been emphasised. Jainism, which lays more emphasis on monks' discipline, attaches unique importance to it. Total abstinence from sexual intercourse is highly extolled here. But the case of a householder-adherent is little bit different. Because in his case, sexual intercourse cannot be totally avoided as it is a part of his married life. Thus Samantabhadra advises a layman to renounce sex at least with another wife and remain content with his own wife.[2]

In the *Ps* Amṛtacandra asks to renounce non-celibacy and defines it as follows: "*Abrahma* is an act of copulation arising out of sexual desire. *Hiṁsā* is inevitable in sexual intercourse as many vitalities are injured at the time of copulation."[3] Thus any desire for sexual intercourse causes *bhāvahiṁsā* and any copulation leads to *dravyahiṁsā*. Any indulgence in sex-passion by unnatural ways also incurs *Hiṁsā*. So a *Śrāvaka* who, out of attachment, cannot renounce sex with his wife should totally abstain from enjoying other females.

---

1. *Atharvaveda*, 11.5.
2. *Ratna. Śrāvaka*, 59.
3. *Ps*, 107-108.

Tattvārthasūtra defines *Abrahma* as copulation.[1] Copulation can be of three types: male-female, male-male and female-female. Defining the vow of celibacy Samantabhadra[2] says, "One who, out of fear of vices, does not go to other's wife, neither makes any one go (for the same), abstains from having intercourse with other's wife, and satisfies himself with his own, does certainly practise *Brahmacaryāṇuvrata.*"

FIVE TRANSGRESSIONS OF THIS VOW[3]

(i) *Smaratīvrābhiniveśa* (intense desire for sexual intercourse)

(ii) *Anaṅgakrīḍā* (unnatural sexual indulgence)

(iii) *Anyapariṇayakaraṇa* (arranging marriage of others)

(iv) *Aparigṛhītetarayorgamana* (association with immorally married woman)

(v) *Ītvarikagamana* (going to an unmarried woman)

5. PARIGRAHATYĀGĀṆUVRATA OR THE VOW OF NON- POSSESSION.

Ps,[4] *Tattvārthasūtra*[5], *Daśavaikālika*[6] etc. explain *aparigraha* as *mūrcchā* or hallucination of possessions. While defining *aparigraha Ratnakaraṇḍa* says, "Non-possession is the absence of desire for getting

1. *Tattvārtha*. 7.11.
2. *Ratnakaraṇḍa-Śrāvakācāra*, 59.
3. *Ps*, 186.
4. *ibid*, 111.
5. *Tattvārtha*, 7.
6. *Daśavaikālika*, 6.20

more after having got the required prospertiy."[1] Amitagati contends that every violence is committed due to possession.[2] Therefore a householder should constantly try to limit his activities towards possessions. Thus attachment is to be understood as *parigraha.*[3] Attachment is an affectionate regard arising out of the operation of *mohakarman*. Secondly, possession does not only mean *parigraha,* it also includes any desire for and attachment towards it. Thus there are two types of *parigraha* : *antaraṅga* and *bahiraṅga*. The first one is of fourteen kinds whereas the second is two-fold. The fourteen internal possessions are attachments, wrong belief, desire for sexual enjoyment with man, with woman, with both, laughter, indulgence, ennui, sorrow, fear, disgust, anger, pride, deceit and greed. External possession is of two types: with reference to living and non-living objects. All these *parigraha* never exclude-s *hiṁsā*. Thus the Jaina preceptors call *Ahiṁsā* as renunciation of *parigraha* and possession of them is *Himsā*. In course of discussion Amṛtacandra raises a vital question: If attachment is *parigraha,* then there may be no difference between a meek young dear and a ferocious cat, both of whom have attachment for food, though of different sorts. He refutes such a question (which is anticipated from others) by saying that there is certainly a difference as to the degree of attachment. It is week in the young deer who lives on green blades of grass; it is strong in the cat which destroys a host of mice. The effect

1. *Ratna. Śrāvaka,* 61.
2. *Amitagatiśrāvakācāra,* 6.75.
3. *Ps,* 116.

is assuredly influenced by the cause, like the difference in attachment for sweetness in milk and sugar. Desire for sweetness is feeble in case of milk which is moderately sweet, and it is just the opposite in case of sugar which is extremely sweet.

For an acquisition of belief in *Tattvārtha*-s etc. he advises to get rid of wrong belief, the four passions of the first degree, which prevent from having Rb. Again having suppressed or destroyed the passions of the second (degree) which certainly obstruct partial conduct, a layman should observe partial vows. All remaining internal attachments should be suppressed or destroyed with self-exertion, through humility, contentment and meditation. Laśtly, he advises to abstain from the attachment towards both living and non-living things. And if one is unable to fully renounce the possessions such as, cattle, corn, servants, buildings, wealth etc., he should at least limit their quantity or number; because renunciation is the only Right Principle.[1]

FIVE TRANSGRESSIONS OF THIS VOW.[2]

(i) *kṣetra-vāstu parimāṇātikramaṇa*

(Exceeding the limits of house and land from their existing shape.)

(ii) *hiraṇya-suvarṇa- pramāṇātikramaṇa*

(Exceeding the limits of gold and silver ornaments.)

(iii) *dhana-dhānya-pramāṇātikramaṇa*

1. *Ps*. 117-128.
2. *ibid*. 187; *Tattvārtha*, 7.24.

(Exceeding the limits of wealth, cattle and corn.

(iv) *dāsa-dāsī- pramāṇātikramaṇa*

(Exceeding the limits of man and woman servant.)

(v) *kupya-bheda-pramāṇātikramaṇa*

(Exceeding the limits of cloths and utencils.)

RĀTRIBHOJANATYĀGA: AN ADDITIONAL VOW TO THE FIVE AṆUVRATAS

For an absolute abstinence from *hiṁsā* Amṛtacandra advises to avoid night-eating. Because, in ordinary light there is every possibility of burning of small insects or mixing of even them with the edibles. Thus it is to be renounced with mind, body and speech as *hiṁsā* is inevitable there.

THE ŚĪLAS OR SUPPLEMENTARY VOWS

The supplementary vows are seven in number and are collectively known as *śīlas*. They include the three *guṇavrata*-s or meritorious vows and the four *śikṣāvrata*-s or disciplinary vows. According to *PS,* the three *guṇavrata*-s are:

(1) *Digviratiśīla,* (2) *Deśaparimāṇaśīla,* (3) *Anarthadaṇḍatyāgaśīla.*

In *Śvetāmbara*!1 tradition*Bhogopabhogaśīla* replaces *Deśaparimāṇaśīla*. The four *śīkṣāvratas,* according to *Ps, are:*

(1) *Sāmāyika*

(2) *Proṣadhopavāsa*

(3) *Bhogopabhoga*

(4) *Atithisaṁvibhāga*

1. *Upāsakadaśāṅga,* 1.11.

Here it may be observed that basically all the *Ācārya*-s have no fundamental difference amongst them selves, and they probably classify these vows differently only due to their personal likings and not on a matter of principle.[1]

According to *Ps*[2], the supplementary vows protect the *aṇuvratas* as the ramparts guards towns. *Samantabhadra,*[3] on the otherhand opines that the *guṇavrata*-s help to increase the capacity of observing the five vows with greater determination and purity. The *śikṣāvratas,* as the name suggests, are helpful in educating the aspirants for the higher life of complete renunciation. Now, in the following pages, we shall deal with the *guṇavrata*-s and *śikaṣāvrata*-s respectively.

GUṆAVRATAS

As has been told earlier, the *guṇavrata*-s are constitutive of three *śīla*-s such as, *digvirati, deśaparimāṇa* and *anarthadaṇḍaśīla*. *Ps* devotes about twelve verses to the discussion of these three vows. It gives more importance to the third one in comparison to the first two. In the first two he advises a householder to limit his area of dwlling so that he can avoid *hiṁsā* to a great extent. Eventhough the bulk of the text on this point is small, it is of high importance.

1. *Bhārgava,* D., Jain Ethics, Delhi, 1968 p. 128.
2. *Ps,* 136.
3. *Ratna. Śrāvaka,* 67.

1. DIGVIRATIŚĪLA

Etymologically *'dig'* means 'direction' and *'virati'* means 'keeping away from'. Thus *'digvirati'* means keeping away from different directions. In actual practice it refers to the choosing of a limited area for one's activities, as less as possible, out of the vast area of this world. When one limits his area he certainly avoids injury occuring beyond those limits. *Ps* asks to fix the limits in all directions through the well-known geographical marks. Then one should limit his activities in all these directions. Practice of this vow leads to a total restraint of *hiṁsā* that occurs beyond the limit fixed and thereby practising complete *ahiṁsā*. *Ratnakaraṇḍaśrāvakācāra* ditto agrees with *Ps*.

TRANSGRESSIONS OF THIS VOW

Ps,[1] Tattvārthasūtra[2] etc. mention the following five *aticāras* of *digviratiśīla*.

(i) *Urdhvadikpramāṇātikramaṇa*-(Exceeding the limit fixed for upward direction by climbing trees or mountains.)

(ii) *Adhodikpramāṇātikramaṇa* - (Exceeding the limit fixed for downward direction by descending into a well or cellar.)

(iii) *Tīryagdikpramāṇātikramaṇa* - (Exceeding the limit fixed for an oblique or curved direction.)

(iv) *Kṣetra-vṛddhi* - (Extending the limits for freedom of movement.)

(v) *Smṛtyantardhāna* - (Transgressing the limits through forgetfulness.)

1. *Ps.,* 188.
2. *Tattvārta,* 7.25.

2. DEŚAPARIMĀṆAŚĪLA

This vow is supplementary to the preceding one. *Deśaparimāṇaśīla* aims at fixing a further limit to the previous limits in terms of time, village, market, house, street etc. That means one shallont, during a certain time, proceed beyond a certain village, market, street or house, or have anything to do with objects beyond that limit. Thus under a more limited territory more *Ahiṁsā* will be practised.[1]

TRANSGRESSIONS OF THIS VOW

The following are the five breaches of this vow as shown in *Ps*,[2] *Tattvārthasūtra*[3] and *Ratnakaraṇḍaśrāvakācāra*.[4]

(1) *Preṣya-prayoga-* Ordering one's servant to do some work outside the limits.

(ii) *Ānayana-prayoga-*Asking somebody to bring something outside the limits.

(iii) *Śabdānupāta* - Making sounds or giving hints to those who are outside the limits to get certain jobs done.

(iv) *Rūpānupāta* - Using signs and gestures to get a work done which is outside one's limit.

(v) *Pudgalakṣepaḥ-* Throwing some article for the same purpose as above.

---

1. *Ps.*, 139-140.
2. *ibid.* 189
3. *Tattvārthasūtra*, 7.26.
4. *Ratna. Śrāvaka*, 96.

3. ANARTHADAṆḌATYĀGAŚĪLA

There is no controversy among the Jain a *ācāryas* regarding the inclusion of this vow under *guṇavratas*. The import of the vow is to abstain from such harmful activities as will do no good to the agent. Samantabhadra advises to avoid such activities even within the limits set under *digvrata* and *deśaparimānaśīla*.[1] Amṛtacandra divides *anarthadaṇḍa* into six types as given below.[2]

1.*Apadhyāna* - This involves hunting, victory, defeat, war, illicit relation with other's wife, theft, etc. All these are to be avoided by a *Śrāvaka*.

2. *Pāpopadeśa* - It means giving sinful advice to a fellow man leaving upon teaching, trade, writing, agriculture, arts and crafts, service and industry. A householder must renounce that.

3. *Pramādacaryā* - An action done without any necessity or legitimate reason comes under this. This includes digging of ground, uprooting of trees, trampling of lawns, sprinkling of water etc., plucking leaves, fruits or flowers. These habits are to be given up.

4. *Hiṁsādāna* - One should be careful instruments of *hiṁsā* such as knife, poison, fire, plough, sword, bow etc. used for injurious acts.

5. *Duḥśruti*-It stands for listening to or reciting such stories which excite passion. One may not listen to or teach such bad stories that increase attachment etc. and are full of absurdities.

---

1. *Ratnakaraṇḍa-Śrārak cāra*, 74.
2. *Ps*, 141-147.

6. *Dyūtakrīḍā* - It refers to gambling. Amṛtacandra advises to renounce gambling from a distance. It is the foremost among all evils, destroyer of contentment, the home of deceit, and the abode of theft and falsehood.

Lastly, he consdudes : "He who deliberately renounces such all unnecessary sins, leads his *ahiṁsā* vow ceaselessly to admirable victory".

Here it may be pointed out that while most of the jaina *ācāryas* like Samantabhadra, Pūjyapāda give five types of *anarthadaṇḍa,* Amṛtacandra adds gambling to them.

2 TRANSGRESSIONS OF ANARTHADAṆḌATYĀGAŚĪLA

The five transgressions which defile the vow of *anarthadaṇḍatyāga,* according to *Ps,* are as follows:

(1) *Kandarpa* - It is associated with the utterance of obscene words.

(2) *Kautkucya* - It is more intense degree of *kandarpa* in which, due to the intense operation of conduct deluding *karmas,* a person performs vulgar and obscene gestures in addition to vulgar and obscene thought and speech.

(3) *Bhogānarthakya* - It refers to the misuse of the articles of use.

(4) *Maukharya* - It stands for non-sensical and purposeless gossip.

(5) *Asamīkṣitādhikaraṇa* - It refers to any act which is done thoughtlessly.[1]

---

1. *Ps.,* 190.

ŚIKṢĀVRATAS

Four vows are included under *Śikṣāvratas* or disciplinary vows. They are (1) *Sāmāyika*, (2) *Proṣadhopavāsa*, (3) *Bhogopabhoga*, and (4) *Atithisaṁvibhāgaśīla*. All *Śvetāmbara* writers and even some *Digambaras* like Kundakunda, Samantabhadra and Āśādhara include bhogopabhoga in guṇavratas. The traditon of *Ps*, Tattvārthasūtra etc. However, puts it in *Śikṣāvratas*. Now we proceed to discuss those four disciplinary vows one by one.

SĀMĀYIKAŚĪLA

Siddhasena Gaṇi[1] explains *Sāmāyika* as an exercise in *samaya*, etymologized as the attainment (*aya*) of equanimity or tranquility of mind (*sama*). Pūjyapāda [2] holds '*samaya*' to be ' the process of becoming one (*ekatvagamana*), of fusion of activities of body, mind and speech with the *Ātman*', and the practice designated to achieve this end is the *sāmāyika*. In practice it means practising equanimous state of mind. Samantabhadra [3] defines *sāmāyika* as relinquishing the five types of sins to the farthest extreme during the time fixed for *sāmāyika*. Amṛtacandra opines that by giving up *'rāga-dveṣa'* affection and repulsion and i.e., observing equanimity in all objects, one should practise *sāmāyika* continuously, which bring about the realisation of the true nature of the self.

1. Commentary on *Tattvārthasūtra*, vii.16.
2. Commentary of Pūjyapāda on *Tattvārtha*, 7.21.
3. *Ratna*. *Śrāvaka*, 97.
4. *ibid*. 149-150.

This *sāmāyika* must be regularly practised at the end of each night and day. If it is performed for many more times it becomes beneficial. Those who attain equanimity, complete the observance of all vows; because they renounce all sinful activities, although their *cāritra-mohakarma* (which does not allow to observe Rc) is in operation.[1] Samantabhadra opines that fastatng facilities *sāmāyika*.[2] In conclusion, observe it may be that *sāmāyika* is nothing but the state of self-absorption.

FIVE TRANSGRESIONS OF THIS VOW

(i) *Vacana - duṣpraṇidhāna* - It refers to the misdirection of speech. That means hasty recitation of a particular text without understanding its meaning.

(ii) *Mano- duṣpraṇidhāna* - Any misconduct of mind by entertaining anger, deceit, pride, envy and such other feelings.

(iii) *Kāya-duṣpraṇidhāna* - It means that while practising *sāmāyika* the body of the practiser should be kept steady.

(iv) *Anādara* - It is explained as lack of zeal in the performance of the vow.

(v) *Smṛtyanuprasthāna* - This means forgetfulness in *Sāmāyika*. Out of forgetfulness it should not be irregular.

---

1. *ibid*. 149-150.
2. *Ratna. Śrāvaka*, 100-101.

PROṢADHOPAVĀSAŚĪLA

Restriction over certain types of food is found in almost all religions. For such activity fast has been considered to be the best means. With the jainas, whether a householder or monk, fast is a common practice. Samantabhadra,[1] Amṛtacandra[2] and others encnciate this vow as renauncing the four kinds of food on the eight hand fourteenth lunar days in each fortnight. The observance of this *vrata* needs performance of meditation, and avoidance of bath, perfumes etc. The procedure of observing *proṣadhopavāsa* differs from one tradition to other in Jainism.

PROCEDURE OF OBSERVING THIS VOW

Amṛtacandra[3] notably lays down the procedure of observing *proṣadhopavāsa*. To strengthen the daily practice of *sāmāyika* discipline, one must observe fasting twice during each fortnight. After renouncing all household works and all worldly attachment one should undertake the vow at the middle of the day preceding to the *proṣadha* (i.e., meditation day). One should then retire to a secluded spot, renounce all sinful activities, abstain from indulgence in all sonsual objects and observe due restraint of body, speech and mind. He should pass the day wrapped in spiritual contemplation, perform *sāmāyika* at sun-set, vanquish sleep by refection on self, and thus pass the night on a mat free from insects. He should rise in the morning,

1. *Ratna. Srāvaka,* 106.
2. *Ps.* 151.
3. *Ibid.* 152-157.

perform the necessary duties of the time and engage himself in *Jana* worship, as prescribed, with *prāsuka* objects (*i.e.* having living beings on them). That day, the second night and the half of the third day should carefully be passed in the manner said above. Thus sixteen *yamas* (*i.e.* forty eight 48 hours) constitute the time of this vow.

In the concluding verses *Ps* gives the result of practising *proṣadha*. It is of the opinion that *bhoga* and *upbhoga* (articles of temporary and permanent enjoyment) are the causes of enjuiny to immobile beings by of all these, *hiṁsā* is assuredly avoided. There is no false-hood because of speech-restrain, no stealing because of abstinence from all misappropriation, no unchastity because of renunciation from sexual intercourse. Having thus got rid of all *hiṁsā*, a *Śrāvaka* practically reaches the sixth stage of a *Mahāvratin*, but does not reach the seventh stage of an *Apramatta*, because *cāritra-mohanīya-karma* still operates there.

TRANSGRESSIONS OF THIS VOW

There are the five breaches of *proṣadhopavāsa* as recorded in *Ps*[1] and *Tattvārthasūtra*[2] and other treatises.

(i) *Anavekṣitāpramārjītamādānam* - It refers to the handling of things without proper examination and sweeping.

(ii) *Saṁstara* - Using seats or beds without proper checking and sweeping.

1. *Ps.*, 192.
2. *Tattvārtha.*, 7.29; also *Ratna*, *Śrāvaka.*, 110.

(iii) *Utsarga* - Passing excrement etc. without examining and sweeping the ground.

(iv) *Smṛtyanupasthāna* - It means forgetting the rules of preaching the vow.

(v) *Anādara* - It refers to the lack of interest in practising the vow.

BHOGOPABHOGAPARIMĀṆAŚĪLA

The word *'bhoga'* pertains to those objects which are capable of being used only once, *e.g.* garland, betel-leaf etc., and the word *'upabhoga'* covers those objects which are capable of being used again and again, *e.g.*, cots, ornaments, cloths etc. This vow implies the limitation in the use of objects of *bhoga* and *upabhoga* in order to minimise attachments to the objects. According to Samantabhadra, a thing may be renounced for the whole life which is called as *yama,* or for a limited period which is called. *niyama.*[1] Thus it seems that *yama* is taken as *guṇavrata* and *niyama* as *śikṣāvrata*. The main idea involved in this vow is that attachment towards and the consumption of objects like meat, honey, intoxicants and objects possessing living organism in them cause hurdle in spiritual development.

Explaining this vow *Ps*[2] advises to renounce the articles of *bhoga* such as vegetables, butter, etc., because they are the birth-s place of numerous *Jīva*. Even non-prohibited objects, if renounced, prove beneficial as they neutralise attachment. Amṛtacandra asks to fix a further limit to the limits already set. Through a continuous practice and

1. *Ratna. Śrāvaka.*, 87.
2. *PS.*, 161-166.

gradual renunciation, true knowledge is obtained. It increases enlightenment and leads to absolute renunciations and perfect conduct; the path of liberation. Throughout his discussion on different vows we see that he aims at a complete avoidance of *hiṁsā* and that is why he inculcates a gradual process of minimising or abstaining worldly objects, as far as possible, as it cuts the very root of attachment.

TRANSGRESSIONS OF THIS VOW

According to *Ps.*[1] *Tattvārthasūtra*[2] these are the five *articāras* of this vow.

1. *Sacittāhāra*:eating articles having life.
2. *Sacittamiśrāhāra* : eating articles mixed with those having life.
3. *Sacittasambandhāhāra*: eating articles which are associated with those having life.
4. *Duṣpakvāhāra*: eating articles not well cooked.
5. *Abhisava*: eating articles that are prepared by fermentation.

Samantabhadra has made substantial contribution in extending the scope of the *aticāra*-s of this vow to *viṣayaviṣato'nuprekṣā, anusmṛti, atitaulya, atitṛṣā* and *atyanubhāva.*[3]

ATITHISAṀVIBHĀGAŚĪLA

Amṛtacandra, in the context of this vow, observes: "for mutual good *i.e.* for the donor and

1. *ibid,* 193.
2. *Tattvārthasūtra,* 7.30.
3. *Ratna.Śrāvaka.,* 90.

the recipient, one possessed of the qualification of a donor, should in a proper manner, give a portion of appropriate things to a Jaina monk.[1]

Then he goes on explaining each of the characteristics enumerated above[2] as follows:

1. Nine-fold manner of donation,

(1) *saṁgraha* or respectful welcome, (2) *Uccasthāna* or offering high seat, (3) *pādodaka* or washing the feet, (4) *arcanā* or worship, (5) *praṇāma* or bowing, (6) *vākśuddhi* or purity of speech (7) *kāya- śuddhi* or purity of body, (8) *manaḥ-śuddhi* or purity of mind and (9) *eṣaṇāśuddhi* or purity of food.

2. Seven qualities of the donor.

(1) *aihikaphalānapekṣā* or disregard for worldly benefit, (2) *kṣānti* or forbearance, (3) *niṣkapaṭatā* or absence of fraud, (4) *anasūyatyam* or absence of jealousy (5) *aviṣādatva* or absence of sorrow, (6) *uditva* or absence of joy and (7) *nirahaṁkāritva* or absence of pride or arrogance.

3. Quality of food to be offered.

Only such things should be given (as food) that help in the sacred studies and also in the due observance of austerities, and which don't bring about attachment, disgust, incontinence, intoxication, pain, fear etc.

---

1. *Ps.* 167.
2. *Ps. 168-174.*

4. Grades of recipients

The recipients are of three grades according to their respective possession of qualities leading to *mokṣa*. They are true believers without vows, with partical vows and with full vows.

5. Merits of giving donations.

In making gifts one comes over greed, which is a form of *hiṁsā*, and hence gifts made to a worthy recipient amount to the renunciation of violence. One who does not observe this is assuredly greedy. When one gives food to a saint which he has prepared for himself, such a thoughtfully offered gift which is made without any disregard or regret or or with suppressed greed, is itself *ahiṁsā*.

TRANSGRESSIONS OF THIS VOW[1]

1) *Paradātṛvyapadeśa* - This refers to the donation of articles belonging to others in one's own name.

2) *Saccittanikṣepa*- placing the food on *saccitta* (*i.e.*, articles having life in them.

3) *Saccittāpadhāna* - giving articles those are covered with *saccitta*.

4) *Kālātikramaṇa* - serving the articles at an improper time.

5) Mātsarya- giving donations with a jealous mind.

---

1. *PS*.194.

SALLEKHANĀŚĪLA

It is a calm resignation and, an unruffled preparedness for meeting death. All religious observances, fastings and austerities would be unavailing and futiles if, at the last noment of life, at the hour of death, one were to lose his balance of mind, equanimity of thought and were afflicted by passion, distress and attachment. One should opt for a voluntary death devoid of attachment or aversion to life. Thus *sallekhanā* is to be adhered to devotedly. *Ps* declares it to be the only thing which would enable one to carry his wealth of piety with him.[1] In fact, *sallekhana* is nothing but practising *samādhi* for a voluntary death. Hence *Ps* ordains that the vow is to be practised well in advance so that one may face death courageously and heroically.

Samādhi, therefore, cannot be mistaken as suicide which is comnitted as result of imbalance of mind purturbed by passions such as anger, pride, frustation etc. Nor also is this death committed by adopting the means like obstruction of respiration, consuming poison or killing by arms and amunitions. Lastly, concluding his discussion on *sallekhanā* Amṛtachandra says that in the practice of *Sallekhanā*, all passions which are the cause of violence, are subdued, and hence *sallekhanā* is said to be leading towards *Ahiṁsā*.

Giving his remarks on the observance of these eight *śīlas*, along with *sallekhanā*, Amṛtacandra, in conclusion, says that he who ceaselessly observes

---

1. Ibid, 175.

all the *śīlas* for the protection of watas, is choosen as a lover by the Lady Liberation.

TRANSGRESSIONS OF SALLEKHANĀ

Ps,[1] *Tattvārthasūtra*[2] give the following five *aticāras* of *Sallekhanaśīla.*

1) *Jīvitāśaṁsā* : desire to live.

2) *Maraṇāśaṁsā* : desire to die.

3) *Suhṛdanurāga* : attachment towards friends.

4) *Sukhānubandha* : revival of past pleasure.

5) *Sanidāna* : expectation of future prosperity.

Regarding the result of understanding and finally renouncing the transgressions of each and every, vow we cannot do better than quoting Aṛtacandra who remarks as follows: one who understands and avoids these transgressions, soon attains the spiritual goal through flawless right faith, vows and *Śīlas.*[3]

AUSTERITIES FOR A HOUSEHOLDER

Austerity is a part of Rc. It is particularly the core of monks' discipline. Still Amṛtacandra prescribes some austerities for householders also for attaining a higher level of spiritual development. He divides it into two types: *bāhya* (external) and *antaḥ* (internal). The first one includes fasting, reduced diet, sleeping and resting in lonely places, renouncing the *rasa*-s (*like* milk, curd, ghee etc.), reducing one's own body and limiting food.

1. *PS.* 195.
2. *Tattvārthasūtra* 7.33.
3. *Ps.* 196.

Internal penance is constitutive of respect, service, expiation, renunciation, study of sacred texts and concentration. Amṛtachandra has merely enumerated these external and internal vows (verse No. 198 and 199), but has not elaborated them. Probably because there is already ample material describing their nature in the works like Tattvārthasūtra prior to Amṛtacandra he did not discuss much on this aspect in order to avoid repetition.

MONKS' DISCIPLINE

Jainism is an ascetic religion from its very beginning whereas the institution of *saṁnyāsa* (total renunciation) is most probably a later addition in Brāhmaṇism. The stage of a householder(*gārhastha*) occupies a lofty place in the latter,[1] whereas in Jainism it is only a means to the higher goal of monkhood. Later on, in Hinduism also, the division of life into four stages (*āśrama*) accorded a proper place to asceticism. Thus asceticism is the marrow of Jainism. It is due to this aspect that in Jaina tradition even a *Śrāvaka* is taught *Yatidharma* (conduct of a monk) prior to *Śrāvakadharma* (householders' discipline) with the intention that he should prepare fully for monks' discipline even in his householder's stage.

A monk devotes his life absolutely to spiritualism. Eventhough he depends upon the society for his bare necessities, he is above all social obligations. His life is predominated by *Niścayanaya* and *Niścayacāritra* rather than *Vyavahāranaya* and

1. *Manusmṛti* 3. 77-78.

Vyavahāra-cāritra. In order to attain perfection, he avoids even smallest deviations in his conduct. Thus the conduct of a monk is an ideal for all aspirants for liberation and it has been dealt with by every Jaina *ācārya* with great care and importance. The *Ps* is not an exception to this. Amṛtacandra gives the *ācāra* of the monks at the end and encourages the householders to follow it because it involves less *hiṁsā* and is more fruitful for observing *Rc*.

GIST OF MONKS' DISCIPLINEAS GIVEN IN THE PS

Having considered one's own position and ability, a householder should practise the conduct of a monk as described in the scriptures. In his treatment of monks' discipline Amṛtacandra prescribes the three *gupti*-s, five *samiti*-s (vigilance), ten *dharma*-s observances), twelve *tapa*-s (meditations) and the ways to get rid of the twenty-two *parīṣaha*-s or sufferings which are as follows:

Equanimity, praising the qualities of the *Tīrthaṅkara*-s, bowing to them, repentance of defects committed and renunciation of possible defects along with giving up the attachment for body are the six daily duties for a monk to be observed (by a *Śrāvaka*). Besides, one should carefully observe the three controls (*gupti*-s): proper control of speech (*vāk*), proper control of body (*kāya*) and proper control of mind (*manaḥ*). Again, careful movement, careful speech, careful eating, careful placing and removal of things, careful evacuation of excrement, are the five *samiti*-s or vigilance in behaviour which are also to be practised. Moreover, forgiveness, humility, straightforwardness, truth, contentment, restraint, austerities, charity, non-attachment and chastity are the *dharma*-s or observances included in monk's discipline. Transitorīness, helplessness, transmigration, loneliness, separateness, impurity, inflow, stoppage and shedding of *karma*-s, Universe, variety of right path, and nature of right path these twelve meditations should be contemplated continuously by a monk. Hunger, thirst, cold, heat, ins-ect bite, nudity, ennui, women, walking, sitting, resting, abuse, beating, begging, non-obtaining, disease, contact with thorny shrobs etc., respect and disrespect, conceipt of knowledge, lack of knowledge and slack-belief are the twenty two sufferings (*pariṣaha*-s) which should be endured without any feeling of harrassment, by one who desires to get rid of all the causes of pain. *Ratnatraya* (Rb, Rk and Rc) should be followed even partially at every moment of time without cessation by a householder desirous of attaining emancipation with a determined continuous effort. One should, when the opportunity for full attachment of *Ratnatraya* is available, adopt the order of saints and make it complete without delay.[1]

A BRIEF SURVEY OF MONK'S DISCIPLINE AS GIVEN IN PS

In the whole discussion the three *'gupti*-s' (-the word is derived from the root *'gup'* meaning to guard, protect or defend-) and the five *'samiti*-s' (-the word coms from the root *'i'* meaning "to go" being attached with the prefix *'sam'* ,are of great

1. Ps., 202-210.

importance. *Vāk-kāya-mono'-gupti* protects a monk from all sins, Kundakunda, in his *Niyamasāra*[1] also prescribes these *gupti-s* for a monk. *Samiti* on the otherhand means vigilance in behaviour. Negligence lies at the root of all sins and therfore constant vigilance is necessary to avoid them.[2] The ten excellent qualities are cultivated with the purpose of spiritual development and not with some wordly purpose. Eventhough the list of vows being overlapping repeats many moral virtues which are already covered by the five great vows, still they are specially helpful in stopping the inflow of Karmic matter. The list of twentytwo sufferings shows that a monk ought to face not only physical pains but also mental hardships. Thus, in any case, he should be non-responding to pain.

RELATION BETWEEN MONKS' DISCIPLINE AND HOUSEHOLDERS' DISCIPLINE.

We have have already noted that a monk practises the vows which is followed with a total renouncement of all sorts of attachment and aversion. He leads a different life which is above all social obligations. Thus he lives in an ideal stage of spiritual elevation.

The position of a householder is little different. He lives in this society for which he is bound to show some obligations. Moreover, while following a code of conduct cannot, he follow it fully as there is every possibility of committing mistake at different steps. Due to his deep involvement in

1. *Niyamasāra*, 66-68.
2. *ibid*. 60-65.

society he is unable to have a complete cessation of attachment etc. Thus the conduct which he follows may be desingated as a beginner's stage in the way of spiritual development which culminates in monks' discipline.

CONCLUSION

The concluding portion of the present work would be divided into two parts. In the first part we shall present its resume in brief while in the last mention will be made of the original contributions of Amṛtacandra's *Ps*.

In the *first Chapter* we dealt with *Rb*. It is comprised of the following sections.

1. Introduction to *Sd*.

2. Various views on *Sd*.

3. *Mokṣa - mārga* from its two-fold standpoint

4. Eight *aṅga*-s of *Sd* from both empirical and transcendental points of view.

5. Place of *Sd* in *Mokṣa-mārga*.

6. Relation between *Sd* and *Sj*.

In the *second Chapter* we discussed Rk by following the same line adopted in the first chapter.

The *third Chapter* being the marrow of the study is the most exhaustive one. After quoting the views of ancient authors on *Sc* we briefly presented householders' discipline and its basis. The twelve vows of the householders have been studied in a thread-bare style. In the epilouge monks' discipline alongwith its importance is also added. After a short analysis of it, its relation with householders' discipline has also been presented.

Now from our study of the *Ps,* we intend to lay down the following points by way of conclusion.

1. Amṛtacandra gives unique importance to *Ahiṁsā* as the basis and essence of all vows and attempts to establish that all vows are nothing but different forms or expressions of *Ahiṁsā* vow only.
2. In his application of *Vyavahāranaya* and *Niścayanaya* to the tenets of householders' discipline, he ditto follows Kundakunda. But he explicitly shows the limitations of the *Vyavahāranaya* and thereby lays more emphasis on the *Niścayanaya* which is an ideal of the former.
3. His inclusion of monks' discipline in *Ps,* which is primarily a *Śrāvakācāra,* is an unique achievement in itself. By that he seeks to show that householders, discipline becomes perfect only when it aims at and ultimately adheres to monks' discipline. The reason, according to him, is that the observance of absolute *Ahiṁsā* and other *vrata-s* is possible in monks' discipline only.
4. Authors like Kundakunda, Samantabhadra etc. include *bhogopabhogaparimāṇaśila* in *guṇavrata*-s while Amṛtachandra, following the *Tattvārthasūtra* places it in *Śikṣāvrata*-s.
5. As *samayagdarśana* implies faith in the dogmas of religion and *Sj* accurate knowledge of those dogmas, many writers, especially among the *Digambara*-s, have found it desirable to preface to their *Śrāvakācāra-s* more or less extensive

summary of Jaina doctrine, particularly to the nature of *jīva* and *karman*. Amṛtacandra also does the same thing in the prologue of the *Ps*. But his unique treatment of *Sj* lies in the fact that like the eight *aṅga-s* of *Sd* he gives the eight aṅga-s of *Sj* such as *grantha, artha* etc. but, of course, the from empirical standpoint only.

Apart from these originalities and differences his treatment of householders' discipline does not essentially differ from that of his predecessors.

Eventhough scholars like R.Williams, A.N. Upadhye, K.C. Sogani, D. Bhargav and others have done some rudimentary researches on Jaina *Śrāvakācāra-s* their comparitive study is still a desideratum. Jaina *Śrāvakācāra-s* provide a rich material for studying its householder community and socio-ethical discipline. It will be interesting to conduct a critical and comparative study of these *Śrāvakācāra-s* with historical perspective. Again, it will also prove to be fruitful to conduct a comparative study of Jaina the Buddhist and Hindu householders' disciplines. The present work is just an humble beginning to such type of research which presupposes the valuable works of the predecessors. That is why it would be proper to conclude this study with Amṛtacandra's words expressed at the end of his *Ps*.

varnaiḥ kṛtāni citraiḥ padāni

tu padaiḥ kṛtāni vākyāni/

vākyaiḥ kṛtaṁ pavitraṁ

śāstram idaṁ na punar asmābhiḥ//

(*Ps*. 226)

Words are (spontaneously) formed through different letters, while sentences are constructed by (different) words. This holy treatise is composed by sentences, not by us.

BIBLIOGRAPHY

1. *ĀCĀRYA* Śrī Kundakunda.

Samayasāra, The Central Jaina Publishing House, Ajirtashrama, Lucknow 1930.

2. *ĀCĀRYA,* Śrī Kundakunda.

Niyamasāra, The Central Jaina Publishing House, Ajitashrama, Lucknow, 1931.

3. *BHARGHAV,* Dayananda. *Jaina Ethics,* Motilal Banarasidass, Delhi, Varanasi, Patna, 1968.

4. *DOSHI,* Sva. Bra. Jīvarāja Gautamcanda.

Ratnakaraṇḍaśrāvakācāra, Jaina Saṅskṛti Saṁrakṣaka Saṅgha, Solapur, 1984.

5. *JAIN,* Adhyātmika Puruṣa Paṇḍita Saranārāma.

Śrīpuruṣārtha - Siddhyupāyaḥ (Mokṣamārgaḥ)

Saharanpur, 1959.

6. *PREMI* Nathuram. *Jaina Sāhitya aur Itihāsa,* Hindi grantha Ratnakar (Pvt.) limited, Bombay, 1956.

7. *SAMGHVI,* Paṇḍ Sukhalāljī.

Tattvārthasūtra, Bhārata Jaina Mahāmaṇḍala, Wardha, 1952.

8. *SOGANI,* Kamal Chand. *Ethical Doctrines in Jainism,* Lalchand Hirachand Doshi, Jaina Saṁskṛti Saṁrakṣaka Saṅgha, Sholapur, 1967.

9. *SURI,* Shrimat Amrita Chandra. *Purushartha Siddhyupaya,* The Central Jaina Publishing House, Ajitashrama, Lucknow, 1933.

10. *UPADHYE* A.N. *Pravacanasāra,* The Parama-Śruta-Prabhāvaka Mandala Shrimad Rajachandra Ashrama, 1984.

11. *WILLIAMS,* R. *Jaina Yoga,* London, Oxford University Press, New York, Toronto, 1963.

श्रीपुरुषार्थसिद्ध्युपायः (मोक्षमार्गः)

तज्जयति परं ज्योतिः समं समस्तैरनन्तपर्यायैः ।
दर्पणतल इव सकला प्रतिफलति पदार्थमालिका यत्र ॥ 1 ॥

परमागमस्य जीवं निषिद्धजात्यन्धसिन्धुरविधानम् ।
सकलनयविलसितानां विरोधमथनं नमाम्यनेकान्तम् ॥ 2 ॥

लोकत्रयैकनेत्रं निरूप्य परमागमं प्रयत्नेन ।
अस्माभिरुपोद्ध्रियते विदुषां पुरुषार्थसिद्ध्युपायोऽयम् ॥ 3 ॥

मुख्योपचारविवरणनिरस्तदुस्तरविनेयदुर्बोधाः ।
व्यवहारनिश्चयज्ञाः प्रवर्तयन्ते जगति तीर्थम् ॥ 4 ॥

निश्चयमिह भूतार्थं व्यवहारं वर्णयन्त्यभूतार्थम् ।
भूतार्थबोधविमुखः प्रायः सर्वोऽपि संसारः ॥ 5 ॥

अबुधस्य बोधनार्थं मुनीश्वरा देशयन्त्यभूतार्थम् ।
व्यवहारमेव केवलमवैति यस्तस्य देशना नास्ति ॥ 6 ॥

माणवक एव सिंहो यथा भवत्यनवगीतसिंहस्य ।
व्यवहार एव हि तथा निश्चयतां यात्यनिश्चयज्ञस्य ॥ 7 ॥

व्यवहारनिश्चयौ यः प्रबुध्य तत्त्वेन भवति मध्यस्थः ।
प्राप्नोति देशनायाः स एव फलमविकलं शिष्यः ॥ 8 ॥

अस्ति पुरुषश्चिदात्मा विवर्जितः स्पर्शगन्धरसवर्णैः ।
गुणपर्यायसमवेतः समाहित समुदयव्ययध्रौव्यैः ॥ 9 ॥

परिणममानो नित्यं ज्ञानविवर्त्तैरनादिसन्तत्या ।
परिणामानां स्वेषां स भवति कर्ता च भोक्ता च ॥ 10 ॥

सर्वविवर्त्तोत्तीर्णं यदा स चैतन्यमचलमाप्नोति ।
भवति तदा कृतकृत्यः सम्यक्पुरुषार्थसिद्धिमापन्नः ॥ **11** ॥

जीवकृतं परिणामं निमित्तमात्रं प्रपद्य पुनरन्ये ।
स्वयमेव परिणमन्तेऽत्र पुद्गलाः कर्मभावेन ॥ **12** ॥

परिणममानस्य चितश्चिदात्मकैः स्वयमपि स्वकैर्भावैः ।
भवति हि निमित्तमात्रं पौद्गलिकं कर्म तस्यापि ॥ **13** ॥

एवमयं कर्मकृतैर्भावैरसमाहितोऽपि युक्त इव ।
प्रतिभाति बालिशानां प्रतिभासः स खलु भवबीजं ॥ **14** ॥

विपरीताभिनिवेशं निरस्य सम्यग्व्यवस्य निजतत्त्वं ।
यत्तस्मादविचलनं स एव पुरुषार्थसिद्ध्युपायोऽयः ॥ **15** ॥

अनुसरतां पदमेतत् करम्बिताचारनित्यनिरभिमुखा ।
एकान्तविरतिरूपा भवति मुनीनामलौकिकी वृत्तिः ॥ **16** ॥

बहुशः समस्तविरतिं प्रदर्शितां यो न जातु गृहणाति ।
तस्यैकदेशविरतिः कथनीयानेन बीजेन ॥ **17** ॥

यो यतिधर्ममकथयन्नुपदिशति गृहस्थधर्ममल्पमतिः ।
तस्य भगवत्प्रवचने प्रदर्शितं निग्रहस्थानम् ॥ **18** ॥

अक्रमकथनेन यतः प्रोत्सहमानोऽतिदूरमपि शिष्यः ।
अपदेऽपि सम्प्रतृप्तः प्रतारितो भवति तेन दुर्मतिना ॥ **19** ॥

एवं सम्यग्दर्शनबोधचरित्रत्रयात्मको नित्यं ।
तस्यापि मोक्षमार्गो भवति निषेव्यो यथाशक्ति ॥ **20** ॥

तत्रादौ सम्यक्त्वं समुपाश्रयणीयमखिलयत्नेन ।
तस्मिन् सत्येव यतो भवति ज्ञानं चरित्रं च ॥ **21** ॥

जीवाजीवादीनां तत्त्वार्थानां सदैव कर्तव्यम् ।
श्रद्धानं विपरीताभिनिवेशविविक्तमात्मरूपं तत् ॥ **22** ॥

सकलमनेकान्तात्मकमिदमुक्तं वस्तुजातमखिलज्ञैः ।
किमु सत्यमसत्यं वा न जातु शकेति कर्त्तव्या ॥ 23 ॥

इह जन्मनि विभावादीन्यमुत्र चक्रित्वकेशवत्वादीन् ।
एकान्तवाददूषितपरसमयानपि च नाकांक्षेत् ॥ 24 ॥

क्षुत्तृष्णाशीतोष्णप्रभृतिषु नानाविधेषु भावेषु ।
द्रव्येषु पुरीषादिषु विचिकित्सा नैव करणीया ॥ 25 ॥

लोके शास्त्राभासे समयाभासे च देवताभासे ।
नित्यमपि तत्त्वरुचिना कर्त्तव्यमनूढदृष्टित्वम् ॥ 26 ॥

धर्मोऽभिवर्द्धनीयः सदात्मनो मार्दवादिभावनया ।
परदोषनिगूहनमपि विधेयमुपबृंहणगुणार्थम् ॥ 27 ॥

कामक्रोधमदादिषु चलयितुमुदितेषु वर्त्मनो न्यायात् ।
श्रुतमात्मनः परस्य च युक्त्या स्थितिकरणमपि कार्यम् ॥ 28 ॥

अनवरतमहिंसायां शिवसुखलक्ष्मीनिबन्धने धर्मे ।
सर्वेष्वपि च सधर्मिषु परमं वात्सल्यमालम्ब्यम् ॥ 29 ॥

आत्मा प्रभावनीयो रत्नत्रयतेजसा सततमेव ।
दानतपोजिनपूजाविद्यातिशयैश्च जिनधर्मः ॥ 30 ॥

इत्याश्रितसम्यक्त्वैः सम्यग्ज्ञानं निरूप्य यत्नेन ।
आम्नाययुक्तियोगैः समुपास्यं नित्यमात्महितैः ॥ 31 ॥

पृथगाराधनमिष्टं दर्शनसहभाविनोऽपि बोधस्य ।
लक्षणभेदेन यतो नानात्वं संभवत्यनयोः ॥ 32 ॥

सम्यग्ज्ञानं कार्यं सम्यक्त्वं कारणं वदन्ति जिनाः ।
ज्ञानाराधनमिष्टं सम्यक्त्वानन्तरं तस्मात् ॥ 33 ॥

कारणकार्यविधानं समकालं जायमानयोरपि हि ।
दीपप्रकाशयोरिव सम्यक्त्वज्ञानयोः सुघटम् ॥ 34 ॥

कर्त्तव्योऽध्यवसायः सदनेकान्तात्मकेषु तत्त्वेषु ।
संशयविपर्ययानध्यवसायविविक्तमात्मरूपं तत् ॥ 35 ॥

ग्रन्थार्थोभयपूर्णं काले विनयेन सोपधानं च ।
बहुमानेन समन्वितमनिह्नवं ज्ञानमाराध्यम् ॥ 36 ॥

विगलितदर्शनमोहैः समञ्जसज्ञानविदिततत्त्वार्थैः ।
नित्यमपि निःप्रकम्पैः सम्यक्चारित्रमालम्ब्यम् ॥ 37 ॥

न हि सम्यग्व्यपदेशं चारित्रमज्ञानपूर्वकं लभते ।
ज्ञानानन्तरमुक्तं चारित्राराधनं तस्मात् ॥ 38 ॥

चारित्रं भवति यतः समस्तसावद्ययोगपरिहरणात् ।
सकलकषायविमुक्तं विशदमुदासीनमात्मरूपं तत् ॥ 39 ॥

हिंसातोऽनृतवचनात्स्तेयादब्रह्मतः परिग्रहतः ।
कार्त्स्न्यैकदेशविरतेश्चारित्रं जायते द्विविधम् ॥ 40 ॥

निरतः कार्त्स्न्यनिवृत्तौ भवति यतिः समयसारभूतोऽयं ।
या त्वेकदेशविरतिर्निरतस्तस्यामुपासको भवति ॥ 41 ॥

आत्मपरिणामहिंसनहेतुत्वात्सर्वमेव हिंसैतत् ।
अनृतवचनादि केवलमुदाहृतं शिष्यबोधाय ॥ 42 ॥

यत्खलु कषाययोगात्प्राणानां द्रव्यभावरूपाणाम् ।
व्यपरोपणस्य करणं सुनिश्चिता भवति सा हिंसा ॥ 43 ॥

अप्रादुर्भावः खलु रागादीनां भवत्यहिंसेति ।
तेषामेवोत्पत्तिर्हिंसेति जिनागमस्य संक्षेपः ॥ 44 ॥

युक्ताचरणस्य सतो रागाद्यवेशमन्तरेणापि ।
न हि भवति जातु हिंसा प्राणव्यपरोपणादेव ॥ 45 ॥

व्युत्थानावस्थायां रागादीनां वशप्रवृत्तायाम् ।
म्रियतां जीवो मा वा धावत्यग्रे ध्रुवं हिंसा ॥ 46 ॥

यस्मात्सकषायः सन् हन्त्यात्मा प्रथममात्मनात्मानम्।
पश्चाज्जायेत न वा हिंसा प्राण्यन्तराणां तु ॥ 47 ॥

हिंसायामविरमणं हिंसापरिणमनमपि भवति हिंसा।
तस्मात्प्रमत्तयोगे प्राणव्यपरोपणं नित्यम् ॥ 48 ॥

सूक्ष्मापि न खलु हिंसा परवस्तुनिबन्धना भवति पुंसः।
हिंसायतननिवृत्तिः परिणामविशुद्धये तदपि कार्या ॥ 49 ॥

निश्चयमबुद्ध्यमानो यो निश्चयतस्तमेव संश्रयते।
नाशयति करणचरणं स बहिःकरणालसो बालः ॥ 50 ॥

अविधायापि हि हिंसां हिंसाफलभाजनं भवत्येकः।
कृत्वाप्यपरो हिंसां हिंसाफलभाजनं न स्यात् ॥ 51 ॥

एकस्याल्पा हिंसा ददाति काले फलमनल्पम्।
अन्यस्य महाहिंसा स्वल्पफला भवति परिपाके ॥ 52 ॥

एकस्य सैव तीव्रं दिशति फलं सैव मन्दमन्यस्य।
व्रजति सहकारिणोरपि हिंसा वैचित्र्यमत्र फलकाले ॥ 53 ॥

प्रागेव फलति हिंसा क्रियमाणा फलति च कृतापि।
आरभ्यकर्तृमकृतापि फलति हिंसानुभावेन ॥ 54 ॥

एकः करोति हिंसां भवन्ति फलभागिनो बहवः।
बहवो विदधाति हिंसां हिंसाफलभुग्भवत्येकः ॥ 55 ॥

कस्यापि दिशति हिंसा हिंसाफलमेकमेव फलकाले।
अन्यस्य सैव हिंसा दिशत्यहिंसाफलं विपुलम् ॥ 56 ॥

हिंसाफलमपरस्य तु ददात्यहिंसा तु परिणामे।
इतरस्य पुनर्हिंसा दिशत्यहिंसाफलं नान्यत् ॥ 57 ॥

इति विविधभङ्गगहने सुदुस्तरे मार्गमूढदृष्टीनाम्।
गुरवो भवन्ति शरणं प्रबुद्धनयचक्रसंचाराः ॥ 58 ॥

अत्यन्तनिशितधारं दुराशदं जिनवरस्य नयचक्रम्।
खण्डयति धार्यमाणं मूर्धानं झटिति दुर्विदग्धानाम्॥ 59 ॥

अवबुध्य हिंस्यहिंसकहिंसाहिंसाफलानि तत्त्वेन।
नित्यमवगूहमानैः निजशक्त्या त्यज्यतां हिंसा ॥ 60 ॥

मद्यं मांसं क्षौद्रं पंचोदुम्बरफलानि यत्नेन।
हिंसाव्युपरतिकामैर्मोक्तव्यानि प्रथममेव ॥ 61 ॥

मद्यं मोहयति मनो मोहितचित्तस्तु विस्मरति धर्मं।
विस्मृतधर्मा जीवो हिंसामविशङ्कमाचरति ॥ 62 ॥

रसजानां च बहूनां जीवानां योनिरिष्यते मद्यं।
मद्यं भजतां तेषां हिंसा संजायतेऽवश्यम्॥ 63 ॥

अभिमानभयजुगुप्साहास्यारतिशोककामकोपाद्याः।
हिंसायाः पर्यायाः सर्वेऽपि च सरकसन्निहिताः ॥ 66 ॥

न विना प्राणविद्यतान्मांसस्योत्पत्तिरिष्यते यस्मात्।
मांसं भजतस्तस्मात् प्रसरत्यनिवारिता हिंसा ॥ 65 ॥

यदपि किल भवति मांसं स्वयमेव मृतस्य महिष्वृषभादेः।
तत्रापि भवति हिंसा तदाश्रितनिगोतनिर्मथनात्॥ 66 ॥

आमास्वपि पक्कास्वपि विपच्यमानासु मांसपेशीषु।
सातत्येनोत्पादस्तज्जातीनां निगोतानाम्॥ 67 ॥

आमां वा पक्कां वा खादति यः स्पृशति वा पिशितपेशीं।
स निहन्ति सततनिचितं पिण्डं बहुजीवकोटीनाम्॥ 68 ॥

मधुशकलमपि प्रायो मधुकरहिंसात्मको भवति लोके।
भजति मधु मूढधीको यः स भवति हिंसकोऽत्यन्तम्॥ 67 ॥

स्वयमेव विगलितं यो गृहणीयाद्वा छलेन मधुगोलात्।
तत्रापि भवति हिंसा तदाश्रयपाणिनां घातात्॥ 70 ॥

मधु मद्यं नवनीतं पिशितं च महाविकृतयस्ताः ।
वल्भ्यन्ते न व्रतिना तद्वर्णा जन्तवस्तत्र ॥ 71 ॥

योनिरुदुम्बरयुग्मं प्लक्षन्यग्रोधपिप्पलफलानि ।
त्रसजीवानां तस्मात्तेषां तद्भक्षणे हिंसा ॥ 72 ॥

यानि तु पुनर्भवेयुः कालोच्छिन्नत्रसाणि शुष्काणि ।
भजतस्तान्यपि हिंसा विशिष्टरागादिरूपा स्यात् ॥ 73 ॥

अष्टावनिष्टदुस्तरदुरितायतनान्यमूनि परिवर्ज्य ।
जिनधर्मदेशनाया भवन्ति पात्राणि शुद्धधियः ॥ 74 ॥

धर्ममहिंसारूपं संशृण्वतोऽपि ये परित्यक्तुं ।
स्थावरहिंसामसहास्त्रसहिंसां तेऽपि मुञ्चन्तु ॥ 75 ॥

कृतकारितानुमननैर्वाक्कायमनोभिरिष्यते नवधा ।
औत्सर्गिकी निवृत्तिर्विचित्ररूपापवादिकी त्वेषा ॥ 76 ॥

स्तोकैकेन्द्रियघातागृहिणां सम्पन्नयोग्यविषयाणांम ।
शेषस्थावरमारणविरमणमपि भवति करणीयम् ॥ 77 ॥

अमृतत्त्वहेतुभूतं परममहिंसारसायनं लब्ध्वा ।
अवलोक्य बालिशानामसमञ्जसमाकुलैर्न भवितव्यम् ॥ 78 ॥

सूक्ष्मो भगवद्धर्मो धर्मार्थं हिंसने न दोषोऽस्ति ।
इति धर्ममुग्धहृदयैर्न जातु भूत्वा शरीरिणो हिंस्याः ॥ 79 ॥

धर्मो हि देवताभ्यः प्रभवति ताभ्यः प्रदेयमिह सर्वम् ।
इति वुर्विवेककलितां धिषणां न प्राप्य देहिनो हिंस्याः ॥ 80 ॥

पूज्यनिमित्तं घाते छागादीनां न कोऽपि दोषोऽस्ति ।
इति संप्रधार्य कार्यं नातिथये सत्त्वसंज्ञपनम् ॥ 81 ॥

बहुसत्त्वद्यातघातजनितादशनाद् वरमेकसत्त्वघातोत्थम् ।
इत्याकल्य्य कार्यं न महासत्त्वस्य हिंसनं जातु ॥ 82 ॥

रक्षा भवति बहूनामेकस्यैवास्य जीवहरणेन।
इति मत्वा कर्त्तव्यं न हिंसनं हिंस्रसत्त्वानाम् ॥ 83 ॥

बहुसत्त्वघातिनोऽमी जीवन्त उपाजयन्ति गुरुपापम्।
इत्यनुकम्पां कृत्वां न हिंसनीयाः शरीरिणो हिंस्राः ॥ 84 ॥

बहुदुःखाः संज्ञपिताः प्रयान्ति त्वचिरेण दुःखविच्छित्तिम्।
इति वासनाकृपाणीमादाय न दुःखितोऽपि हन्तव्याः ॥ 85 ॥

कृच्छ्रेण सुखावाप्तिर्भवन्ति सुखिनो कृताः सुखिन हताः।
इति तर्कमण्डलाग्रः सुखिनां घाताय नादेयः ॥ 86 ॥

उपलब्धिसुगतिसाधनसमाधिसारस्य भूयसोऽभ्यासात्।
स्वगुरोः शिष्येण शिरो न कर्त्तानीयं सुधर्ममभिलषिता ॥ 87 ॥

धनलवपिपासितानां विनेयविश्वासनाय दर्शयतां।
झटितिघटचटकमोक्षं श्रद्धेयं नैव खारपटिकानां ॥ 88 ॥

दृष्ट्वापरं पुरस्तादशनाय क्षामकुक्षिमायान्तम्।
निजमांसदानरभसादालभनीयो न चात्मापि ॥ 89 ॥

को नाम विशति मोहं नयभङ्गविशारदानुपास्य गुरून्।
विदितजिनमतरहस्यः श्रयन्नहिंसां विशुद्धमतिः ॥ 90 ॥

यदिदं प्रमादयोगादसदभिधानं विधीयते किमपि।
तदनृतमपि विज्ञेयं तद्भेदाः सन्ति चत्वारः ॥ 91 ॥

स्वक्षेत्रकालभावैः सदपि हि यस्मिन्निषिद्ध्यते वस्तु।
तत्प्रथममसत्यं स्यान्नास्ति यथा देवदत्तोऽत्र ॥ 92 ॥

असदपि हि वस्तुरूपं यत्र परक्षेत्रकालभावैस्तैः।
उद्भाव्यते द्वितीयं तदनृतमस्मिन् यथास्ति घटः ॥ 93 ॥

वस्तु सदपि स्वरूपात् पररूपेणाभिधीयते यस्मिन्।
अनृतमिदं च तृतीयं विज्ञेयं गौरिति यथाश्वः ॥ 94 ॥

गर्हितमवद्यसंयुतप्रियमपि भवति वचनरूपं यत्।
सामान्येन त्रेधा मतमिदमनृतं तुरीयं तु ॥ 95 ॥

पैशून्यहासगर्भं कर्कशमसमञ्जसं प्रलपितं च।
अन्यदपि यदुत्सूत्रं तत्सर्वं गर्हितं गदितम् ॥ 96 ॥

छेदनभेदनमारणकर्षणवाणिज्यचौर्यवचनादि।
तत्सावद्यं यस्मात्प्राणिबधाद्याः प्रवर्तन्ते ॥ 97 ॥

अरतिकरं भीतिकरं खेदकरं वैरशोककलहकरं।
यदपरमपि तापकरं परस्य तत्सर्वमप्रियं ज्ञेयम् ॥ 98 ॥

सर्वस्मिन्नप्यस्मिन्प्रमत्तयोगैकहेतुकथनं यत्।
अनृतवचनेऽपि तस्मान्नियतं हिंसा समवतरति ॥ 99 ॥

हेतौ प्रमत्तयोगे निर्दिष्टे सकलवितथवचनानां।
हेयानुष्ठानादेरनुवदनं भवति नासत्यम् ॥ 100 ॥

भोगोपभोगसाधनमात्रं सावद्यमक्षमा मोक्तुम्।
ये तेऽपि शेषमनृतं समस्तमपि नित्यमेव मुञ्चन्तु ॥ 101 ॥

अवितीर्णस्य ग्रहणं परिग्रहस्य प्रमत्तयोगाद्यत्।
तत्प्रत्येयं स्तेयं सैव च हिंसा बधस्य हेतुत्वात् ॥ 102 ॥

अर्था नाम य एते प्राणा एते बहिश्चराः पुंसां।
हरति स तस्य प्राणान् यो यस्य जनो हरत्यर्थान् ॥ 103 ॥

हिंसायाः स्तेयस्य च नाव्याप्तिः सुघटा एव सा यस्मात्।
ग्रहणे प्रमत्तयोगो द्रव्यस्य स्वीकृतस्यान्यैः ॥ 104 ॥

नातिव्याप्तिश्च तयोः प्रमत्तयोगैककारणविरोधात्।
अपि कर्मानुग्रहणे नीरागाणामविद्यमानत्वात् ॥ 105 ॥

असमर्था ये कर्तुं निपानतोयादिहरणविनिवृत्तिं।
तैरपि समस्तमपरं नित्यमदत्तं परित्याज्यम् ॥ 106 ॥

यद्वेदरागयोगान्मैथुनमभिधीयते तदब्रह्म।
अवतरति तत्र हिंसा वधस्य सर्वत्र सद्भावात् ॥ **107** ॥

हिंस्यन्ते तिलनाल्यां तप्तायसि विनिहिते तिला यद्वत्।
बहवो जीवा योनौ हिंस्यन्ते मैथुने तद्वत् ॥ **108** ॥

यदपि क्रियते किंचिन्मदनोद्रेकादनङ्गरमणादि।
तत्रापि भवति हिंसा रागाद्युत्पत्तितन्त्रत्वात् ॥ **109** ॥

ये निजकलत्रमात्रं परिहर्तुं शक्नुवन्ति न हि मोहात्।
निःशेषशेषयोषिन्निषेवणं तैरपि न कार्यम् ॥ **110** ॥

या मूर्च्छानामेयं विज्ञातव्यः परिग्रहो ह्येषः।
मोहोदयादुदीर्णो मूर्छा तु ममत्वपरिणामः ॥ **111** ॥

मूर्छालक्षणकरणात् सुघटा व्याप्तिः परिग्रहत्वस्य।
सग्रन्थो मूर्छावान् विनापि किल शेषसंगेभ्यः ॥ **112** ॥

यद्येवं भवति तदा परिग्रहो न खलु कोऽपि बहिरंगः।
भवति नितरां यतोऽसौ धत्ते मूर्छानिमित्तत्वम् ॥ **113** ॥

एवमतिव्याप्तिः स्यात्परिग्रहस्येति चेद्भवेन्नैवम्।
यस्मादकषायाणां कर्मग्रहणे न मूर्छास्ति ॥ **114** ॥

अतिसंक्षेपाद्द्विविधः स भवेदभ्यन्तरश्च बाह्यश्च।
प्रथमश्चतुर्दशविधो भवति द्विविधो द्वितीयस्तु ॥ **115** ॥

मिथ्यात्ववेदरागास्तथैव हास्यादयश्च षड्दोषाः।
चत्वारश्च कषायाश्चतुर्दशाभ्यन्तरा ग्रन्थाः ॥ **116** ॥

अथ निश्चित्तसचित्तौ बाह्यस्य परिग्रहस्य भेदौ द्वौ।
नैषः कदापि सङ्गः सर्वोऽप्यतिवर्त्तते हिंसां ॥ **117** ॥

उभयपरिग्रहवर्जनमाचार्याः सूचयन्त्यहिंसेति।
द्विविधपरिग्रहवहनं हिंसेति जिनप्रवचनज्ञाः ॥ **118** ॥

हिंसापर्यायत्वात्सिद्धा हिंसान्तरङ्गसंगेषु ।
बहिरंगेषु तु नियतं प्रयातु मूर्छैव हिंसात्वम् ॥ **119** ॥

एव न विशेषः स्यादुन्दररिपुहरिणशावकादीनाम् ।
नैवं भवति विशेषस्तेषां मूर्छा विशेषेण ॥ **120** ॥

हरिततृणांकुरचारिणि मन्दा मृगशावके भवति मूर्छा ।
उन्दरनिकरोन्माथिनि माज्जरि सैव जायते तीव्रा ॥ **121** ॥

निर्वाधं संसिद्धयेत्कार्यविशेषो हि कारणविशेषात् ।
औधस्य खण्डयोरिह माधुर्यप्रीतिभेद इव ॥ **122** ॥

माधुर्यप्रीतिः किल दुग्धे मन्दैव मन्दमाधुर्ये ।
सैवोत्कटमाधुर्ये खण्डे व्यपदिश्यते तीव्रा ॥ **123** ॥

तत्त्वार्थाश्रद्धाने निर्युक्तं प्रथममेव मिथ्यात्वम् ।
सम्यग्दर्शनचौराः प्रथमकषायाश्च चत्वाराः ॥ **124** ॥

प्रविहाय च द्वितीयान् देशचरित्रस्य सन्मुखायातः ।
नियतं ते हि कषायाः देशचरित्रं निरुन्धन्ति ॥ **125** ॥

निजशक्त्या शेषाणां सर्वेषामन्तरंगसंगानाम् ।
कर्त्तव्यः परिहारो मार्दवशौचादिभावनया ॥ **126** ॥

बहिरंगादपि संगाद्यस्मात्प्रभवत्यसंयमोऽनुचितः ।
परिवर्जयेदशेषं तमचित्तं वा सचित्तं वा ॥ **127** ॥

येऽपि न शक्यस्त्यक्तुं धनधान्यमनुष्यवास्तुवित्तादिः ।
सोऽपि तनूकरणीयो निवृत्तिरूपं यतस्तत्त्वम् ॥ **128** ॥

रात्रौ भुंजानानां यस्मादनिवारिता भवति हिंसा ।
हिंसाविरतैस्तस्मात्त्यक्तव्या रात्रिभुक्तिरपि ॥ **129** ॥

रागाद्युदयपरत्वादनिवृत्तिर्नीतिवर्तते हिंसां ।
रात्रिं दिवमाहरतः कथं हि हिंसा न संभवति ॥ **130** ॥

यद्येवं तर्हि दिवा कर्तव्यो भोजनस्य परिहारः ।
भोक्तव्यं तु निशायां नेत्थं नित्यं भवति हिंसा ॥ **131** ॥

नैवं वासरभुक्तेः भवति हि रागाधिको रजनिभुक्तौ ।
अन्नकवलस्य भुक्तेः भुक्ताविव मांसकवलस्य ॥ **132** ॥

अर्कालोकेन विना भुञ्जानः परिहरेत् कथं हिंसां ।
अपि बोधिते प्रदीपे भोज्यजुषां सूक्ष्मजीवानाम् ॥ **133** ॥

किं वा बहुप्रलपितैरिति सिद्धं यो मनोवचनकायैः ।
परिहरति रात्रिभुक्तिं सततमहिंसां स पालयति ॥ **134** ॥

इत्यत्र त्रितयात्मनि मार्गे मोक्षस्य ये स्वहितकामाः ।
अनुपरतं प्रयतन्ते प्रयान्ति ते मुक्तिमचिरेण ॥ **135** ॥

परिधय इव नगराणि व्रतानि किल पालयन्ति शीलानि ।
व्रतपालनाय तस्माच्छीलान्यपि पालनीयानि ॥ **136** ॥

प्रविधाय सुप्रसिद्धैर्मर्यादां सर्वतोऽप्यभिज्ञानैः ।
प्राच्यादिभ्यो दिग्भ्यः कर्तव्या विरतिरविचलिता ॥ **137** ॥

इति नियमितदिग्भागे प्रवर्तते यस्ततो बहिस्तस्य ।
सकलासंयमविरहाद् भवत्यहिंसाव्रतं पूर्णम् ॥ **138** ॥

तत्रापि च परिमाणं ग्रामापणभवनपाटकादीनाम् ।
प्रविधाय नियतकालं करणीयं विरमणं देशात् ॥ **139** ॥

इति विरतो बहुदेशात् तदुत्थहिंसा विशेषपरिहारात् ।
तत्कालं विमलमतिः श्रयत्यहिंसां विशेषेण ॥ **140** ॥

पापर्द्धिजयपराजयसंगरपरदारगमनचौर्याद्या ।
न कदाचनापि चिंत्याः पापफलं केवलं यस्मात् ॥ **141** ॥

विद्यावाणिज्यमषीकृषिसेवाशिल्पजीवानां पुंसाम् ।
पापोपदेशदानं कदाचिदपि नैव वक्तव्यम् ॥ **142** ॥

भूखननवृक्षमोट्टनशाड्वलदलनाम्बुसेचनादीनि ।
निष्कारणं न कुर्याद्दलफलकुसुमोच्चयानपि च ॥ 143 ॥

असिधेनुविषहुताशनलांगलकरवालकार्मुकादीनाम् ।
वितरणमुपकरणानां हिंसायाः परिहरेद्यत्नात् ॥ 144 ॥

रागादिवर्द्धनानां दुष्टकथानामबोधबहुलानां ।
न कदाचन कुर्वीत श्रवणार्जनशिक्षणादीनि ॥ 145 ॥

सर्वानर्थप्रथमं मथनं शौचस्य सद्म मायायाः ।
दूरात् परिहरणीयं चौर्यासत्यास्पदं द्यूतम् ॥ 146 ॥

एवं विधमपरमपि ज्ञात्वा मुञ्चत्यनर्थदण्डं यः ।
तस्यानिशमनवद्यं विजयमहिंसाव्रतं लभते ॥ 147 ॥

रागद्वेषत्यागान्निखिलद्रव्येषु साम्यमवलम्ब्य ।
तत्त्वोपलब्धिमूलं बहुशः सामायिकं कार्यम् ॥ 148 ॥

रजनीदिनयोरन्ते तदवश्यं भावनीयमविचलितम् ।
इतरत्र पुनः समये न कृतं दोषाय तद्गुणाय कृतम् ॥ 149 ॥

सामायिकश्रितानां समस्तसावद्ययोगपरिहारात् ।
भवति महाव्रतमेषामुदयेऽपि चारित्रमोहस्य ॥ 150 ॥

सामायिकसंस्कारं प्रतिदिनमारोपितं स्थिरीकर्तुं ।
पक्षार्द्धयोर्द्वयोरपि कर्त्तव्योऽवश्यमुपवासः ॥ 151 ॥

मुक्तसमस्तारम्भः प्रोषधदिनपूर्ववासरस्यार्धे ।
उपवासं गृहणीयान्ममत्वमपहाय देहादौ ॥ 152 ॥

श्रित्वा विविक्तवसतिं समस्तसावद्ययोगमपनीय ।
सर्वेन्द्रियार्थविरतः कायमनोवचनगुप्तिभिस्तिष्ठेत् ॥ 153 ॥

धर्मध्यानाशक्तो वासरमतिवाह्य विहितसांध्यविधिं ।
शुचिसंस्तरे त्रियामां गमयेत्स्वाध्यायजितनिद्रः ॥ 154 ॥

प्रातः प्रोत्थाय ततः कृत्वा तात्कालिकं क्रियाकल्पं ।
निर्वर्तयेद्यथोक्तं जिनपूजां प्राशुकैर्द्रव्यैः ॥ 155 ॥

उक्तेन ततो विधिना नीत्वा दिवसं द्वितीयरात्रिं च ।
अतिवाहत्प्रयेत्नादर्द्धं च तृतीयदिवसस्य ॥ 156 ॥

इति यः षोडशयामान् गमयति परिमुक्तसकलसावद्यः ।
तस्य तदानीं नियतं पूर्णमहिंसाव्रतं भवति ॥ 157 ॥

भोगोपभोगहेतोः स्थावरहिंसा भवेत्किलामीषाम् ।
भोगोपभोगविरहाद् भवति न लेशोऽपि हिंसायाः ॥ 158 ॥

वाग्गुप्तेर्नास्त्यिनृतं न समस्तादानविरहतः स्तेयम् ।
नाब्रह्म मैथुनमुचः संगो नांगेऽप्यमूर्छास्य ॥ 159 ॥

इत्थमशेषितहिंसः प्रयाति स महाव्रतित्त्वमुपचारात् ।
उदयति चारित्रमोहे लभते तु न संयमस्थानम् ॥ 160 ॥

भोगोपभोगमूला विरताविरतस्य नान्यतो हिंसा ।
अधिगम्य वस्तुतत्त्वं स्वशक्तिमपि तावपि त्याज्यौ ॥ 161 ॥

एकमपि प्रजिघांसुर्निहन्त्यनन्तान्यतस्ततोऽवश्यं ।
करणीयमशेषाणां परिहरणमनन्तकायानाम् ॥ 162 ॥

नवनीतं च त्याज्यं योनिस्थानं प्रभूतजीवानां ।
यद्वापि पिण्डशुद्धौ विरुद्धमभिधीयते किञ्चित् ॥ 163 ॥

अविरुद्धा अपि भोगा निजशक्तिमपेक्ष्य धीमता त्याज्याः ।
अत्याज्येष्वपि सीमा कार्यैकदिवानिशोपभोग्यतया ॥ 164 ॥

पुनरपि पूर्वकृतायां समीक्ष्य तात्कालिकीं निजां शक्तिं ।
सीमन्यन्तरसीमा प्रतिदिवसं भवति कर्तव्या ॥ 165 ॥

इति यः परिमितभोगैः सन्तुष्टस्त्यजति बहुतरान् भोगान् ।
बहुतरहिंसा विरहात्तस्याहिंसा विशिष्टा स्यात् ॥ 166 ॥

विधिना दातृगुणवता द्रव्यविशेषस्य जातरूपाय ।
स्वपरानुग्रहहेतोः कर्तव्योऽवश्यमतिथये भागः ॥ **167** ॥

संग्रहमुच्चस्थानं पादोदकमर्चनं प्रणामं च ।
वाक्कायमनःशुद्धिरेषणाशुद्धिश्च विधिमाहुः ॥ **168** ॥

ऐहिकफलानपेक्षा क्षान्तिर्निष्कपटतानसूयत्वम् ।
अविषादित्वमुदित्वे निरहङ्कारित्वमिति हि दातृगुणाः ॥ **169** ॥

रागद्वेषासंयममदद्दुःखभयादिकं न यत्कुरुते ।
द्रव्यं तदेव देयं सुतपःस्वाध्यायवृद्धिकरम् ॥ **170** ॥

पात्रं त्रिभेदमुक्तं संयोगो मोक्षकारणगुणानाम् ।
अविरतसम्यग्दृष्टिः विरताविरतश्च सकलविरतश्च ॥ **171** ॥

हिंसायाः पर्यायो लोभोऽत्र निरस्यते यतो दाने ।
तस्मादतिथिवितरणं हिंसाव्युपरमणमेवेष्टम् ॥ **172** ॥

गृहमागताय गुणिने मधुकरवृत्त्या परानपीडयते ।
वितरति यो नातिथये स कथं न लोभवान् भवति ॥ **173** ॥

कृतमात्मार्थं मुनये ददाति भक्तमिति भावितस्त्यागः ।
अरतिविषादविमुक्तः शिथिलितलोभो भवत्यहिंसैव ॥ **174** ॥

इयमेकैव समर्था धर्मस्वं मे मया समं नेतुं ।
सततमिति भावनीया पश्चिमसल्लेखना भक्त्या ॥ **175** ॥

मरणान्तेऽवश्यमहं विधिना सल्लेखनां करिष्यामि ।
इति भावनापरिणतो नागतमपि पालयेदिदं शीलम् ॥ **176** ॥

मरणेऽवश्यं भाविनि कषायसल्लेखनातनुकरणमात्रे ।
रागादिमन्तरेण व्याप्रियमाणस्य नात्मघातोऽस्ति ॥ **177** ॥

यो हि कषायाविष्टः कुम्भकजलधूमकेतुविषशस्त्रैः ।
व्यपरोपयति प्राणान् तस्य स्यात्सत्यमात्मवधः ॥ **178** ॥

नीयन्तेऽत्र कषाया हिंसाया हेतवो यतस्तनुतां ।
सल्लेखनामपि ततः प्राहुरहिंसा प्रसिद्ध्यर्थम् ॥ 179 ॥

इति यो व्रतरक्षार्थं सततं पालयति सकलशीलानि ।
वरयति पतिंवरेव स्वयमेव समुत्सुका शिवपदश्रीः ॥ 180 ॥

अतिचाराः सम्यकत्वे व्रतेषु शीलेषु पञ्चक्तवेपञ्चेति ।
सप्ततिरमी यथोदितशुद्धिप्रतिबन्धिनो हेयाः ॥ 181 ॥

शङ्का तथैव कांक्षा विचिकित्सा संस्तवोऽन्यदृष्टीनां ।
मनसा च तत्प्रशंसा सम्यग्दृष्टेरतिचाराः ॥ 182 ॥

छेदनताडम्नबंधाः भारस्यारोपणं समधिकस्य ।
पानान्नयोश्च रोधः पंचाहिंसाव्रतस्येति ॥ 183 ॥

मिथ्योपदेशदानं रहसोःभ्याख्यानकूटलेखकृती ।
न्यासापहारवचनं साकारमन्त्रभेदश्च ॥ 184 ॥

प्रतिरूपकव्यवहारः स्तेननियोगस्तदाहृतादानम् ।
राजविरोधातिक्रमहीनाधिकमानकरणे च ॥ 185 ॥

स्मरतीव्राभिनिवेशानंगक्रीडान्यपरिणयनकरणम् ।
अपरिगृहीतेतरयोर्गमने चेत्वरिकयोः पञ्च ॥ 186 ॥

वास्तुक्षेत्राष्टापदहिरण्यधनधान्यदासदासीनां ।
कुप्यस्य भेदयोरपि परिणामातिक्रियाः पञ्च ॥ 187 ॥

ऊर्ध्वमधस्तात्तिर्यक्व्यतिक्रमाः क्षेत्रवृद्धिराधानं ।
स्मृत्यन्तरस्य गदिताः पञ्चेति प्रथमशीलस्य ॥ 188 ॥

प्रेषस्य संप्रयोजनमानयनं शब्दरूपविनिपातौ ।
क्षेपोऽपि पुद्गलानां द्वितीयशीलस्य पञ्चेति ॥ 189 ॥

कन्दर्पः कौत्कुच्यं भोगानर्थक्यमपि च मौखर्यम् ।
असमीक्षिताधिकरणं तृतीयशीलस्य पञ्च इति ॥ 190 ॥

वचनमनःकायानां दुःप्रणिधानमनादरश्चैव ।
स्मृत्यनुपस्थानयुताः पञ्चेति चतुर्थशीलस्य ॥ 191 ॥

अनवेक्षिताप्रमार्जितमादानं संस्तरस्तथोत्सर्गः ।
स्मृत्यनुपस्थानमनादरश्च पञ्चोपवासस्य ॥ 192 ॥

आहारो हि सचित्तः सचित्तमिश्रस्सचित्तसम्बन्धः ।
दुष्पक्वोऽभिषवोऽपि च पञ्चामी षष्ठशीलस्य ॥ 193 ॥

परदातृव्यपदेशः सचित्तनिक्षेपतत्पिधाने च ।
कालस्यातिक्रमणं मात्सर्यं चेत्यतिथिदाने ॥ 194 ॥

जीवितमरणांशसे सुहृदनुरागः सुखानुबन्धश्च ।
सनिदानः पञ्चैते भवन्ति सल्लेखनाकाले ॥ 195 ॥

इत्येतानतिचारानपरानपि संप्रतर्क्य परिवर्ज्य ।
सम्यक्त्वव्रतशीलैरमलैः पुरुषार्थसिद्धिमेत्यचिरात् ॥ 196 ॥

चारित्रान्तर्भावात् तपोऽपि मोक्षांगमागभे गदितम् ।
अनिगूहितनिजवीर्यैस्तदपि निषेव्यं समाहितस्वान्तैः ॥ 197 ॥

अनशनमवमौदर्यं विविक्तशय्यासनं रसत्यागः ।
कायक्लेशो वृत्तेः संख्या च निषेव्यमिति तपो बाह्यम् ॥ 198 ॥

विनयो वैयावृत्त्यं प्रायश्चित्तं तथैव चोत्सर्गः ।
स्वाध्यायोऽथ ध्यानं भवति निषेव्यं तपोऽन्तरंगमिति ॥ 199 ॥

जिनपुंगवप्रवचने मुनीश्वराणां यदुक्तमाचरणं ।
सुनिरूप्य निजां पदवीं शक्तिं च निषेव्यमेतदपि ॥ 200 ॥

इदमावश्यकषट्कं समतास्तवनवन्दनाप्रतिक्रमणं ।
प्रत्याख्यानं वपुषो व्युत्सर्गश्चेति कर्तव्यम् ॥ 201 ॥

सम्यग्दण्डो वपुषः सम्यग्दण्डस्तथा च वचनस्य ।
मनसः सम्यग्दण्डो गुप्तीनां त्रितयमंवगम्यम् ॥ 202 ॥

सम्यग्गमनागमनं सम्यग्भावा तथैषणा सम्यक् ।
सम्यग्ग्रहनिक्षेपो व्युत्सर्गः सम्यगिति समितिः ॥ 203 ॥

धर्मः सेव्यः क्षान्तिर्मृदुत्वमृजुता च शौचमथ सत्यम् ।
आकिंचन्यं ब्रह्म त्यागश्च तपश्च संयमश्चेति ॥ 204 ॥

अध्रुवमशरणमेकत्वमन्यताशौचमास्त्रवो जन्म ।
लोकवृषबोधिसंवरनिर्जराः सततमनुप्रेक्ष्याः ॥ 205 ॥

क्षुत्तृणा हिममुष्णं नग्नत्वं याचनारतिरलाभः ।
दंशो मसकादीनामाक्रोशो व्याधि दुःखमङ्गमलम् ॥ 206 ॥

स्पर्शश्च तृणादीनामज्ञानमदर्शनं तथा प्रज्ञा ।
सत्कारपुरस्कारः शय्या चर्य्या वधो निषद्या स्त्री ॥ 207 ॥

द्वाविंशतिरप्येते परिषोढव्याः परीषहाः सततं ।
संक्लेशमुक्तमनसा संक्लेशनिमित्तभीतेन ॥ 208 ॥

इति रत्नत्रयमेतत्प्रतिसमयं विकलमपि गृहस्थेन ।
परिपालनीयमनिशं निरत्ययां मुक्तिमभिलषिता ॥ 209 ॥

बद्धोद्यमेन नित्यं लब्ध्वा समयं च बोधिलाभस्य ।
पदमवलम्ब्य मुनीनां कर्त्तव्यं सपदि परिपूर्णम् ॥ 210 ॥

असमग्रं भावयतो रत्नत्रयमस्ति कर्मबन्धो यः ।
स विपक्षकृतोऽवश्यं मोक्षोपायो न बन्धनोपायः ॥ 211 ॥

येनांशेन सुदृष्टिस्तेनांशेनास्य बन्धनं नास्ति ।
येनांशेन तु रागस्तेनांशेनास्य बन्धनं भवति ॥ 212 ॥

येनांशेन ज्ञानं तेनांशेनास्य बन्धनं नास्ति ।
येनांशेन तु रागस्तेनांशेनास्य बन्धनं भवति ॥ 213 ॥

येनांशेन चरित्रं तेनांशेनास्य बन्धनं नास्ति ।
येनांशेन तु रागस्तेनांशेनास्य बन्धनं भवति ॥ 214 ॥

योगात् प्रदेशबन्धः स्थितिबन्धो भवति तु कषायात् ।
दर्शनबोधचरित्रं न योगरूपं कषायरूपं च ॥ 215 ॥

दर्शनमात्मविनिश्चितिरात्मपरिज्ञानमिष्यते बोधः ।
स्थितिरात्मनि चारित्रं कुत एतेभ्यो भवति बन्धः ॥ 216 ॥

सम्यक्चारित्राभ्यां तीर्थंकराहारकर्मणो बन्धः ।
योऽप्युपदिष्टः समये न नयविदां सोऽपि दोषाय ॥ 217 ॥

सति सम्यक्त्वचरित्रे तीर्थंकराहारबन्धकौ भवतः ।
योगकषायौ नासति तत्पुनरस्मिन्नुदासीनम् ॥ 218 ॥

ननु कथमेवं सिद्ध्यति देवायुःप्रभृतिसत्प्रकृतिबन्धः ।
सकलजनसुप्रसिद्धो रत्नत्रयधारीणां मुनिवराणाम् ॥ 219 ॥

रत्नत्रयमिह हेतुर्निर्वाणस्यैव भवति नान्यस्य ।
आस्रवति यत्तु पुण्यं शुभोपयोगोऽयमपराधः ॥ 220 ॥

एकस्मिन् समवायादत्यन्तविरुद्धकार्ययोरपि हि ।
इह दहति घृतमिति यथा व्यवहारस्तादृशोऽपि रूढिमितः ॥ 221 ॥

सम्यक्त्वचरित्रबोधलक्षणो मोक्षमार्ग इत्येषाः ।
मुख्योपचाररूपः प्रापयति परमपदं पुरुषम् ॥ 222 ॥

नित्यमपि निरुपलेपः स्वरूपसमवस्थितो निरुपघातः ।
गगनमिव परमपुरुषः परमपदे स्फुरति विशदतमः ॥ 223 ॥

कृत्कृत्यः परमपदे परमात्मा सकलविषयविषयात्मा ।
परमानन्दनिमग्नो ज्ञानमयो नन्दति सदैव ॥ 224 ॥

एकेनाकर्षन्ती श्लथयन्ती वस्तुतत्त्वमितरेण ।
अन्तेन जयति जैनीनीतिर्मन्थानेत्रमिव गोपी ॥ 225 ॥

वर्णैः कृतानि चित्रैः पदानि तु पदैः कृतानि वाक्यानि ।
वाक्यैः कृतं पवित्रं शास्त्रमिदं न पुनरस्माभिः ॥ 226 ॥

INDEX